WHY GOVERNMENTS GROW

Volumes published in this series:

Edited by
Charles Lewis Taylor

WHY GOVERNMENTS GROW
Measuring Public Sector Size

Published in cooperation with the
International Political Science Association and
the International Institute for Comparative Social Research
Science Center, Berlin

SAGE PUBLICATIONS
Beverly Hills / London / New Delhi

For information address:

SAGE Publications, Inc.
275 South Beverly Drive
Beverly Hills, California 90212

SAGE Publications India Pvt. Ltd.
C-236 Defence Colony
New Delhi 110 024, India

SAGE Publications Ltd
28 Banner Street
London EC1Y 8QE, England

Printed in the United States of America

Library of Congress Cataloging in Publication Data

Main entry under title:

Why Governments Grow

(Advances in political science ; 3)

1. Expenditures, Public—Addresses, essays, lectures.
2. Government spending policy—Addresses, essays, lectures.
I. Taylor, Charles Lewis. II. Series.
HJ2005.M42   1983   336.3'9   83-14390
ISBN 0-8039-2124-1

FIRST PRINTING

CONTENTS

ACKNOWLEDGMENTS

Political scientists, economists, sociologists, and official statisticians from Germany, the United States, Britain, Australia, Denmark, and the Netherlands met in Berlin in the summer of 1981 to discuss problems in the measurement and explanation of the size and growth of the public sector. Most of the papers delivered at that conference are being published here. The intention of the organizers of the conference was to bring together scholars and government officials who would take a variety of approaches to measurement and explanation. Therefore this book, as the conference before it, is not a single integrated view of the public sector but is instead a collection of views, some of them complementary and some of them contradictory. The purpose of the conference was to foster an exchange of these views; the purpose of the book is to present the components of this exchange.

Support for the conference was provided by the International Institute for Comparative Social Research in the Wissenschaftszentrum—Berlin. Its director, Karl W. Deutsch, was the guiding inspiration for the meeting. Appreciation is due to him and the Wissenschaftszentrum for making both conference and book possible and to Ottokar Runze for providing a marvelous baroque meeting room at the Schloss Hotel Gerhus. Thanks must also be given to Ina Frieser and Konstanza Prinzessin zu Löwenstein for their assistance with the conference and to Tricia Inlow, Steven Kraft, Doris Linkous, Susan Rose, and my wife Mary Frances for their cheerful help with the myriad of editing details.

—Charles Lewis Taylor
Wissenschaftszentrum—Berlin

FROM THE SERIES EDITOR

Advances in Political Science: An International Series reflects the aims and intellectual traditions of the International Political Science Association: the generation and dissemination of rigorous political inquiry free of any subdisciplinary or other orthodoxy. Along with its quarterly companion publication, the *International Political Science Review*, this series seeks to present the best work being done today (1) on the central and critical controversial themes of politics and/or (2) in new areas of inquiry where political scientists, alone or in conjunction with other scholars, are shaping innovative concepts and methodologies of political analysis.

Political science as an intellectual discipline has burgeoned in recent decades. With the enormous growth in the number of publications and papers and their increasing sophistication, however, has also come a tendency toward parochialism along national, subdisciplinary, and other lines. It was to counteract these tendencies that political scientists from a handful of countries created IPSA in 1949. Through roundtables organized by its research committees and study groups, at its triennial world congresses (the next of which takes place in July 1985 in Paris), and through its organizational work, IPSA has sought to encourage the creation of both an international-minded science of politics and a body of scholars from many nations (now from more than 40 regional associations) who approach their research and interactions with other scholars from an international perspective.

Measuring the Public Sector, edited by Charles Lewis Taylor, is the third volume in *Advances in Political Science: An International Series*. Like its predecessors it is comprised of original papers that focus in an integrated manner on a single important topic—in this case, procedures for measuring the growth of government and interpretations of the meaning of the relevant data. At the same time its authors, from various countries and social systems and trained in various academic disciplines, take rather different approaches to the central theme. Together the papers in the volume contribute significantly to our understanding of one of the most important political phenomena of our time.

The volume also represents a new stage in the series' international collaborative orientation, this time between IPSA and the International Institute of Comparative Social Research, Science Center Berlin (Wissenschaftszentrum—Berlin). The conference at which the papers were originally presented was developed and financed by the IICSR; the Wissenschaftszentrum also commissioned and supported financially Professor Taylor's editorial labors. IPSA and the series editor are grateful to the Wissenschaftszentrum—Berlin and its president, Meinolf Dierkes, for their generous assistance; to Karl W. Deutsch, director of the IICSR, for encouraging the collaboration; and especially to Konstanza, Prinzessin zu Löwenstein, for facilitating both the conference and the publication.

PART I

Introduction:
Multiple Approaches to
Measurement and Explanation

CHARLES LEWIS TAYLOR

Government for many ordinary people is big, getting bigger, and ought to be cut down to size. The problem, one would suspect, is not that most people believe that they are receiving too many services, although they may feel that other people are. Rather, it is primarily that there are too many taxes to pay and too many bureaucrats to support. This popular concern is reflected in numerous academic studies that argue that the expansion of the public sector limits the choice properly belonging to the individual, that compare productivity in the public sector unfavorably with productivity in the market sector, that perceive the public sector as nonproductive and supported by the production of the private market sector, that examine the regulatory policies of governments as costs for the private sector, and that seek a variety of explanations for the perceived rapid growth in the public sector. Although other studies argue that in a democracy at least people do tend to get the level of services they desire and that attention should be given primarily to institutional reforms that enhance free and efficient fiscal choice, the problem of why government grows remains one for explanation.

A large number of analyses have attempted with varying degrees of success to produce carefully documented explanations of government growth. In a seminal analysis David Cameron (1978) examined several of the more important of these. Perhaps the most famous is that produced by Adolf Wagner (1883/1958). Wagner propounded a law of the increasing extension of state activity by which he asserted that the public economy expands in direct relation to expansion in the economy of a country. Cameron notes the work of Peacock and Wiseman (1967) and of Wildavsky (1975) that throws doubt upon Wagner's conclusion and that indicates no relationship or the opposite relationship respectively between public sector growth and general economic growth. In addition to these economic explanations, Cameron identifies a fiscal explanation. Downs (1960) argues that since public goods are inherently nondivisible so that costs and benefits cannot be directly linked and since each citizen has to pay for some programs from which no benefits are derived, public officials can spend large amounts of money only when the real costs can be concealed. Buchanan and Wagner (1977) then argue that complex and indirect payment structures produce a fiscal illusion leading to public outlays that are higher than would be the case with simple payment structures. According to the fiscal explanation, therefore, the public sector grows most in those countries having the greatest reliance on indirect taxes and social insurance contributions.

A third type of explanation identified by Cameron is political in nature. Periodic electoral competition brings promises to cut taxes and to increase spending by political parties and candidates who wish to win votes (Key, 1949; Kramer, 1971; Tufte, 1975, 1978; Nordhaus, 1975; Lindbeck, 1976). Moreover, incumbents are in a position to give some earnest of their promise. Hence countries with frequent elections are likely to have larger increases in their public sectors than countries with less intense electoral competition. The ideological orientation of governments in power has also been suggested as an explanation of public sector growth; leftist parties are perceived as more favorable to extension of governmental intervention in the economy than are parties of the center or right. Hibbs (1978), Davis and associates (1966, 1974), and Wildavsky (1975) suggest that priorities and policies vary over time as the partisan composition of government changes. Explanations based upon institutional structures of government compose a fourth type identified by Cameron. Downs (1964), Niskanen (1971), Wildavsky (1974), and Tarschys (1975) demonstrate that bureaucracies have internal pressures for expansion. A number of autonomous bureaucracies within a government are likely to produce greater public sector growth than is a single centralized controlling authority (Heidenheimer, 1975).

Countries are, of course, dependent upon the outside world in a number of ways and a fifth type of explanation takes this fact into account. Aggregate demand, especially in small economies, is partially a function of demand in the world market for domestically produced goods. Governments' abilities to manage aggregate demand and to control unemployment and capital formation are thereby limited. Their abilities to control production and pricing and to resist inflationary pressures from outside are also limited by the penetration of the domestic market by external producers. Lindbeck (1976) argues that governments can reduce these effects from the outside by increasing the scope of the public economy. Social insurance, tax systems, unemployment compensation, subsidies to maintain full employment, and other methods are responses to external dependence. Hence countries whose economies are most exposed to the international economy are the ones most likely to experience the greatest growth in their public sectors.

Cameron examines each of these types of explanation, using revenue data for eighteen OECD countries, and finds that the two variables most important for the explanation of the expansion of the public economy are the partisanship of government and the openness of the economy. He finds little or no evidence for the other explanations. The dominance of leftist parties in government he finds to be a sufficient condition for a large increase in the public sector but not a necessary one. Several countries without long experiences of leftist governments also had large public sector growths. All of these had relatively open economies. Indeed, Cameron found, the best explanation for why some countries expanded their public sectors rapidly and others did not was to be found in the varying degrees of exposure to and dependence upon external producers and consumers. Governments must use a variety of policies to shelter their economies from the competitive risks of the international economy. One of the most effective of these, especially for the small developed economies that are particularly open to the outside world, is a policy of income supplements in the form of social security schemes, health insurance, unemployment benefits, job training, employment subsidies to firms, and industrial capital—in short, an expansion of the public sector.

Cameron and Lindbeck before him have performed a major service in emphasizing the linkages that exist between individual national economies and the international economy. Indeed, explanations of public sector growth must take these into account if we are fully to understand the dynamics of that growth. Nevertheless, there is still a great deal of work to be done before a complete explanation of public sector expansion (and contraction) will have been found. Cameron's work, as important as it is in comparing explanations, is limited with respect to time, countries, and indicators. The empirical data come from only one and a half postwar decades and from the experience of only eighteen highly developed, capitalist countries. The measurement of the public sector is limited to revenue as a percentage of gross domestic product.

Any general theory of public sector growth must explain developments in countries that may be very different from those for which good data are easily available. In many ways the interesting questions are concerned with the comparisons of developed and less developed countries, of centrally planned and free market economies. A general theory must be based upon a much longer range of experience. Gordon Tullock (1982) has pointed out that government as a share of the nonagricultural economy 300 years ago was probably almost everywhere much larger than it is today. A "dense web of government controls" was extended over the entire economy. This web, he argues, began to collapse all over Europe in the early eighteenth century and its breakdown was most complete in the United States. Later, toward the end of the nineteenth century, this process began to be reversed and government growth has been most rapid since World War II. In Tullock's view all of the old theories to explain these changes have been demolished and no success-ful new ones have been created.

The chapters in this book go some way toward addressing some of the implications of these observations and toward considering new theories. A few deal with time spans longer than the postwar period. Others are con-cerned with the public sector in centrally planned economics. However, it has not been possible within the scope of a single collection of papers to cover all relevant topics. Instead, concentration has been directed toward the other major difficulty for theories of explanation for public sector growth, namely measurement.

Considerable attention has been given to explanations of the growth of government, or the public sector, or the public economy, but a great deal less has been devoted to what these are. It is necessary to have an exact notion of what is to be measured and why if explanation is to be valid, but arriving at this notion is not a simple task. Certainly the conception and measurement of the public sector should be broadened from the simple notion of revenues received by the government or even a consideration of both revenues and expenditures. The number of personnel employed, the extent of services per-formed, the quantity of laws enacted, and the degree of regulations pre-scribed are a few of the possible additional indicators for measurement. Attention not simply to central government but to all general government activity including semigovernment actors broadens the concept even more. A large portion of American public sector growth in the past three decades, for example, has been in the expansion of contractual services and in the increase of activity at the state and local levels. If those are excluded from the measurement of the public sector, the analysis is distorted.

Most of the chapters in this book speak to these questions. They explore the most appropriate concepts and indicators for identifying and measuring the public sector and its components. One of the most salient perceptions throughout this book is that the concept of the public sector is neither simple nor unidimensional. Richard Rose suggests in Chapter 9 that the concept must be disaggregated not only between state and government and between government and public sector, but also among functions and dimensions of each of these. This multidimensional set of concepts cannot be measured along a single continuum. Some aspects of government may grow while others stand still or even decline. Jürgen Kohl documents some of these variable rates of growth for a hundred-year period in eight Western European countries in Chapter 11 and Frank Gould looks at varying rates of change since 1950 in six developed countries in Chapter 12. Both of these investigations employ government expenditures to measure the public sector.

The public sector, as mentioned above however, is more than simply public finance. Rose urges the measurement of legislation, organizations, and programs also. These are considerably more difficult to measure than finances or public employment, but a comprehensive view of the public sector is impossible without indicators of this kind. Laws can be counted although no laws are of the same significance when enacted and their useful lives vary. Few laws get repealed, but many are eventually ignored. In principle, organizations can also be counted, but they differ in size, power, and purpose and their innovative and productive periods are shorter than their total life spans. Programs and policies are perhaps the least easily measured of the proposed indicators. Nevertheless, it is undeniable that the very difficulties in measurement point to the very great importance of these indicators in determining what is actually happening in the various components of the public sector.

Guy Peters and Martin Heisler, in Chapter 10, join Rose in examining several alternatives to budget data in the disaggregation of the concept of the public sector. They emphasize particularly the regulatory policies of government. Government regulation imposes public and private costs that do not show up as public expenditures. So also do informal regulation through mandated self-regulation, the use of "guidelines" and "jawboning," negative tax expenditures, various kinds of contracts, and government insurance schemes. These instruments are used by governments to exercise control over society. The costs that are incurred by the private sector in conforming to the changing scope and content of these instruments do not get counted in the usual measurements of government. The measurement of these costs and the effects of control is very difficult, but the effort must be made if we are to obtain a true picture of the size and scope of the public sector.

The particular contribution of the fourth section of this book, therefore, is to emphasize the need for a variety of indicators to catch a large array of movements in order to make very specific and very accurate statements about how big government is and how rapidly it is growing. It is not entirely surprising that this section has least to offer in completed empirical results. The chapters are conceptually the most ambitious and, as the authors of both of them admit, there is an enormous amount of work yet to be done in conceptualization, in indicator construction, and in data gathering.

The other chapters deal with the more traditional indicators of national accounting, government budgets, and government employment. The underlying assumption, of course, is that measures such as revenues or expenditures as a percentage of the gross domestic product or public employment as a proportion of total employment give us a good, or at least preliminary, idea of the relative size of public sectors across time and across countries. Nevertheless, a great variety of approaches is possible even within this underlying assumption.

Indeed, the fundamental question of the boundaries of the public sector is still open. Karl Deutsch argued in the Berlin conference that absolutely everything not fully private ought to be considered a part of the public sector. The private was taken to mean those areas of life in which government with its authoritative decision making is involved in no way whatsoever. The measurement of the size of this nonprivate arena is important, Deutsch asserted, in order to compare countries in terms of their inclinations toward the public as opposed to the private organization of national life. Omitting the enormous market-type activities of government and ignoring throughput, Deutsch asserted, biases the analysis when the political significance of the public sector is being examined. By throughput Deutsch referred to the total income and total expenditures of government including transfers among all departments, agencies, semipublic bodies, and nationalized industries.

As for the Rose, Peters, and Heisler positions, there are considerable measurement difficulties in what Deutsch suggests. Net revenues and expenditures for nationalized industries are not difficult to obtain, but the measurement of throughput is a much more complicated matter. Indeed, economists have avoided efforts along this line, feeling that it involves too much double counting. There is also a question of what kind of denominator could be used for a ratio to be employed in comparisons. The scheme for collecting comparable cross-national data on government expenditure and revenue, developed by the International Monetary Fund (IMF), is expressly limited to the nonmarket activities of government and to net receipts and expenditures. When government is not taxing but selling, when it is providing goods and services with direct payment in return, it is considered by the IMF to be engaged in the market economy. These transactions are therefore excluded from the IMF data published in the *Government Finance Statistics Yearbooks*. Slowly the detail reported in this annual source is being expanded and more and more attention is being given to the multiple levels of government. It is becoming a valuable source of traditionally defined indicators of government size.

There are multiple ways of looking at the traditional data. The public sector, for example, can be examined as a competitor for the use of disposable income produced by the market sector. The development of the market sector is one of the dominant forces underlying the growth of expenditures in the public sector; production from the market must support the nonproductive activities of the public sector. The market produces goods and services sold through a market mechanism and continuity of production is dependent upon adequate income from market sales. The public sector is dependent upon grants rather than market prices. The value of the market sector can be seen as a financial base that provides funds for public expenditure. Hence the ratio of nonmarketed purchases to marketed output measures the pressure on the market sector from government-financed incomes and expenditures. Henny van der Wielen examines the interaction of the public and market sectors in the Netherlands using this model in Chapter 4. In Chapter 5 Walter Eltis also analyzes both conventional national account statistics and statistics revised to reflect more clearly the actual burden of the public sector on the private in Britain.

Measurement of the public sector becomes more complicated if comparisons are made across types of economic systems. Western-based notions of the public sector are difficult to apply in the centrally planned economies of Eastern Europe, where the government owns nearly all the means of production and where nearly everyone works for the government. The conceptual and statistical frameworks used there are stated not in terms of the government sector versus the private sector but in terms of productive versus nonproductive activities. If the public sectors of East and West are to be compared with each other, some effort must be made to find common definitions. Gertrude Schroeder and John Pitzer, in Chapter 6, examine the growth of government in the Soviet Union and other Eastern European countries in terms both of national accounts and of employment data. Donna Bahry, on the other hand, in Chapter 7 makes use of Soviet budget data to examine public expenditure in the Soviet Union. She finds that in spite of its alleged advantage in considering externalities in planning public goods, the Soviet Union has not had an upward spiral in expenditures since World War II. This is partially due to the countervailing trends in individual expenditure categories and partially due to devolution in financing public programs. Although these programs are within the public sector, social consumption goods become less public, that is, less available to individuals outside the factory or farm that finances them. This indicates an important change in the Soviet Union. These two studies are presented in this book in order to provide a greater appreciation of what must be involved in measuring the public sector than can be obtained from Western developed economies alone.

The primary example of the measurement of public employment in this book is provided by Richard Eichenberg in Chapter 8. Eichenberg examines public employment in twelve Western European democracies since the middle of the nineteenth century. He presents a few of his results here and he discusses the difficulties and ambiguities involved in defining the bureaucracy and in matching data to the resulting concepts. Eichenberg's data suggest that war experience is one of the primary stimuli for public sector expansion. Otherwise there has been a slow incremental increase in public employment over the last century. Significantly less work has been done on public employment than on public expenditures and revenues. A great deal has yet to be accomplished in concepts and indicators.

Most of the chapters in this book are focused on the problem of measurement, not because measurement in itself is sufficient, but because it is both a legitimate and necessary step along the way to explaining government size and growth. The intimate connection between measurement and explanation is apparent in these papers. Each is based upon some underlying conception of what is behind public sector growth. Some of these conceptions are more explicit than others and the movement from measurement to explanation has gone further in some than in others. Nevertheless, any good measurement system must necessarily be based upon some notion of what is important to be analyzed and therefore of what is important to an explanation.

For this reason, of course, it is unlikely that the boundaries of the public sector and the significant details of its internal divisions will ever be agreed upon once and for all. Different analyses have different purposes and this is as it should be. The requirements set by these differing purposes involve varying sets of indicators. A carefully constructed, generally accepted set of definitions could close more analytical doors than it would open. Measurements still need to be chosen with particular questions in mind.

Some of the chapters in this book have a more direct interest in explanations of public sector growth. Jürgen Kohl, in Chapter 11, examines structures of public finance in four major Western European and four Scandinavian countries in the period between 1870 and 1970. He combines the extended time perspective of historical research with the comparative perspective of multicountry analysis. He discusses some of the problems involved in public expenditure classification, examines the changing priorities in the structure of public expenditure, and suggests two models of development change which might appropriately be applied to the data. Frank Gould, in Chapter 12, also disaggregates public expenditure into categories for six postwar developed economies. He finds that these categories have grown at different rates and are influenced in different ways by varying factors. He examines annual time-series data on general government public expenditure disaggregated by central versus local government; by current versus capital goods, services, and transfers; and by functions. Two main growth areas are identified: transfers primarily by the central government and local government expenditures on goods and services. These two analyses measure the public sector and its components and then attempt to find patterns in the data and to make use of the potentialities that they offer for explanation of public sector growth.

The final two chapters in Section V are more explicitly theoretical in their orientation. Franz Lehner and Ulrich Widmaier, in Chapter 13, present a sociological explanation of the development of the public sector in capitalist societies. Market failure, growth of government, and government failure are explained in terms of socioeconomic structure and organization. It is suggested that major factors for explanation are density of economic organization, societal differentiation, and the scope and density of the organization of interests. A careful argument is made for the crucially important sociological influences on government. That is, market failure is defined not in the narrow sense of economic efficiency. Efficient economic markets may produce prices, income distributions, or conditions of competition that are unacceptable to significant parts of the population. This lack of social or political acceptance leads to demand for government intervention. Consideration of these noneconomic forces is a valuable addition to the search for the causes of government growth and decline. Lehner and Widmaier make suggestions for the empirical testing of their arguments, but they have not been able to undertake these tests.

Manfred Schmidt, in Chapter 14, is able to go further in empirical testing. Schmidt examines the growth of the tax state, as measured by current revenues from taxes and social security contributions taken as a proportion of gross domestic product, in twenty-one postwar industrial democracies. He finds that the causal mechanisms shaping the rate of expansion of the tax state vary over time. Its rapid expansion in the 1950s was the result of a politics of convergence; less-developed tax states tended to catch up with the more developed ones. In the 1960s and early 1970s party politics became more important in the determination of which tax states grew most rapidly. From 1974 extraparliamentary politics became the primary explanatory factor. Schmidt is able to add to the discussion of causes of public sector growth the flexibility of changing explanations over time. What is still needed, of course, is the integration of the changing explanations into a more complex single explanation.

That is exactly what is needed in the fields of public finance, public choice, and comparative political analysis. As Meltzer and Richard (1981) have observed, there is as yet no generally accepted explanation of the increase in the size of the public sector and, for that matter, no single accepted measure of the size of government. This is not for a lack of effort. Larkey and associates (1981) provide a very long bibliography of research on theorizing about the growth and decline of government, and Brunner (1978) presents a useful essay on the subject. The chapters in this book are offered in the hope that they will contribute to the search for an explanation that will make sense to scholars studying the problem.

Finally, underlying most of the studies in this book is the concern, if not the assumption, that the public sector is getting out of control in most developed countries. Perhaps the consideration of the proper scope of the public sector is best dealt with in Chapters 2 and 3. In the first of these R. A. Musgrave proposes that the size of the public sector is correct if the social goods provided are of the amount that would be bought and paid for voluntarily by consumers if availability could be made contingent on price payments, that is, if Lindahl prices could be charged. He examines several hypotheses that have been advanced to show that excess provision of services beyond that obtained under Lindahl pricing occurs, but he rejects these as unconvincing and as unsupported by the data. Voters in the long run, he says, get the level of services they desire. The public sector is the size that it is because that is the size that the voters want it to be.

Jonathan Pincus and Geoffrey Brennan disagree. Endowments and relative prices may change with changes in public expenditure, they argue, and these have consequences on the composition and distribution of final output. The prime consequence is to be seen not in a shift toward items of government expenditure and away from other items, but in terms of a shift away from private consumption items that are heavily taxed to those more lightly taxed. Moreover, for government-provided goods and services other than the traditional ones such as defense and justice, it is possible to buy additional amounts in the private market, but the excess provision cannot be sold. For example, one can buy private education in addition to that offered publicly, but one cannot sell one's right to public education. The expansion of the public sector, therefore, limits choice that properly belongs to the individual. The issue, like the others, cannot be settled in this book. Nevertheless, the arguments are presented with the hope that they will contribute to the ongoing political, economic, and social analyses of the role of government in the modern world.

REFERENCES

BRUNNER, K. (1978) "Reflections on the political economy of government: the persistent growth of government." Schweizerische Zeitschrift fuer Volkswirtschaft und Statistik 114: 649-680.

BUCHANAN, J. M. and R. E. WAGNER (1977) Democracy in Deficit: The Political Legacy of Lord Keynes. New York: Academic Press.

CAMERON, D. (1978) "The expansion of the public economy: a comparative analysis." American Political Science Review 72: 1243-1261.

DAVIS, O. A., M. A. H. DEMPSTER, and A. WILDAVSKY (1974) "Toward a predictive theory of the federal budgetary process." British Journal of Political Science 4: 419-452.

——— (1966) "A theory of the budgetary process." American Political Science Review 60: 529-547.

DOWNS, A. (1964) Inside Bureaucracy. Boston: Little, Brown.

_____ (1960) "Why the government budget is too small in a democracy." World Politics 12: 541-563.

HEIDENHEIMER, A. J. ET AL. (1975) Comparative Public Policy. New York: St. Martin's Press.

HIBBS, D. A., Jr. (1978) "On the political economy of long-run trends in strike activity." British Journal of Political Science 8: 153-175.

KEY, V. O. (1949) Southern Politics. New York: Knopf.

KRAMER, G. H. (1971) "Short-term fluctuations in U.S. voting behavior, 1896-1964." American Political Science Review 65: 131-143.

LARKEY, P. D., C. STOLP, and M. WINER (1981) "Theorizing about the growth and decline of government: a research assessment." Journal of Public Policy 1: 157-220.

LINDBECK, A. (1976) "Stabilization policy in open economics with endogenous politicians." American Economic Review 66: 1-19.

_____ (1975) "Business cycles, politics, and international economic dependence." Skandinaviska Enskoven Bank Quarterly Review 2: 53-68.

MELTZER, A. H. and S. F. RICHARD (1981) "A rational theory of the size of government." Journal of Political Economy 89: 914-927.

NISKANEN, W. A. (1971) Bureaucracy and Representative Government. Chicago: Aldine-Atherton.

NORDHAUS, W. D. (1975) "The political business cycle." Review of Economic Studies 42: 160-190.

PEACOCK, A. R. and J. WISEMAN (1967) The Growth of Public Expenditure in the United Kingdom. London: Allen & Unwin.

TARSCHYS, D. (1975) "The growth of public expenditures: nine modes of explanation." Scandinavian Political Studies 10: 9-31.

TUFTE, E. (1978) Political Control of the Economy. Princeton: Princeton University Press.

_____ (1975) "Determinants of the outcome of midterm congressional elections." American Political Science Review 69: 812-826.

TULLOCK, G. (1982) "Public choice and government growth." Center for Study of Public Choice, Virginia Polytechnic Institute and State University, Working Paper CE 11-1-82.

WAGNER, A. (1883) "The nature of the fiscal economy," reprinted in Richard A. Musgrave and Alan R. Peacock (1958) Classics in the Theory of Public Finance. London: Macmillan.

WILDAVSKY, A. (1975) Budgeting: A Comparative Theory of Budgetary Processes. Boston: Little, Brown.

_____ (1974) The Politics of the Budgetary Process. Boston: Little, Brown.

PART II

How Large Should the Public Sector Be?

CHAPTER 1

THE PUBLIC SECTOR
Some Concepts and Indicators

KARL W. DEUTSCH

What is the public sector—and why does its growth or its shrinking matter? Why does it make any difference? Why do we want to know about it?

As a matter of definition we may call the public sector the opposite of the private sector. If so we assume that the two form a complete partition: What is not in the one sector must be in the other. From the viewpoint of structure, the private sector consists of the realm of private property. The public sector elements are not protected and conserved by private property rights and habits, deeply anchored in the culture and often in the family system. Private or family property in one form or another is thousands of years old. By contrast, a large part of public property is of relatively recent origin and its changes have created few, if any, deep-set habits.

Contemporary events in the modern private sector in most countries are largely steered by market processes of supply and demand, and among them particularly by the tendency of mobile capital to flow to places where its owners may expect the highest rates of reproduction. This is sometimes abbreviated and simplified in popular Marxist formulations by simply saying that capital seeks places of its highest reproduction. This is semantically wrong. Capital does not seek anything, people do. However, one could argue that from a macro point of view capital could be shown to tend to flow there, but even that is not correct. Observably capital goes where human beings expect it to be reproduced at a higher rate. Capital went to Iran but was not in fact reproduced at a very high rate for the creditors of the Shah. In the end they lost their money. What happened in Iran is only one of the many cases where people made dubious investments, such as lending money to the Turkish Sultan, the Russian Tsar, or to any number of other dubious debtors in the course of history. It is not so, therefore, that capital behaves with the rationality that the phrase "seeks this or that place" would seem to imply.

In any case the movements in the private sector are steered by people's subjective expectations, that is, by expectations developed in the interplay with the distribution of past events and experiences and therefore to some limited degree with objective probability. Events in the public sector are mainly steered by political processes, including administrative bureaucratic ones. In the private sector property rights decide; there money talks and votes. It generally functions as the medium of decision and it is very unequally distributed among individuals and groups. In the public sector political power and influence are the general media that those in power may use to change the values of those they influence to more closely resemble their own. Power and influence are also unequally distributed, but their distribution is not necessarily the same as that of money. In general, productive resources such as land, capital, labor, and information are difficult to mobilize and reallocate quickly on a very large scale in the private sector. Property rights, diversities of interests, private contracts and commitments, and the inclination of competing owners to a secrecy all stand in the way. Many of these obstacles to structural change or rapid and large-scale allocation also exist in the public sector but to a much lesser degree. We may hypothesize that for either warfare or social reform and social change, public sector resources on the average are more easily disposable by governments. They can be reallocated more easily by governments, by reformers, or by revolutionaries.

That does not imply that the private sector ordinarily is devoid of change. The economist Joseph Schumpeter spoke of the "creative destruction" that occurs as a result of market competition. On the scale of generations and centuries the results of such market changes may be very large indeed, as they were in the course of the Industrial Revolution in Britain and Western Europe. On a shorter time scale there are few if any changes in the private markets that can compare in speed and scope of their effects with the introduction of general elementary education or of a social security system (that is, an old age pension or a national health insurance) or with the raising of large military forces. All such large-scale changes happened largely in the public sectors of the countries concerned in the 1930s and 1940s and later.

The size of the public sector ought to be correlated, therefore, with the capabilities of governments and of political systems and over long periods with the salience of politics and the levels of political participation. Whether in fact this is so, empirical studies will have to show. In the meantime many people have assumed it. Some saw the public sector as replacing private greed by disinterested public service. Others saw it as replete with bureaucratic inefficiency and waste. Max Weber saw bureaucracy as rational; Northcote Parkinson saw it as the opposite. Socialists of the democratic persuasion often have hoped that the growth of the public sector would bring a new social order—socialism—nearer. Radicals often have believed that revolution and dictatorship would work through a drastically restructured, planned, and growing public sector leading to the same result. Opponents of socialism have seen the growth of the public sector most often as a sign of "creeping socialism," if not "the road to serfdom," as the economist Friedrich von Hayek once called it. In this way persons with radically different values have read in the growth or shrinking of the public sector a portent of their hopes or fears.

If the size of the public sector is an indicator of its potential influence on the rest of the society within a state—and if it thus matters to the people's subjective expectations about a wide variety of economic, political, social, and cultural developments, and perhaps to the objective probabilities of some of these developments—how is that sector to be defined and measured in a systematic and verifiable manner?

How Much Precision Is Indispensable?

It may be useful from the outset to think of the public sector as a probabilistic factor and not as something that determines precisely what will happen to some other process, but as a factor that has something to do with the likelihood of the speed, direction, and order of magnitude of other processes. In short, the public sector is not a measure of quantitative and qualitative social change; it is at best a factor and at least an indicator. The public sector, so defined, indicates probabilities of other social changes, and as with all indicators, the correlation between the indicator and the indicated is not perfect. We do not live in a deterministic world where every factor completely determines every other; we live in a probabilistic world.

To this comes a second point: In order to find out what the likely risks or opportunities of social and political development and change are, we must make judgments based on incomplete data; dubious information; and, to some extent, information that is not completely verifiable. Luckily, comparability is not, like virginity, an all-or-nothing property. There are degrees of comparability. There are margins of error and I would like to recall once again the proposition by the Indian statistician, P. A. Mahalanobis, that one needs information only to the degree of accuracy that is critical for the decision that one has to make. If I want to know whether I should take an umbrella along because rain is likely—and because I wish to go out and not to get drenched—it is enough if I know that there is a fair chance of rain. I do not need perfectly accurate, deterministic information. If I know whether I should take out insurance at a particular level for a certain contingency against which I want to be protected, once again I make a judgment of likelihood, and I may, depending on my own values, add a small or large safety margin to it.

All of us, citizens, governments, and social scientists, also have to act often under the pressure of time. In this respect we are not really situationally too different from the emergency ward physician. A patient is brought in; he is bleeding and he is making indistinct moans. Within a few minutes we may get a temperature reading, a quick and imperfect X-ray, the heart rate, even a cardiogram; but we will know that our information is very incomplete. We may know that the symptoms do not completely fit any one of the standard symptoms, and we may not have the exact history of just what happened to the person before he was brought to the hospital. If we wrote a memo saying that we are going to find comparabilities very limited and that "more research is needed," we might just as well order a coffin. Instead, we have to act and do the best we can with the information in hand within the time available.

In times of war people engaged in intelligence research have to do much the same thing. They may be asked whether a particular port is available for landing and whether it will be lightly or heavily defended. Within a few days a landing attempt will be made or cancelled. The information is incomplete; it is not completely comparable. There are various gaps in the data, and yet the best possible judgment has to be made. Then the decision maker—comparing the uncertain probabilistic prediction or statement of fact, comparing this with his own scale of values (landing early may or may not be very important)—must make the decision.

These examples illustrate a general principle. In medical, military, and safety engineering research, as well as in political and social science, one seeks unceasingly the best and most complete knowledge, but one also must search for incomplete and imperfect knowledge that can be applied under the pressure of need and of time so as to improve human chances for survival. To improve even that imperfect knowledge surely is a worthwhile task. Assumptions about facts and suppositions about one's own values are then the two sets of data that must be combined in the process of decision making. In order to find out where society is going, what is going to happen to the highly industrialized countries in particular, but even to the world in general, we must therefore do the best we can to find the least inaccurate, the least misleading, the least unusable indicators, including those that may suggest best what is happening to the government sector. If we do that then we may consider even a whole scale of such indicators.

Eight Indicators of the Public Sector

(1) The first, and it is difficult to estimate, is the *total social product of society*, which should include, for instance, the unpaid work of housewives or the unpaid work of children who learn in school. Remember, if somebody

would use an electric device or connect two copper wires in a computer, this is called work and goes into the gross national product. Two grey cells connecting in a baby's head do not enter the gross national product, although the learning that goes on in the heads of children is still considerably larger in every generation than any amount of copper connections joined in computers.

(2) Another concept is the *monetized or monetizable set of goods and services*. This is what we call the *gross national product* (GNP); we ordinarily take that which appears on the market and add an estimate for the market value of crops that peasants consume at home. The reason why we do not do that with the housewives is probably that a government knows how to get grain away from peasants. It has often enough been done. However, there is no good way of getting a housewife's labor away from her family. Governments as a rule have not been temerarious enough to try and the efforts of scholars to add further corrections for nonmonetary income to such estimates have remained limited.

(3) We may then go on to a subset of the gross national product, the *public sector*, which involves anything and everything within the GNP not on the market.

(4) We go finally down to the government sector, a part of the public sector devoted to administrative, political, and military purposes. The government budget and the public sector budget are two indicators of what one might call the discretionary income of nations. George Katona has pointed out that the market becomes very difficult in a country where a large number of individual consumers have a discretionary income, income not wholly taken up by basic needs and fixed obligations so that people can choose whether to spend it or not, and if they spend it, what to spend it on and where. The government sector indicates something about the discretionary income of nations and of political systems. The larger the share of the government sector and the larger the GNP is, the more resources the nation could reallocate, if desired, for politically chosen purposes.

Having said that much about the public sector in general, let us consider very quickly some particular bodies of data.

(5) There is the *central government revenue*, which is usually smaller than the central government expenditures. The difference may consist of foreign loans or subsidies or plain inflation. In general, if one takes government revenues one will get lower figures than if one takes government expenditures.

(6) We then find beyond the central government the *general government*, or the total aggregate of central government, provincial or state government, and municipal governments. We may again distinguish general government revenues and general government expenditures. We usually find that data are excluded when definitions are chosen for ideological reasons (more about this will be said later).

(7) The next step would be to take the *general government* budget, let us say revenues once again, *plus the revenues of public institutions*, such as the post office, the social security administration, the national science foundation, the atomic energy commission, the national health service (in Britain), and so on. If for ideological reasons a government wishes to make a government and a country look more private than it is, it excludes these data from the government budget and adds only the net gain or the net loss, for example, the net deficit of the post office. It may do the same with many other public institutions; thus the turnover of the public sector is artificially diminished because to the government turnover data are added only the net gain or losses of the public agencies. By coupling two different things together, a market-oriented regime may make the government sector seem smaller. Many Western countries follow this practice. Communist countries, which favor the public sector, add cooperatives of farmers and cooperatives of craftsmen to the "socialist sector" with the result that the so-called socialist sector is inflated. Depending on their ideology, people fiddle with the figures in one direction or in the other, but the figures can be manipulated in any direction. In order to be positively comparable it would be better to always count the total turnover of the public institutions either on the revenue side or on the expenditure side.

(8) Finally, we can go still further and add to the general government and the public institutions the nationalized industries. This is seen in mining in Great Britain, or in many countries, the railroad, the telegraph and telephone companies, or, in France, the Renault factory, which is public. (When one sees a Peugeot, one sees private enterprise. If a Renault car should overtake it, one would be seeing creeping socialism.)

The widest concept of the public sector is the general government revenues or expenditures on the revenue/expenditure side, respectively, plus the public institutions plus the nationalized industries. It is this large definition that in its turn may serve as one indicator for the capacity of a government to influence the total rates of waste and investment in its country.

I should not go one step further, as Kenneth Galbraith sometimes has proposed; Galbraith speaks of quasi-public industries that are privately owned but serve one single public customer. Most intercontinental rockets are bought by governments. There is nobody else buying spacecraft or artillery. By and large space industries or armaments industries in fact exist for single customers within a nation—monopsonists—and in the world market they compete under conditions of oligopoly.

From Indicators to More Questions

One thing to be done with these data is the computation of *centralization ratios*. What is the ratio of central government revenue to expenditures, to total general government revenue and expenditure, or even to the total public sector? You could refine that and in the agencies ask which of these are again nationally central, like social security, which of these are state or regional or communal. Communal water works presumably belong to the decentralized part of the public sector, while the U.S. Department of Energy belongs to the central part of the public sector. For different kinds of political analysis one could use the data most appropriate for each.

The Public Sector
on Conflicts Over
Rates of Wages and Investments

In the private enterprise markets of the nineteenth century, wage rates were largely set by the forces of the market. External costs in social suffering, in public health, in illegitimacy and political instability eventually led people to move away from it. In the dictatorships of communist Eastern Europe, wage rates are set essentially by the political processes of centralized bureaucratic dictatorships. To some extent the wages had to be set in both West and East in such a way as to attract enough young people into entering the occupations in sufficient numbers to meet economic and social needs. To some extent, therefore, there remains the possibility of a "candidates' strike" or refusal of young people to try to enter certain occupations. In other words, there is one irreducible market there under each economic system. It is the market of young job entrants, or career choices that no government or economic system can completely control.

In the pluralistic democracies of Western Europe and North America wages setting by consensual bargaining developed. While there is a good deal of political theater involved in this—going down to the deadline, negotiating dramatically at midnight, stopping the clock, threatening strikes, taking a strike vote of the membership—nevertheless, wages are most often set by agreement among the parties, with the government being a more or less visible or discrete partner behind the scenes.

However, it works in so imperfect a way that we have come to what today we call the "crisis of the welfare state." For while labor by and large rarely engages in very prolonged, bitter-end strikes about wages, another kind of strike—the investors' strike—may have become more frequent.

The higher the wages in a country, the more welfare oriented its network of social security. The larger its nonmilitary public sector, the less inclined are investors to invest their money in that country. They prefer Hong Kong, Singapore, South Korea, Taiwan, and Brazil, in a pinch. In short, they prefer countries with low wages and dictatorial governments. When you read that the child mortality rate is above one hundred per thousand in a country but that the return rate on private investment is ten percent and that the probability of creditors getting paid looks good, many newspapers call this regime "beneficial," at least in their business pages.

Perhaps it may become possible some day to settle a large part of the amounts and rates of investment by negotiations among the relevant interest groups and agencies, private and public. This might include the investible resources of medical and insurance funds of all kinds, private and public. Then it might be possible to have a much steadier rate of employment than we have today. This is in part a function of the size of the public sector and in part a function of the willingness of what in Germany are called the social partners—the labor unions and the private enterprise firms—to cooperate. Austria has a particularly large public sector; it has to some extent succeeded in coordinating the investment practices of the health insurance organizations, of the retirement funds, of the trade unions, and of the various public agencies. It is claimed—there are people who know the Austrian economy much better than I do—that as a result it has mitigated the business cycle to some degree.

Once again, how practical such practices in the future will be I do not know, but the hypothesis that the size of the public sector would make a major difference in making such policies practicable or not is relevant to this book. The efforts of Austria and France from Metternich to Kreisky and from Colbert to Mitterand may tell us something about it. It is quite possible that in some other country the leadership toward a more stable and agreed-upon rate of investment will be taken by some of the very large corporations such as insurance companies. We do not know.

We would like to know, apart from whatever happens on the private sector side, how big the public sector is now, how big it has been in past decades, how large it seems likely to become in the next ten, twenty, or 30 years. Such empirical knowledge is an important condition for the development of better and more relevant theories in regard to these problems.

CHAPTER 2

THE GROWTH OF GOVERNMENT
Do the Figures
Tell Us What
We Want to Know?

GEOFFREY BRENNAN
JONATHAN PINCUS

Less than seven percent of gross national product (GNP) of the United States passed through the government budget in 1900; by 1970 the percentage was well over thirty and rising. In constant value terms total public spending rose sixtyfold in seventy years; per capita spending rose from about $60 per head to $1200 (at 1958 prices). The American story is by no means unique; virtually every country, independent of constitutional stance and of ideological color, exhibits a similar pattern. In the United Kingdom and in the Federal Republic of Germany, for example, public sectors that had respectively absorbed about seven and twelve percent of GNP in 1890, absorbed about forty percent each in 1970. Tax rates that our grandparents would have rebelled at are now the norm. A spectacular political and economic transformation seems to have gone on, for which many competing explanations exist.[1]

This chapter directs attention to questions that are logically prior to explanations of the growth of government: What is it that needs to be explained? What precisely do budget figures tell us, and what remains speculative? Most important, what exactly do we want to know? These are not trivial issues. Many analysts have drawn conclusions from the data that may not be

AUTHORS' NOTE: We wish to thank Peter G. Warr for impressing on us the importance of "crowding out." Our chapter generalizes and extends his analysis in Warr (1982).

justified after more careful study. Also, simple, obvious, and significant conclusions, readily drawn from the figures, have been substantially ignored. Our simple framework for the analysis of the public sector helps to focus on what is central, clarifies what is of interest, and isolates some of the problems with taking the data at face value.

What Do We Want to Know?

Government growth impinges on the well-being of individuals in society. It is therefore interesting not intrinsically (like sex) but for its *consequences*. The justification for this "consequentialist" approach is twofold. First, if our concerns are ultimately normative, some consideration of the effects of government growth seems obligatory. Second, if the purpose is to explain government growth by political and economic forces, whether those forces are expressed as the interests of particular groups or as aspects of abstract categories such as efficiency or justice, one needs to know the extent to which the effects of government growth were in fact such as to improve the lot of the interests in question or to further justice or efficiency.

We claim that the important consequences of public expenditure growth are on the composition of total production as among different commodities (the product mix) and on the distribution of the total product as among different individuals.

These consequences can be illustrated using the matrix table of Table 2.1. The entries depict the level of output, x_i, consumed by each individual, j. Each column involves a different consumption item; each row depicts a different individual. The consumption items, the x_is, constitute in principle everything from which the individual derives satisfaction, and include all those items purchased directly in markets, those acquired by barter, and those distributed by the state. Protection from foreign aggression, protection from crime, street lighting, education, and health are included as x_is,

TABLE 2.1   Consumption Pattern

| | *Consumption Items* | | | | | | |
Individuals	x_1	x_2	x_3	x_4	x_5	x_n	*Total Income*
1							
2							
...					...		
S						x^j_i	
TOTAL							*National Income*

along with food, clothing, entertainment, leisure activities, and electricity. Column sums equal the total consumption of the various goods for the society of S individuals: if Mr. 1 consumes 3 oranges, and Mr. 2 consumes 6, they consume 9 oranges between them. Clearly, we cannot add across columns in the same way: 3 oranges, 2 haircuts, and 6 medical treatments do not directly add to any meaningful total. Accordingly, in forming row totals we need to weigh items by their prices to obtain an aggregate consumption expenditure figure for each individual measured in standard dollar units. The value of this aggregate consumption expenditure figure represents the individual's income, and the sum of such incomes determines total (national) income.[2]

We will rank individuals so that individual 1 is the richest and individual S the poorest in the initial period (1900, perhaps). Although the relative income positions of those individuals may change, this ranking represents a convenient means of ordering the individuals who make up the group and assists the analysis of changes in income distribution.

Our central object is to compare the matrix in Table 2.1 at different times so as to investigate how changes in the level of government-budgeted spending have influenced the composition of consumption and its distribution between individuals. These things will typically change over time without any contributing change in government spending, but in order to focus strongly on the consequences of government expenditure growth, it is crucial to conduct a conceptual experiment for which any incidental changes are abstracted. That is, we treat a change in the level of budgeted government spending as an initiating (exogenous) change and examine the effects on the matrix in Figure 9.1, holding all other parameters in the system constant.

Parameter constancy does not deny the possibility of individuals adjusting their consumption patterns in response to the change in public spending or involve ignoring the taxation side of fiscal transactions. It does, however, abstract from any changes in the level or distribution of income, or in individuals' tastes, that are not consequent upon the public expenditure change. We aim for a conceptually closed experiment.

The Basic Analytics

How might the change in the level of budgeted public expenditure induce changes in the entries in the matrix in Table 2.1 after all relevant adjustments have been made? The government expenditure increase might change tastes, it might change endowments, or it might change relative prices. Having ruled changes of the first type as being outside our scope, we are solely concerned with the second and third categories.

Endowments are those things that individuals have legal rights to hold, to consume, or to exchange as a matter of law, such as their labor, their accumulated wealth, and so on. Government can affect endowments by appropriating an individual's property and giving it to someone else. Or, government may remove some of individuals' endowment and return it in another form: for example, levy a tax on their consumption of privately provided goods, and return it to them in the form of defense. Consequently, when the government alters the composition or distribution of total output in Table 2.1 via a direct "expenditure operation"—either a transfer of cash or direct provision of some good—without affecting relative prices, the result is a change in endowments.

"Relative prices" are the terms at which an individual can transform endowments into another bundle of economic quantities that are presumably more preferred. Such transformation represents the essence of economic activity. For example, individuals may possess an endowment of labor time, part of which they transform into goods via money by exchanging some for wages and part of which they consume directly as leisure. The terms at which they transform time into goods constitute the price of goods relative to time, or what we normally refer to as the individual's wage rate. Changes in that wage rate and in other prices, such as the price of butter relative to jam, will induce corresponding changes in the individual's consumption pattern because the individual will tend to buy more of the cheaper things and less of the more expensive.

Now such relative price changes are the sine qua non of economists' analysis of markets and of institutional changes more generally. Changes in endowments, by contrast, tend to be ignored, for good reasons. A change in the composition of individuals' endowment in a market setting has no effect as such on the composition of those individuals' final consumption. The bundle of goods that they most prefer is independent of the composition of the bundle they start with.

A simple example might elucidate this claim. Suppose Mr. S can freely exchange one apple for one orange in the market. The first time S comes to market, endowed with ten apples and six oranges, he trades two of his apples for two oranges and retains eight of each for consumption. The eighth apple is worth just more than an extra orange to him, but a ninth apple is worth just less than an extra orange to him, otherwise he would have consumed at least nine apples and at most seven oranges. S next time comes to market with sixteen apples only. By assumption, his tastes have not changed and he can still get one orange in exchange for each apple he gives up. He will again end up consuming eight apples and eight oranges: The eighth apple will still be worth slightly more to him than a ninth orange. He will, of course, do more trading, but the composition of his preferred consumption bundle will remain unaffected by the change in the composition of his endowments.

The economist's instincts therefore are to ignore changes in endowments as a way in which changes in the composition of final output can be wrought.

The relevant analytical rule is: *Cherchez the relative price effects* (see section below). Now, the claim that this focus on relative prices is the appropriate analytic method when examining changes in public expenditures is neither obvious nor wholly correct. There is one important case where a change in endowments does translate into a corresponding change in the final consumption mix. Nonetheless, in a significantly large number of cases the change in endowments may have either no effect at all on the composition of final consumption or it may alter that composition in a perverse way.

We need now to distinguish among categories of final consumption. First, are goods provided wholly in the market; the state is not directly involved, and expenditure on such goods appears nowhere in public budgets. Second, goods are directly subsidized by the state and are featured to that extent in public budgets. Suppose the state subsidizes the use of fertilizers at the rate of x per pound. Budgeted public subsidy expenditure will not typically represent total expenditure on fertilizers; fertilizers will still cost something to the subsidized users. The characteristic feature of this category is that the public activity alters the price of the subsidized activity relative to the prices of other things.

The third category deals with the bulk of public expenditure, that is, goods and services that the government provides directly such as defense, law and order, public transport, and public education. These public expenditures do change endowments, but need not directly affect the relative prices of the expenditure items themselves. Because of the overwhelming predominance of this category, most of the ensuing pages deal with it.[3]

Government Expenditure Growth and Private Expenditure Adjustment

What effects do changes in the level of public expenditures on items in this third category have on the composition of final consumption? Immediately, it is useful to make further tripartite distinction:

(1) Those goods (such as national defense and space research) that are provided *solely by the state*.
(2) Those goods that are provided by the state but are such that individuals can purchase additional quantities of them in the open market (possibly in another form). For example, protection from crime may be partly provided via state police services, and partly via guard dogs, burglar alarms, watchmen, and other market-provided services. This group of goods we can characterize as being subject to *private supplementation*.
(3) Those goods that are provided by the state and that can be consumed only in place of some alternative marketed source of similar service. For example, one cannot live in a government-provided house and a privately owned house simultaneously nor can one typically supplement government housing with

privately owned extensions (though one may be able to supplement housing services by expenditure on furnishings or garden). One cannot, likewise, attend government and private schools simultaneously. Private and public provision are *substitutes*.

The effect of a change in public expenditure in each of these subcategories is quite different.

Consider goods in the first group, where there is no private supplementation or substitution. If the government increases its defense spending (the price of defense held constant), there is an immediate corresponding increase in the consumption of defense by all individuals. The only significant analytical questions about goods solely supplied by government are whether the expenditure increase reflects an output increase or a price increase and whether increases in population size imply corresponding increases in aggregate consumption; we set these important issues aside. Our first conclusion is that changes in endowments due to public expenditure increase will imply a corresponding change in the final consumption mix *if the public expenditure in question falls into the first group* (goods solely supplied by government).

This is not the case, however, for items in the second or third groups. Where there is private supplementation or substitution, changes in the level of public provision lead to adjustments in the level of private provision that may offset part, all, or more than all the public increment. For particular individuals the change in endowments may either leave their total consumption unchanged, or increase it in part, or reduce it.

In fact, a great deal of public spending, especially in areas where it has grown most rapidly, falls precisely within these latter groups. Almost all of the social welfare budget (government provision of health, education, housing, direct payments) and most of the remainder of nondefense public spending are subject to private supplementation or substitution of various kinds. In all these cases, the change in endowments as such has no effect on final total consumption of the good; all effects on final total consumption are due to the relative price consequences or concomitants of public provision. Some examples below illustrate.

Our categories 1 through 3 cut across the economist's technical distinction between "public goods" and "private goods." A public good is like Norman Lindsay's magic pudding and is not diminished in its capacity to give nourishment even though another individual has supped upon it. The public sector provides both kinds of goods: in fact, rather more of private (housing) than of public goods (defense). It is possible for the state to force a private good into our first category by banning private supply, or taxing it out of existence, or subsidizing the publicly provided output so that private supply is negligible. Tertiary education is a case in point in some but not all Western

countries. Equally, consumption of genuinely public goods may be supplemented by the market purchase of privately provided goods that provide an
essentially equivalent service. An increase in the level of public supply will
reduce the purchase of the private equivalent, and hence this case fits our
second category notwithstanding the technically public nature of government supply.

Crime Protection and Private Supplementation

Consider protection from crime. Market-provided guard dogs, night
watchmen, burglar alarms, locks, privately owned guns, and security services supplement the services of government-provided police. Suppose that
the curve $D_K D_K$ (in Figure 2.1) depicts the aggregate demand curve for
crime-prevention services for some individual, K. Suppose further that
some quantity, Q_0, of these services is provided free by the state; individuals
are able to buy supplementary private crime-prevention services, of the kind
already referred to, at a per unit price of P.[4] Given the demand curve, $D_K D_K$,

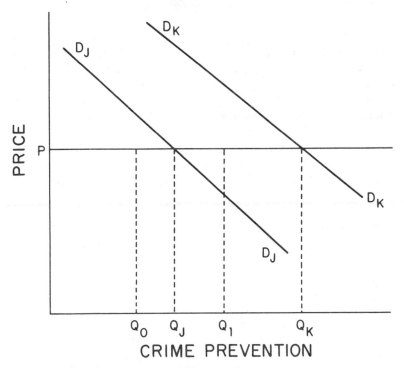

FIGURE 2.1

we know that K will purchase an additional $(Q_K - Q_0)$ units of crime prevention in the market; the final $(Q_K$th$)$ unit purchased is worth exactly \$P to K.

Let us suppose that the government increases its supply of crime prevention services by hiring more police so that the total public expenditure rises. Then the level of publicly provided output rises from Q_0 to Q_1, but the level of aggregate consumption of crime-prevention services by K remains unchanged at Q_K; the additional $(Q_1 - Q_0)$ units provided by the government *simply replace units currently provided in the market.*[5] The quantity of output provided in the market falls from $(Q_K - Q_0)$ to $(Q_K - Q_1)$; but that last unit of service that K buys will still be worth \$P to him or her. The change in public spending on crime prevention does not increase the aggregate level of consumption, so that in terms of the entry representing K's consumption of crime prevention in the matrix indicated in Table 2.1, there is virtually no effect. (Of course, individual K may be made better off or worse off by the change, depending on the taxes he or she is obliged to pay to finance the expansion of the state police. This effect will show up not in his or her consumption of crime prevention services specifically, but rather in his or her aggregate consumption expenditure (the final column in Figure 2.1) and will be spread across all consumption items.)

Now consider individual J, whose demand for crime prevention is given by the curve D_JD_J in Figure 2.1. When public output is Q_0, J supplements privately to reach Q_J; the last unit is worth \$P to J. If public provision and J's consumption rise to Q_1, the last unit of service is worth less than \$P to J, who would wish to sell off the excess, $Q_1 - Q_J$. If resale were impossible (and it often is), once public provision exceeds Q_J private supplementation ceases, and crime prevention becomes like defense or space research to him; a change in *endowment is a change in final consumption.* In these circumstances total consumption of crime prevention services (the final sum of the relevant column) must also rise, but, of course, not by the full amount of the public sector increase.

TABLE 2.2   Total Consumption of Crime Prevention

Individual	Levels of Public Provision		
	Q_0	Q_1	Q_2
1	q_1	q_{1-}	Q_2/S
2	q_2	q_{2-}	Q_2/S
...	...	...	...
S − 1	q_{s-1}	Q_1/S	Q_2/S
S	Q_0/S	Q_1/S	Q_2/S
Total	T_0	$T_0 + q$	Q_2

NOTES: For convenience it is assumed that public provision is consumed equally. Q_0 eliminates private supplementation by person S only, so that $(q_s - 1 > Q_0/S)$; Q_1 eliminates private supplementation by person S − 1; Q_2 eliminates all private supplementation. The change $Q_1 - Q_0$ greatly exceeds q. Q_2 exceeds $T_0 + q$.

In order to sketch the consequences in Table 2.2, we assume that poorer individuals (S and S−1) privately purchase little crime prevention,[6] and that higher income individuals pay higher taxes than do lower income individuals (hence the negative signs after q_1 and q_2 in column three). When public provision increases from Q_0 to Q_1, aggregate consumption increases by much less; therefore the proportionate increase in budgeted government spending greatly exaggerates the actual effect until (as at public expenditure level Q_2) all private supplementation has been eliminated. Until then the major effect seems to be a tendency for aggregate consumption to be redistributed in favor of lower income groups, though as indicated in Note 5 even this is debatable.

Education and Private Substitution

The characteristic feature of the cases to be examined here is that the relevant private provision is a substitute for, rather than a supplement to, public provision.[7] Of course, there may be some private supplementation in the education case: tutors, encyclopedias, educational aids. Furthermore, in some (enlightened?) settings, governments may provide education vouchers that individuals can spend freely on the education of their choice. However, it is much more common that individuals attend either a government school or a private school. If the latter, they or their parents purchase their education in the market; they then forego consuming government schooling without a concomitant reduction in tax liabilities.

Consider Figure 2.2. In this diagram K has demand for education given by the curve $D_K D_K$ and can purchase education in the market at price P_E. The government initially provides free education up to the level E_G. (The horizontal axis can be thought of as measured in some objective quality units; we abstract from difficulties of measurement.) Ideally, K would like to purchase E_K units. To do so he or she must forego the benefits of publically provided education entirely. Thus the extra cost to K of consuming E_K units is all of $P_E \cdot E_K$, whereas the extra benefits are derived only from the additional $(E_K - E_G)$ units of education. These benefits are given by the area under K's demand curve over the range E_G to E_K, shaded in Figure 2.2. Individual K will choose to consume education privately only if the area of the triangle ABC exceeds the market value of government provided education, $E_G \cdot P_E$. In Figure 2.2 this is so and hence K does buy education privately (in amount Q_K).

Now suppose that government expands its supply of education to E'_G. Then, the area of triangle A′B′C is no longer larger than $E'_G \cdot P_E$, so K now uses the publicly provided schooling. In doing so, however, K's consumption of education in toto falls from E_K to E'_G. Therefore, unlike the case of private supplementation examined above where the public expenditure in-

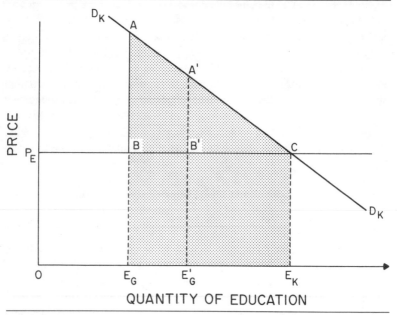

FIGURE 2.2:

crease may leave total consumption virtually unchanged, in the case of private substitution the public expenditure increase can actually reduce total consumption.

For individuals who consume publicly provided education both before and after the public spending increase, the expansion of public provision *does* increase consumption (as in the case of defense). However, due to reduced consumption by other individuals (such as K), the overall effect of the public sector expansion on total consumption is unclear. Certainly, we would expect that the public sector expansion would lead to more equal consumptions of education; more individuals will consume E'_G units of education than consumed E_G units. Thus we can indicate in Table 2.3 the likely changes in the relevant columns of matrix 1 attributable to public sector expansion: the change in the distribution of total consumption toward equality (at E'_G), and the ambiguity in the net effect on total education consumption by the entire community in response to the increase in public spending on education.

Distribution:
A Case of Private Supplementation

The central conclusions of the discussion to this juncture are that insofar as the increase in government spending represents a change in *endowments*

TABLE 2.3 Total Consumption of Education (secondary, for example)

Individual	Before Public Sector Expansion	After Public Sector Expansion
1	Q_1	Q_1
2	Q_2	$E_G^{\cdot}\,(<Q_2)$
3	Q_3	$E_G^{\cdot}\,(<Q_3)$
...	...	...
$s-1$	E_G	$E_G^{\cdot}\,(>E_G)$
s	E_G	$E_G^{\cdot}\,(>E_G)$
Total	E_T	$E_{T\pm}$

NOTE: Equal public provision is assumed.

with no direct effect on relative prices, the aggregate effect on total consumption of the publicly provided goods for the community as a whole remains ambiguous where there is private substitution, and will be predictably small where there is private supplementation. Only where there is neither private substitution nor private supplementation (as in the defense case, or where government provision of, say, police is already so large that no one buys from private suppliers) will an increase in public provision involve a corresponding increase in aggregate consumption.[8] However, in all interesting cases increases in public provision will lead to a less dispersed *distribution* of aggregate consumption. The normative significance of reducing dispersion is by no means clear if dispersion in individuals' consumption levels are attributable to differences in tastes, not incomes.[9] However, when we note this tendency, and the extent of direct redistribution through the tax-transfer system, it is tempting to focus attention on the effects that government growth may have had on the distribution of aggregate consumption, that is, on the final column in Figure 2.1, and ignore effects on the consumption of aggregate consumption as being too ambiguous.

In recognition of this temptation, it is perhaps important that we carry the logic of the general argument of our analysis a little further. To do so we should note that private redistribution is possible and does indeed go on, both through the agency of nongovernmental charitable institutions and through direct transfers between individuals (Becker, 1974; Abrams and Schmitz, 1978; Warr and Wright, 1981).

For example, total gifts to charitable institutions approximated $25 billion in the United States in 1974, representing about one and two-thirds percent of the GNP, compared with the eight percent of GNP expended by the government on social welfare programs. Left out of account is what one would surmise is a very significant amount of direct interpersonal redistribution, both intrafamily and otherwise, on which reliable figures are unavailable.

Redistribution, therefore, is a public activity that fits substantially into the second subclass of our third general category—public provision with private supplementation—so that the increase in public transfers will be offset in some degree by corresponding reductions in private transfers. To some extent, of course, private giving may be oriented toward ends rather different from public transfers,[10] but it would be somewhat surprising if public transfers did not substitute for private transfers over some range. Regrettably, there is little conclusive empirical evidence, only casual observation, on the effects of changes in the level of public transfers on private giving, partly because estimates of total private giving are so poor. Public support for the aged does seem to have in some measure simply replaced the private support of elderly parents by their children, once a common feature of family life. Likewise, the network of small-scale local philanthropy that seems to have operated to some extent during the Depression appears to have largely disappeared, probably in response to increased unemployment relief payments by government. Just as in the crime prevention case, adjustments in private supplementation may have offset much of the expansion in public activity. The effects of government growth on the dispersion of individuals' consumptions, both directly via tax-transfer programs and indirectly via changes in the distribution of consumption of publicly provided goods, may have been less than might first appear.

Cherchez the Relative Price Changes

The previous sections showed that changes in the level of budgeted public spending, to the extent that they represent changes only in endowments, may not translate into significant changes in either the composition of total consumption or the distribution of total consumption between individuals, things that are the focus of normative and analytic concern. By contrast, we know that changes in relative prices *do* affect the composition of total consumption in entirely predictable ways. If, therefore, we are to trace out the implications of government growth for the composition of total consumption, it seems natural to look first at the more direct and obvious relative price changes that government expenditure growth entails.

Some public spending does, to be sure, affect relative prices directly. Voucher schemes in which the government matches private expenditure over some range, subsidies for farm production, and rent subsidies all alter relative prices and induce unambiguous increases in the production and consumption of the subsidized goods. However, the vast bulk of direct budgeted expenditure is not of this type.

What of the regulation side of government activity? Requirements that cars have pollution control devices, that entry into certain professions or occupations be restricted, that production processes meet certain standards, that all workers be paid at or above a certain real wage—all these change relative prices. Likewise, tariffs that protect domestic industries from foreign competition (or import quotas with similar effects) serve to change relative prices and involve corresponding major restructuring of the composition of aggregate consumption. Yet none of these policies appears directly in the budgeted expenditure figures. While it may be tempting to surmise that the extent and significance of such regulation have increased along with the level of budgeted government expenditure, any such conclusion remains a conjecture; it is not, by any means, logically implied by budget figures.[11]

There is a simple and obvious point to be made here. Even if the budgeted expenditure data give us little feeling for relative price effects, they do indicate a spectacular increase in the relative price effects that emerge on the tax side as a natural consequence of expenditure growth. Virtually all taxes operate through markets; they are imposed at various points in the processes of production and exchange and invariably change the relative prices of alternative activities. For example, a tax on labor income is a tax on the productive factor, labor, and can be avoided (at a cost) by both the buyers of labor (who might be induced to shift to other productive factors) and the sellers of labor (who might choose to work less on taxed activities). Taxes induce behavioral adjustments designed to reduce tax liabilities; the relative prices of taxed and tax-free activities or goods or factors will have changed.

Suppose the level of government-expenditure crime protection increases eightfold over a period of time. The taxes to pay for this increase are levied on beer; but the extra taxes that the average taxpayer pays simply come back to him or her in the form of savings in private expenditure on crime protection. Assume that there is no effect on his or her aggregate consumption of crime prevention services, and there is no loss of income available to spend on other things. There is simply enormous effect on the price of beer relative to other consumption items, which will in turn change the individual's consumption pattern. The prime effects of government expenditure growth on the composition of output are, therefore, not to be seen in terms of a shift in favor of the items of government expenditure and away from other consumption items *but in terms of the shift away from those private consumption items that are relatively heavily taxed in favor of those consumption items that are relatively lightly taxed.* This conclusion represents the major thrust of our entire discussion here. In the light of our specification of what it is that we really want to know, the main object of interest is not so much the nature and composition of budgeted public expenditure increases as such, but rather the nature of the relative price effects induced by the tax changes necessary to make those public expenditure increases possible.

With this in mind it may be useful to conclude with a brief catalogue of the major relative price changes that an increase in total revenue collections entails (noting that it is the change in marginal tax rates, not average tax rates, that is relevant in determining the relative price effects and that the precise effects will depend on the particular tax structure).

(1) Leisure-effort trade-off and the underground economy. The general effect of an increase in the overall level of tax rates is to increase the price of all marketed goods vis-à-vis leisure, home production, or goods exchanged outside formal markets.[12] Thus, we would expect individuals to work less hard because of the tax increase: shorter hours of work, longer vacations, earlier retirement, choice of more congenial rather than onerous or odious jobs; more relaxation on the job, less enthusiasm for promotion. Because of progressive tax rate structures, paid work would tend to be shared more evenly within the family unit. We would expect a significant growth in home production, do-it-yourself activities, and in the underground economy (where individuals use money or barter, but do not report the results to tax authorities). Recent estimates for the United States have put the underground economy at an aggregate expenditure level of $600 billion, more than one-fifth of GNP. Other predictable effects are an increased tendency to underreport income and to engage the services of tax experts.

(2) Savings. It is widely believed by public finance experts that the standard tax structure discriminates against savings and encourages current consumption. This effect is exacerbated by increased tax rates (Nellor, 1981) and is more likely to occur under inflationary circumstances. Moreover, distortions due to the differential treatment of interest, dividend income and capital gains, and to the simultaneous taxation of corporate dividends under the personal and company income taxes must involve enormous adjustments in the composition of the capital stock as tax rates increase.

(3) Housing. Virtually every income tax, in exempting the inputed rent on owner-occupied dwellings, discriminates between renters and home owners in favor of the latter, encouraging individuals to keep more of their wealth as owner-occupied housing.

(4) Income-tax concessions, deductions, and exemptions. Income tax law provides a considerable array of deductions, exemptions, and concessions, often for expenditure on health, for contributions to approved charitable institutions, and commonly for expenditures incurred in earning income (in which there is typically some consumption element). As tax rates rise there is a corresponding tendency to reorient one's expenditure toward these favorably treated expenditure items.

The existence and magnitude of these tax effects are well known to public finance experts (although the net effect of so many competing and overlapping considerations is not simple to unravel, particularly in the presence of other relative price changes attributable to regulations). Our point here is that in understanding the consequences of budgeted public expenditure increases (of very considerable magnitude), the simple and obvious effects on the tax side have been almost totally ignored. Instead, analysts have focused on the consequences of expenditure change per se and as we have seen, these remain very much a matter of conjecture and speculation; they can in no way be induced directly from a mere inspection of the budget figures.

Conclusion

We have not dealt here with *all* the problems of interpreting government growth statistics. Among others, for example, is the relation between expenditure levels and real output levels in the public sector. Nor have we discussed the question of whether per capita expenditure or absolute expenditure represents the appropriate indicator of public output. The focus of our discussion has been, rather, the specification of what it is about public expenditure growth that one ought really to be interested in: what is normatively relevant, and what bears on *explanations* of what has happened. We have argued that changes in the levels of budgeted public expenditures are interesting only to the extent that such changes have consequences. The consequences in question are twofold. First, there may be attendant changes in the *composition* of final output; second, there may be changes in the *distribution* of final output.

With respect to composition we have argued that changes in the level of budgeted public expenditures have much less effect directly on the composition of final output than the figures themselves suggest. This is because such expenditures represent a change in endowments and because in many relevant cases there is scope for adjustments in the level of analogous supplementary private activity, adjustments that will in some measure offset (perhaps, more than offset) the change in public provision. Changes in the composition of final output are effected more readily by changes in relative prices than by changes in endowments. Such relative price changes tend to be wrought less by direct expenditures (in the form of explicit subsidies) and more by regulation (in growth which is not signified by budgeted expenditure share statistics) and by taxes.

Changes in the level of budgeted public expenditures, while not necessarily directly affecting the composition of final output, do seem to have had predictable effects on its distribution. However, once changes in the level of private supplementation in the area of interpersonal redistribution are allowed for, the prospect of any significant net effect on the distribution of final output also seems somewhat speculative. We might conjecture that there has been some effect of government expenditure growth in reducing dispersion in the distribution of total consumption, increasing as public provision progressively displaces private provision.

The only unambiguous effects of public expenditure growth seem to be those effects on the composition of output that are attributable to dramatically increased tax rates. These are effects that show up predominantly in areas of *private* expenditure where the expenditure activities of governments are least conspicuous. Strangely, these tax-side effects have been almost totally ignored in the growth of government literature. This fact is strange because they seem to be the only effects that can be induced directly and unambiguously from the figures.

NOTES

1. We intend investigating these in a subsequent paper.

2. One of the columns can be treated as savings (measured in dollars) so that our definitions can conform to familiar accounting definitions of "income."

3. In the terms of this categorization goods produced by the state, but sold in the market at a price that entirely covers costs, are treated in the first category. Who *produces* the goods in the technical sense matters less than whether decisions about price and output are taken politically—and hence are ultimately constrained by electoral process—or are taken as a matter of market calculation and are constrained by market processes. For example, a state electricity authority marketing its output without government subsidy is treated equivalently to a private firm. There may be some important differences between public and private enterprises; but for the purpose of the coarse-grained distinctions relevant at this level of analysis, it makes more sense to designate public authorities operating on market principles as private firms. To the extent that the public authority operates with some financial support from tax revenues, that support will treated as a subsidy and that component only will emerge in the second category.

4. The final output might be measured as the number of crime-free days, or the inverse of the probability of being the victim of assault or theft, or some such. Since our prime purpose here is illustrative, the precise terms do not matter so much.

5. Technically, we are assuming that private supply is competitive. A. Fels and P. G. Warr pointed out replacement is half as big when private supply is monopolized.

6. This is not self-evident. Crime has locational dimensions: If richer individuals buy some freedom from crime by living in relatively crime-free areas, demand for crime prevention services (public and private) may be somewhat higher for lower income individuals. Moreover, by deliverage policy, or because police try to minimize dangers to themselves, publicly provided crime prevention services may be concentrated in areas where the affluent live, work, and play. On private supplementation of crime-prevention services in response to relative price effects, see Charles Clotfelter (1977). Clotfelter's purposes are different from ours here, and his empirics are rather inconclusive.

7. See Sam Peltzman (1973) for the complete argument and evidence; Yoram Barzel (1973) presents a figure like our Figure 2.1.

8. The term "corresponding increase" is used advisedly. The precise relation between the increase in public output and the increase in aggregate consumption for the community as a whole will differ according to the nature of the good in question. The good is a pure public good if adding an extra individual to the community of consumers does not reduce at all the consumption of the good by other individuals: In this case, increase *production* of the public good by an amount G, *by each individual*, and aggregate community consumption increases by $S \cdot G$. If, by contrast, the publicly provided good is purely private in the technical sense, then an increase in consumption of the public supply by any one individual (with production unchanged) automati-

cally reduces consumption by some other individual: in this case, any increase in production of G implies an increase in *aggregate* consumption for the community as a whole by the same amount, G. There are, of course, intermediate cases. Although this matter of the publicness/ privateness characteristics of the publicly provided good is germain here, we depress its status to a footnote because of space constraints.

9. Many might approve of the suppression of dispersion due to income differences, but wish to respect differences in individuals' tastes (in allocating equal incomes, for example).

10. For example, some individuals may give privately for prestige, or out of moral conviction or spiritual discipline.

11. For some evidence that the degree of regulation has increased in the United States, see Weidenbaum (n.d.).

12. We should emphasize again that in our setting there is net income effect due to taxation in aggregate.

REFERENCES

ABRAMS, B. A. and M. D. SCHMITZ (1978) "The 'crowding-out' effect of governmental transfers on private charitable contributions." Public Choice 33, 1: 29-37.

BECKER, G. S. (1974) "A theory of social interactions." Journal of Political Economy 82, (November/December): 1063-1093.

BARZEL, Y. (1973) "Private schools and public school finance." Journal of Political Economy 81 (January/February): 174-186.

CLOTFELTER, C. (1977) "Public services, private substitutes and the demand for protection against crime." American Economic Review 67 (December): 867-877.

NELLOR, D. (1981) Timing and Expectation in the Theory of Taxation. Ph.D. dissertation, Virginia Polytechnic Institute and State University.

PELTZMAN, S. (1973) "The effect of government subsidies-in-kind on private expenditures: the case of higher education." Journal of Political Economy 81 (January/February): 1-27.

WARR, P. G. (1982) "Private benevolence and distribution weights for benefit-cost analysis." Research School of Pacific Studies, Canberra.

——— and B. D. WRIGHT (1981) "The isolation paradox and the discount rate for benefit-cost analysis." Quarterly Journal of Economics 95 (February): 129-145.

WEIDENBAUM, M. with R. DE FINA (n.d.) "The cost of federal regulation of economic activity." Study for the American Enterprise Institute, AEI Reprint 88.

CHAPTER 3

WHEN IS
THE PUBLIC SECTOR
TOO LARGE?

RICHARD A. MUSGRAVE

The major theme of this book is how to measure the growth of the public sector and how to explain the causes of this growth. My particular focus is not so much on whether the public sector has grown and why but on whether it has grown too much.[1] This is in line with recent trends in fiscal theory that have focused on the question of public sector failure, a sharp reversal from traditional concern from Pigou in the 1920s to J. M. Keynes with his social goods theory of the 1950s and 1960s, which viewed budget policy as a remedy to private sector failure. Together with this shift in concern, fiscal theory has moved from a normative analysis of what constitutes efficient public sector behavior to a positive examination of how the public sector in fact behaves. The proposition, now widely advanced, that the public sector has become too large straddles both spheres; if the public sector is said to be too large, there must be some norm of correct size against which the actual behavior can be measured. Deviant behavior cannot be defined without a concept of normal behavior, lest it be merely a value judgment on the part of the particular observer. In this chapter I will interpret the public sector in the sense of budgetary activity only, that is, the revenue-expenditure process of government. I thereby omit the important field of regulation, although it readily could be included since the issues are quite similar in nature.

Is the Provision of Public Goods Excessive?

To be of analytical interest, the proposition that the public sector is too large must reflect more than the preferences of the particular observer. It must be taken to imply that public sector activity is greater than would be expected if the process of collective decision making operated correctly. The crux of the matter, as noted before, is that actual performance must be compared with some norm. In so doing I will distinguish two major budgetary functions: (1) the provision of public or social goods and (2) adjustments in the state of distribution. As we shall see, this distinction cannot always be drawn closely, but it is convenient, especially since defining a normative standard for the first is simpler than for the second.

Budgetary provision for social goods means that the decision to allocate resources to their production has to be made through the budgetary process, involving budgetary finance on the one side and quasi-free supply to the users on the other. Put very briefly, this arrangement is needed because the resulting benefits are largely external and are received in common. This being the case, individuals will not purchase such goods voluntarily but will choose to act as free riders. Hence, a political process is needed by which the provision of social goods and their financing is decided upon. This, however, does not imply that such goods must be *produced* by the government. The issue of public enterprise is quite separate from that of budgetary provision; pencils used by civil servants may be purchased from a private firm or the government may produce pencils in a public enterprise and sell them to private users. Only the issue of budgetary provision is dealt with here.

The question of whether or not the provision of social goods is too large, therefore, involves the preceding question of how the proper level of provision can be defined. One answer accepted by most public finance economists is that the level is correct if the social goods provided are such as would be bought and paid for voluntarily by consumers if availability could be made contingent on price payments. Putting it differently, the cost would be covered if so called Lindahl prices were charged, that is, if each consumer were called upon to pay in line with his or her marginal evaluation of the benefits. Or, provision would be correct if paid for by benefit taxes thus defined. Hypotheses of excess provision thus implied that for some reasons the budget will turn out to be larger than this rule would call for. Various hypotheses have been advanced as to why this should be the case and these will be considered presently.

It should be noted that the finding of a rising or falling expenditure share by itself cannot be taken as evidence of overexpansion or underexpansion. Obviously, the proper share will depend on income elasticities, price elasticities, changes in relative prices, and demographic and technological factors affecting the mix of public and private goods in the desired composition of output.

Voting bias. Perhaps the central hypothesis is that majority voting inherently leads to overexpansion. Suppose that the costs of a project are to be shared equally. The majority, which passes the project, will consider only its part of the cost, say fifty-one percent of the total, leaving the remaining forty-nine percent out of consideration. Thus a project is agreed to that would not be accepted if full costs were allowed for. At closer consideration this is not a valid argument. Majority voting may pass projects that under Lindahl pricing would be rejected, but it may also reject projects that under Lindahl pricing would be passed. Thus the budget may be either too large or too small. To establish a presumption regarding the direction of bias, it must be shown that the transaction costs of coalition forming (or the willingness to undertake such costs) are larger for proponents than for opponents. This may tend to be the case, but it is by no means obvious and it may well differ for various issues. Obviously, voting outcomes cannot be perfect with regard either to composition or to size of the budget. Much will depend upon the voting procedure and budgeting arrangements, but no simple a priori judgment on direction is possible.

Underestimation of tax burden. A second hypothesis is that voters underestimate their tax bill, and hence the cost of public services, either because taxes are not visible as in the case of product taxes or because direct taxes are hidden through withholding. To this it might be added that taxpayers consider the amount paid only, while overlooking the deadweight losses that are attached. These points have merit although one should not overlook the fact that in some countries vast sums are spent on political advertising aimed at dramatizing and exaggerating the existence of oppressive tax burdens.

Problems of fiscal illusion arise on the expenditure as well as the tax side of the budget. Expenditure benefits that are received indirectly and without effort may be accepted as given by nature, such as sunshine, without being linked to tax payments. Altogether I do not find it evident whether the net effect of fiscal illusion makes for an excessive or a deficient budget level. What is evident is that direct and visible taxes are superior to indirect taxes, and that efficient choice calls for a visible linkage between tax and expenditure measures.

Monopolistic bureaucrats. While the preceding considerations relate to voting behavior, another type of bias is said to be generated by autonomous behavior of bureaucrats aimed at maximizing the size of their bureaus. The bureaucrat—for example, the division chief—is said to confront the sponsor—the congressional committee, for example—with an all-or-nothing offer of some public service at a level so that total benefits equal total costs rather than the more efficient (and lower) level at which marginal costs and benefits are equated. The sponsor is assumed to accept this offer so that overexpansion follows.

This model of bureaucratic behavior is of interest, but it leaves me uneasy in various respects. For one thing it is unrealistic to interpret the behavior of the public executive purely in terms of profit maximization, in analogy to the private firm. Surely considerations of the public interest also enter. Even allowing for a tendency to identify the bureau's interest with the public interest, the analogy to profit-maximizing behavior of the private sector monopolist goes too far. For another, officials acting in their own interest may find it advantageous to limit the activities of their own particular bureaus so as to gain favor with their superiors, thereby advancing to better positions, perhaps the direction of a larger bureau. Finally, and most important, the budgetary position for any particular bureau is determined as a part of a general budgetary process in which competing claims are balanced. While this process is far from perfect, it nevertheless imposes a general equilibrium framework in which the individual bureaus must operate, which is inadequately allowed for by the monopoly model.

A related argument views the bureaucrat as maximizing his or her bureau by setting the agenda on which the public or legislature is permitted to vote. By directing the vote toward the largest budget for which a majority can still be obtained, the outcome will exceed that which would be preferred by the median voter. Once more the question is whether the bureaucrat does in fact possess this power or will be overridden by the voting group.

Inefficiencies. Next is the consideration that government operations tend to be inefficient because bureaucrats have tenure and, unlike the competition on the market, cannot be fired or run into bankruptcy. Whatever the comparative levels of inefficiency in the public and private sectors, note that inefficiency is not the same as excessive budget size. If the provision for public services is inherently inefficient, this means that the cost of supplying a given service level is higher. Assuming a functioning voting system, outlay will then be larger or smaller depending on whether demand is inelastic or elastic to price.

Services qua redistribution. Redistribution policy is considered in the later part of this chapter, but brief notice is taken here of how redistributional objectives may influence the level at which public services are provided. Two aspects are noted.

First, proponents of redistribution may consider the provision of public services a second-best mechanism for achieving redistributional objectives that for political reasons could not be achieved through a direct tax transfer process. Even generally available public services tend to be redistributive if they grant equal, absolute benefits independent of income, as they involve a larger proportional gain to low income recipients. Moreover, the financing of general public services through taxes that are more progressive than justified on a benefit-received basis involves redistribution. As long as the level of taxation is low (so that incremental burdens may be imposed at the top) expansion of the public service budget becomes a vehicle of redistribution, leading to overexpansion. Seen in the historical context, this may well have been a greater source of overexpansion than voting bias or bureaucratic power, but now the argument may work in the opposite direction. Fear of redistribution of finance may prevent acceptance of public services otherwise desired.

Second, redistributional objectives may legitimately involve the provision of public services, and thus are not a cause of overexpansion. Such is the case where donors are willing to concur in redistribution if the recipient is required to use his or her funds in a particular way. This type of redistribution via paternalistic giving thus ties together the public service and redistributional aspects, and we shall return to this later on.

Macro diversions. Finally, there is the possibility that the actual provision of public services will depart from the correct level due to diversions caused by macro policy considerations. In the early stages of Keynesian depression economics, there was a strong tendency to argue that public expenditures (hence the supply of public services) should be used as a means of employment creation. This tends to create an excess budget, as compared to the level of public services appropriate in a full employment context. Moreover, this distortion is not necessary because the same employment effects could be accomplished by tax reduction. Exactly the same holds, with reverse sign, in the current setting of inflation. Reduction in public services is advocated to reduce demand, even though the same objective could be accomplished by increasing taxes. On these grounds the budget tends to be overextended in periods of sustained unemployment and deficient in periods of sustained inflation. This simple relationship, of course, is complicated by the coexistence of unemployment and inflation in the current setting.

Similar tendencies are reinforced by the fact that deficit finance (called for in depression) tends to understate the cost of public services, especially at the margin, thus inviting excess provision. Once more, the opposite holds in the case of surplus finance (called for, in principle at least, under inflation) where the cost of public services appears as overstated. Finally, a tendency for excess budgeting arises under conditions of inflation, where without indexing there results an automatic increase in the effective rate of income tax. Thus legislators are enabled to raise expenditures without having to increase nominal tax rates. Program expansion that otherwise would not be possible becomes so; indexing of tax brackets will prevent this.

More generally, the impact of inflation on the level of public services relative to the GNP will depend on the behavior of relative prices (e.g., defense equipment versus consumer goods), relative wage rates in the public and private sectors, the pattern of indexing of social security benefits, and so on. This raises the interesting methodological question of whether the ratio of public expenditures to GNP should be computed in nominal or deflated terms.

Conclusions. Having established a criterion for the correct level of public services, it is only reasonable to expect the level of public services to rise with GNP. There is no evident presumption whether it should rise more or less rapidly, so that the share increases or declines. In any particular period this will depend on demographic and technological factors. Various factors have been examined suggesting that there is an endemic bias toward overexpansion. Closer consideration, however, shows that these hypotheses are not convincing on a priori grounds. Nor do the overall data lend strong support to the hypotheses of cumulative expansion. Taking the American case, government purchases as a percentage of GNP are now about what they were in 1960 and below their 1970 level. Purchases for civilian programs only have risen but at a distinctively declining rate. Adjusted for inflation, the civilian purchase share has in fact declined. Current developments also point in that direction. As demonstrated vividly by recent events, the political process is quite capable of reversing what are considered excesses in budgetary expansion and voters are by no means as helpless as much of the recent literature suggests. Rather, voters will get in the long run the level of public services they desire. The difficulties and defects, I suspect, lie more in the mix of public services than in their overall level.

The Scope of Redistribution

It is a rather curious fact that most of the recent literature has dealt with the hypotheses of overexpansion of the public services, even though the major dynamics in budget expansion have been related to redistribution. As noted before, redistribution has been a factor in the growth of public services, but even more it has taken the form of transfer programs.

As in the case of purchases, a judgment that the transfer share has become too large has to be related to some norm or concept of correct level. Unfortunately the definition of such a norm is more difficult than for the provision of public services. In the latter case a criterion is provided by how well consumer preferences are met given the distribution of income. In the former case one has to go back to what the distribution of income should be or to what constitutes legitimate mechanisms by which it can be changed. Views as to the appropriate levels of redistribution will differ depending on whether one starts from a Lockean premise of entitlement, a Rawlsian premise of maxi-min, or the notion of a social welfare function that assigns decreasing social value to successive income increments without disregarding welfare losses that redistribution imposes.

Suppose that the social contract is such as to (1) establish entitlement to earnings while (2) rendering such entitlement subject to adjustment through majority rule. The correct level of redistribution will then depend on both the redistribution of earnings and the desire of voters (on both the donor and recipient sides) to engage in redistribution. Preferences regarding redistribution change over time depending on the social and political climate of the period. As I see it, the rise of the welfare state over the last fifty years has been the reflection of such a change, just as current attitudes suggest a reversal in this trend. As individuals we may have our own views as to what is and what is not desirable, but this differs from holding that one trend or another is correct in an objective sense. The scientific observer, however, may examine whether (1) the actual process of redistribution reflects voter preferences, (2) it does in fact accomplish the desired objective, and (3) it does this in the most efficient fashion.

Redistribution choice. As noted before, the literature in public choice has been more concerned with the provision of public services than with redistribution. In approaching the problem one might begin with the expectation that majority rule will tend to establish an egalitarian distribution so that failure to arrive at this result suggests a deficient level of redistributive activity. In line with this hypothesis it has been suggested that the past trend toward increased redistribution (especially in the American setting) may be explained by an upward shift in voting participation at the lower end of the income scale, and that this might be expected to continue in future years. However, it is easy to see how the extension of the redistribution process becomes more difficult as the group of losers rises in size relative to the gainers. This, it would seem, is precisely the situation in which we may now find ourselves, leading to a slowdown or reversal in the redistribution process.

There are other brakes to redistribution. Individuals are not wholly risk averse; some at the lower end of the scale may not wish to lose the chance to move upward. People also realize that the size of the pie depends on its division, so that excessive redistribution may be counterproductive. Finally, the further the process of redistribution is carried, the greater will be the leakages that arise and result in arbitrary shifts not in line with the initial redistribution goals.

Excessive redistribution. Economic analysis in particular can point to various considerations that need to be allowed for in considering whether or not the prevailing level of redistribution is excessive. One is the fact that levels of taxation imposed at the upper end of the income scale may be pushed so far as to reduce revenue, thereby lowering the amount of income that can be transferred to the lower end of the scale. Tax rates pushed beyond the point of maximum revenue may be said to be excessive not because they result in too much but in too little redistribution. Such at least is the case if the goal of redistribution policy is to generate transfers, but it need not be the case if concern is with narrowing differentials only. Another consideration is that the redistribution process in itself imposes an efficiency cost or dead-weight loss that must be allowed for in assessing the social gains to be derived from redistribution.

Failure to make this allowance will result in excessive redistribution: excessive, that is, relative to whatever level would be proper given a particular social welfare function. Economists have recently emphasized this aspect in developing a theory of optimal taxation. The basic difficulty in all of this is that leisure cannot be taxed, so that a person may substitute leisure for income in response to high marginal rates of tax. The problem would not arise if it were possible to tax potential rather than actual income.

A related problem arises with the impact of redistributive policy on economic growth. A redistributive tax-transfer system may reduce the rate of growth, thereby retarding productivity gains and lowering future earnings at both ends of the income scale. Failure to consider this relationship may give rise to an excessive level of redistribution. At the same time such effects may be exaggerated by opponents of redistribution, thereby leading to the opposite result.

Redistribution instruments. Economists have traditionally argued that redistribution through transfers is more efficient than redistribution in kind because it leaves the recipient free to choose how to use the funds. More recently, it has been shown that this need not be the case. Deadweight losses may be reduced by the choice of an appropriate mix of selective product taxes and subsidies. While important to the theory of welfare economics, this is not as yet a very practical approach and in any case does not explain the extensive use of transfers in kind that are to be found in actual budget policies, for example, low cost housing, health services, and so on. Rather, the importance of such programs reflects the preferences of donors who are willing to agree to transfers provided that the recipient is bound to use the funds as they prescribe. Paternalistic giving plays an important role in redistribution policy, interacting as noted above with the provision for public services. The difficulties of determining what constitutes an appropriate level of redistribution are transmitted into setting the appropriate level of public services.

Conclusion

There is no simple way to determine if budgetary activity at any particular time and in any particular place is excessive. The test should be whether or not its prevailing scope is larger than it would be if (1) the democratic process did indeed succeed in expressing the true preferences of the people and (2) this choice were based upon a full awareness of all hidden as well as apparent costs and benefits involved. Application of this test is difficult for the provision of public goods and services and it is even more difficult for redistributive activity.

There are, to be sure, limits to budgetary activity in the market economy. Provision for public goods and redistribution reduce the share of income available for private use. Without reflecting at all on the usefulness of public services or on the gains to transfer recipients, this inevitably means that the share of income available as compensation for individual effort is curtailed. Labor supply (in the market economy at least) as well as saving and invest-ment are affected. Expansion of the budget carries an efficiency cost and if carried far enough eventually becomes incompatible with the functioning of the market. All this is correct but no more so than the proposition that the market cannot function and an efficient and fair order cannot be secured without the contribution of the public sector. The danger to the functioning of a well-ordered society lies in both extremes and not just on the upper border. Somewhere within this band the democratic process must be relied upon to choose what it considers the desirable level. Designing appropriate institutional frameworks can contribute much to this task; but the goal of reform should be to permit free and efficient fiscal choice (Musgrave, 1981a).

NOTE

1. For a fuller discussion see Musgrave (1981a).

REFERENCES

MUSGRAVE, R. (1981a) "Fiscal functions: order and politics." Acceptance Paper, Frank E. Seidman Distinguished Award in Political Economy, P. K. Seidman Foundation, Memphis, Tennessee.
_____ (1981b) "Leviathan cometh—or does he?" in H. Ladd and N. Tideman (eds.) Tax and Expenditure Limitations. Washington, DC: Urban Institute.

PART III

Using Aggregate Data
to Measure
the Public Sector

CHAPTER 4

THE PUBLIC SECTOR'S INTERACTION WITH THE MARKET SECTOR
The Netherlands

HENNY van der WIELEN

During the last two decades the public sector[1] in the Netherlands has grown rapidly, surpassing the expansion in most other Organization for Economic Cooperation and Development (OECD) countries. For this relatively strong growth many explanations have been offered. One of them suggests that the growth is the result of the insufficient growth in capital-widening investments, which in turn is the result of the rapid expansion of the public sector. The thought underlying this idea of a "boomerang effect" is that the continuing increase in the burden of taxation and social insurance contributions is put largely upon industry, since the growth of the public sector is based upon something other than an actual shift in preferences toward public sector goods and services. (Or if there is such a shift, the economic subjects are unwilling to pay for them.) As a consequence of industry's increased burden, profitability declines and with it the propensity to invest. This in turn leads to a decreased absorption of the supply of labor and, in the end, to job losses. Since in Western welfare states the unemployed are financially supported by the governments temporarily—or in the case of the Netherlands, indefinitely—this development brings about an increase in public sector expenditure and, sooner or later, a rise in the burden of taxation and social insurance contributions. The vicious circle outlined here can be aggravated if the disposable income of public servants and recipients of public sector benefits is linked to disposable wage increases in the private sector. This is what happens in the Netherlands.

In other words, public sector expenditure is largely determined by developments outside the public sector (i.e., in the market sector). This public sector expenditure, however, is spent directly or indirectly on goods and services produced by the market sector. The income that remains after this claim on production has been paid for becomes available for distribution in the market sector. The growth of this disposable income and the manner in which its distribution among wages and profits is resolved has consequences for the continuity of production in the market sector. In view of these considerations, attempts have been made to establish criteria by which the various claims on goods and services produced in the market sector can be allocated (see Kessler, 1979; Nederlandsch Bank, 1979, 1980; Sociaal-Economische Raad 1978, 1979).

In order to obtain insight into the process described here, a number of factors are of crucial importance:

- a workable definition of public sector goods and services as opposed to market sector goods and services;
- the assessment of the number of persons (both active and nonactive) dependent on the public sector for their income and of the number of persons involved in the production of market sector goods and services;
- a comparison of the various groups' increases in disposable income within the context of their collective scope, that is, the growth of the production of market sector goods and services.

This chapter will take a closer look at (1) the shortcomings of current statistics with respect to these factors, which hinder the analysis of the interaction between the public sector and the market sector; (2) the manner in which attempts have been made in the Netherlands in recent years to make up for these shortcomings, and especially the most appropriate denominator for measuring the size and growth of the public sector and the criteria for a consistent allocation of market sector resources; and (3) the developments in the Netherlands since the mid-1960s.

Inadequate Statistics

Before turning to the shortcomings in the data, it should be said that for the purpose of highlighting the interaction between market and public sectors, market sector goods and services are defined as those goods and services whose distribution is effected through the market mechanism. The continuity of the production depends on sufficient market yields, which in turn depend upon the development of disposable income, that is, income after taxes and social insurance contributions, which is spent on market sector goods and services only. Public sector goods and services are defined as those goods and services whose distribution is organized by the government and whose production is financed out of public means. Thus the definitions are linked with the concept of disposable income. For that reason a large number of institutions active in health care, old age care, culture, and recreation, which can be designated to be in the semipublic sector, are regarded here as part of the public sector because the distribution and financing of their services are in the care of the government.

The existing data proved largely to be inadequate to evince the assumed interaction between the public sector and the market sector. This inadequacy was manifest notably in three distinct ways.

In the first place the existing subdivision of public sector expenditure turned out to be rather impractical for use. In accordance with international usage, public sector expenditure in the national account statistics and the budgets are divided into the following categories: (1) public servants' wages, (2) expenditure on goods and services, (3) income transfers and interest payments, and (4) capital transfers and loans. The income transfers, by far the most rapidly increasing expenditure item, make up numerous expenditure categories. Not only are expenditures included that are meant to form a direct income for those who receive them—for example, unemployment benefits and old age pensions—but also included are transfers to nursing and convalescent homes and grants to cultural or recreational institutions for the financing of wages and for goods and services. These transfers also provide income to the personnel of these institutions. Finally, income transfers include supplementary income to receipients, such as family allowance benefits and the like. As a result of the multipurpose nature of income transfers, it is not easy to obtain insight into the number of persons dependent on the public sector for their income or into the amount of income received by them.

In the second place the nursing and convalescent homes and cultural or recreational institutions mentioned above are regarded as part of the enterprise sector in the national accounts. Separate data on their output, employment, and financing are available only to a limited degree.

In the third place data are missing on disposable incomes (i.e., incomes after taxes and social insurance contributions) of the various socioeconomic categories: workers, recipients of a transfer income, and entrepreneurs. These data are essential if an accurate picture is to be obtained of the extent to which the public sector competes for the available funds with the various claims for disposable income made by the market sector.

In the following paragraphs a method of compensating for these statistical shortcomings as it has been developed over the last couple of years is discussed. It goes without saying that, due to the lack of basic data, such a method can only produce some approximations of the data required.

Method

In order to show the interaction between the market sector and the public sector, the following adaptations had to be made to the statistical material. The public expenditures had to be regrouped and a semipublic sector had to be demarcated. The burden of taxation and social insurance contributions had to be divided over the relevant groups. Finally, it was necessary to say something about an appropriate denominator and about some rules for allocation.

The number of persons dependent on the public sector for their income. A distinction can be made among the following groups:

- public servants—their number is published in the national accounts;
- persons receiving benefits on account of loss of income; these include the unemployed, the elderly, and persons incapacitated for work, with the provision that persons who are unemployed for half a day or who are fifty percent incapacitated for work are included for only fifty percent. The sick, insofar as they received sickness benefits through a public sector provision, are also included in this category. In the Netherlands statistics on the number of persons receiving benefits on account of loss of income are not readily available. They have to be compiled from figures supplied by very different sources. This situation is complicated further by the fact that as a result of the many benefit schemes existent, people often receive partial incomes through various programs. There are cases on record in which persons receive income via five different schemes. It is hardly surprising that this gives rise to statistical problems;
- workers in the semipublic sector; these are not employed by public authorities but by firms that are largely financed by the public authorities. The number of persons employed in the semipublic sector can only be determined when the semipublic sector has been clearly defined. We will now go into this definition in greater detail.

Demarcation of the semipublic sector. Various criteria, such as the nature of the service provided or the legal form of the institution concerned, are used to demarcate the semipublic sector. Each of these criteria yields different results. In this chapter the source of finance is the criterion. Firms whose continuity is dependent upon public sector contributions, and not upon sufficient market yields, are designated the semipublic sector. All remaining firms form the market sector, that is, the sector that produces goods and services sold via a market mechanism; here the continuity of production depends on sufficient market yields. For example, state enterprises that sell their products to cover their operating costs and do not depend on transfers from the government are incorporated with the market sector.

As to public sector contributions (the criterion for the demarcation of the semipublic sector), only income transfers are taken into account. It goes without saying that the public authorities give financial support to firms in many ways, for example, price-reducing subsidies and capital transfers. Yet the definition of the semipublic sector is expressly limited to finance in the form of income transfers. This form of financing usually involves direct regulation of the level of production, so that the price mechanism does not play a role in determining the volume of production, while other forms of public sector support only involve indirect influence over the level of production. Through price-reducing subsidies, for example, an attempt is made to increase the attractiveness of certain goods compared with other goods and thus to boost sales. Admittedly the direct connection between demand and the sacrifice made is to some extent affected, but it is not served; the market mechanism still functions.

The semipublic sector is made up primarily of health care; old age care; social welfare; and services related to culture, recreation, and research. Insofar as these services rely on mixed financing, that is, a part is made up of contributions by the consumer and the remainder consists of income transfers by the public sector, their activities are considered to fall within the semipublic sector proportionate to the share of the income transfers in the total financing of production. The advantage of this definition is that the exploitation costs of the semipublic sector are by definition equal to the public authority grants it has received. This means that when public and semipublic sectors are consolidated, the total amount of public expenditure will remain unchanged, thus preserving the link with the traditional presentation of public sector expenditure.

The share of public sector income transfers in the total output of the benefitted institutions is calculated with the help of the input/output tables of the national account statistics. Two categories can be distinguished: (1) medical and veterinary services and (2) culture, recreation, and social work. The public authority's share of the financing of the first was seventy-seven percent in 1980 (sixty-four percent in 1963), and its share of the second was sixty-nine percent in 1980 (forty percent in 1963). Wages paid in the semipublic sector, as well as expenditure on goods and services, can be approximated by applying the calculated percentage shares to the total wages paid in these sectors and to their total expenditures on goods and services respectively. Finally, employment in the semipublic sector can be estimated in the same manner; the percentage share is applied to the total number of employees in the two categories named above.

Income per capita. The average gross income per earner in the public sector can be calculated simply by dividing total remuneration by the number of persons. Real gross income per capita is obtained by deflating the resulting figure with the price index. Of course, this does not give us information about the actual income earned by any specific public servant. If, for example, the average age of public servants were to fall, the average income per public servant would show a tendency to decrease simply because young public servants tend to earn less than older ones. A marked increase in the number of public servants with a higher level of education will have the opposite effect. A similar phenomenon can be discerned with regard to social benefits per recipient. For example, over a period of time an unemployed person shifts automatically from a scheme with higher to one with lower benefits.

Other public sector expenditure. The following categories of public sector expenditure have now been distinguished:

a. wages paid to public servants, specifying the number of such persons and the gross wage per person;
b(i). wages paid to persons employed in the semipublic sector, specifying the number employed and the gross wage per person;
b(ii). benefits paid to the recipients of social welfare, specifying the number of recipients and the gross benefit per recipient.

The following income transfers remain:

b(iii). income transfers that serve to supplement income, for example, family allowances, study grants, and tenant-related rent subsidies;
b(iv). net amount paid in income transfers abroad, under EEC arrangements, for example;
b(v). semipublic sector expenditure on goods and services: Such expenditure is a direct claim on goods and services produced by the market sector.

The following transfers remain as well:

c. expenditure on goods and services by the public sector itself;
d. interest paid on the public sector debt;
e. miscellaneous expenditure, such as capital grants and loans to industry and public housing loans.

The Distribution of the Burden of Taxation and Social Insurance Contributions.

So far, the public sector receipts have been taken to be taxation and social insurance contributions. The public sector also obtains income from private persons through sources such as fines, school and university fees, duties, and disposal fees. The Netherlands public sector also receives large amounts in natural gas royalties and the like.

Taxes and social insurance contributions paid by the public sector. As already stated, the purpose of this chapter is to analyze the extent to which public sector expenditure lays a claim on goods and services produced by the

market sector. Such an analysis requires that the amounts paid in taxes, social insurance contributions, and the like, by public sector employees and the
beneficiaries of social welfare be deducted from the relevant public sector
expenditure items. For this to be done it is necessary to know the amounts
paid by the various categories. However, the information available is
sketchy so that such taxes and social insurance contributions must be estimated as nearly as possible. This is done in the following way.

The total of the relevant taxes and social insurance contributions are allocated to the public sector and the market sector on the basis of the wages
subject to income tax and to social insurance contributions. In doing so account is taken of the differences in average income and of progressive rates of
taxation. Account has also been taken of the amounts the recipients of social
insurance benefits have paid in taxation and in social insurance contributions.

Income transfers by the personal sector (fines, duties, and so on) are ap-
portioned to the total number of income earners in proportion to the number
employed in the public sector plus the number receiving social insurance
benefits and social welfare, and the number employed in the market sector.

The amounts thus obtained are then deducted from the payments shown
under a and b (i) through b (iii) above so that it becomes possible to calculate
the average disposable wage per public sector employee and the average
disposable benefit.

Taxes and social insurance contributions paid by the market sector. All
remaining taxes, social insurance contributions, duties, and so on (including
the natural gas royalties) are by definition paid by the market sector. Employees' taxes, and so on, are calculated in the same way as taxes from public
sector personnel and dependents. The taxes and social insurance contributions that have not been imputed are then allocated to the other incomes
(mainly incomes from profit). Thus it becomes possible to calculate the average disposable labor income per capita and the disposable capital incomes.

Certain public sector expenditures have the effect of easing the burden of
taxation and social insurance contributions on the market sector. For example, in the Netherlands the public authorities grant subsidies to investors.
These subsidies are generally paid by way of a deduction from the amount
due in taxation. From the macroeconomic point of view such investment
subsidies must be regarded as easing the burden of taxation and social insurance contributions.

National Income as
the Denominator and Rules
for Distribution

It is customary in international analyses to relate various magnitudes including public sector expenditure, public sector receipts, and the financial

deficit to the national income or the national product. There are, however, several disadvantages in using national income as the denominator.

First, it insufficiently reflects the interaction between the market sector and the public sector. After all, national income also includes the value added (wages paid) by the public sector. Second, national income, and this relates to the first problem, does not provide the financing base for public sector expenditure, nor does it give a satisfactory indication of the income available for distribution. Thus the analysis presented in this chapter shows public sector expenditure expressed as a percentage of the value added by the market sector (at market prices). The value added by the market sector equals national income minus the value added by the public and semi-public sectors.

Moreover, owing to the lack of data on taxes and social insurance contributions paid by recipients of transfer incomes, the volume of the public sector is often overestimated if expressed as a percentage of net national income. Transfer incomes are not included in net national income; the taxes and social insurance contributions paid from these incomes do not form a burden on primary incomes. Overestimation of the public sector, expressed as a percentage of net national income, can then be made equal to the amount in taxes and social insurance contributions paid from the transfer incomes.

As already noted, net public sector expenditure must be financed from the value added (output) by the market sector; the remainder must be divided between labor income and profits. In other words, claims are laid on the output of the market sector (in real terms) by

(1) income earners consisting of persons entitled to income on the grounds of labor performed (in the market sector or public sector) or persons entitled to benefits;
(2) public sector expenditure, other than mentioned under (1);
(3) profits.

If the growth in output of the market sector is to be distributed in such a way that the relative shares of these three categories remain constant, it is possible to formulate a simple rule: the improvement in the disposable income per capita (employed and unemployed) should equal the growth in production of the market sector per income earner/recipient.[2] The growth of other public sector expenditure in real terms may not exceed the growth in output. Only in this way can growth in profits be guaranteed that will not fall short of the growth in output. Given a satisfactory level of profit, this is a necessary condition for the continuity of the production in the market sector and thus for a viable basis to finance the public sector.

For example, if output increases by three percent per year and the number of persons one and one-half percent, then disposable income may rise by one and one-half percent per capita. If the other public sector expenditure increases by three percent in volume terms, then disposable profits will also increase by three percent. Assuming that the share of disposable profits must rise because investment must be stimulated, then the increase in disposable income per capita will have to be less than the growth in output per capita and/or it will also be necessary to reduce the share of the other public sector expenditure.

Results for the Netherlands

Expressed as a percentage of the value added by the market sector, public sector expenditure in the Netherlands has increased by nineteen percentage points over the past seventeen years, a much sharper increase than in most of the other OECD countries. The increase in revenues was slightly lower, causing the public sector's financial deficit to increase. In the ten years preceding the first oil crisis, the growth of market sector output still averaged six percent per annum, after which it fell to an average of one percent in the next seven years (Table 4.1). After having remained constant in the ten-year period first referred to, the number of persons employed in the market sector declined by an average of three-fourths percent per annum in the subsequent period.

Public sector expenditure on incomes. Over seventy-five percent of the rise in the relative volume of public sector expenditure over the past seventeen years (1963-1980) has been attributable to net expenditure on incomes,

TABLE 4.1   Public Sector Expenditure and Revenues on a Transaction Basis

	1963	1973	1980	1964/1973	1974/1980
	As Percentage of Value Added by Market Sector			*Average Percentage Change Per Annum in Real Terms**	
(1) Net expenditure on incomes	19.7	27.3	34.5	9½	4½
(2) (number of persons)				(3¾)	(3¾)
(3) (real income per person)				(5½)	(½)
(4) Goods and services bought	13.0	11.8	14.2	5	3½
(5) Other expenditure	10.0	10.8	13.2	7	4
(6) Total expenditure	42.7	49.9	61.9	8	4
(7) Receipts from market sector	38.5	49.0	54.3	9	2½
(8) Financial deficit (−)	−4.2	−0.9	−7.6		
(9) Value added by market sector	100	100	100	6	1

*Deflated by the rise in domestic selling prices in industry. For the recipients of net expenditure on incomes, the rise in prices of personal consumption is more relevant.

that is, payments of salaries to persons employed in the public sector and the semipublic sector plus benefits paid on account of loss of income after deduction of taxes and social insurance contributions paid by these two categories. During the two periods distinguished (1964-1973 and 1974-1980) the increase in real terms in net expenditure on incomes was on average three and one-half percentage points per annum higher than the growth of output of the market sector. (Compare lines 1 and 9 of Table 4.1).

The rise in net expenditure of incomes in real terms has been due to two causes: (1) the increase in the number of persons receiving an income from the public sector and (2) the increase in real disposable income per person.

The increase in the number of persons receiving an income from the public sector has been equal in the two periods considered, averaging three and three-quarters per annum. However, measured in man years this meant a substantially sharper increase from 1974 to 1980. After all, the annual growth of the *total* number of persons receiving an income in one way or another (roughly the population aged fifteen years and over) has remained more or less constant; however, in the 1970s the loss of employment in the market sector was about 25,000 man years per annum. The persons thus losing their jobs, plus those making their entry in the labor market, have had to claim benefits on account of loss in income unless they found a job in the public or semipublic sector. The ratio of the number of persons receiving an income from the public sector to the number employed in the market sector thus rose from fifty-five percent in 1963 to eighty percent in 1973 and one hundred and ten percent in 1980 (see Table 4.2).

TABLE 4.2 Number of Persons Dependent for Their Income on the Public Sector

	1980	1964/1973	1974/1980
	Thousands of Man Years	Average Rise Per Annum, in Thousands of Man Years	
(1) Persons employed by public sector	660	8	13
(2) Persons employed by semi-public sector	350	13	14
(3) Recipients of benefits on account of loss of income	2,760	68	97
(4) Persons dependent for income on public sector	3,770	89	124
(5) Persons earning their income in the market sector	3,400	2	−25
(6) Total number of income earners/recipients	7,170	91	99

TABLE 4.3   Growth of Market Sector Output and Growth of
**   Income Per Person**

	1964/1973	1974/1980
	Average Percentage Change in Real Terms	
(1) Market sector output*	6	1
(2) Total number of income earners and recipients	1½	1½
(3) Output per income earner/recipient	4½	−½
(4) (Disposable income per person in public sector)	(5½)	(½)
(5) (Disposable labor income per person in market sector)	(4½)	(1)½

*Adjusted for changes in the terms of trade.

The rise in the income per capita in the public sector also contributed to the increase in the claim on goods and services produced by the market sector. Table 4.3 shows that the rise in the disposable income per capita in the public sector did in fact slow down considerably over the years, but that it was nonetheless on average about one percentage point higher than the growth available per capita.

Goods and services bought and other public sector expenditure. Goods and services bought and other public sector expenditure also contributed between 1974 and 1980 to the rise in the relative claim by the public sector on output; between 1964 and 1973 it had been more or less neutral. It is true that the rate of increase in real terms both of expenditure on goods and services by the public sector and of other expenditure had fallen considerably in comparison to between 1964 and 1973, but this decline was much less than the fall in market sector output. (Compare lines 4, 5, and 9 in Table 4.1).

Disposable income in the market sector. To finance the rise in public sector expenditure, the burden to taxation and social insurance contributions borne by the market sector rose considerably. In the seven years between 1974 and 1980 this burden, expressed in terms of value added by the market sector, rose by sixteen percentage points and the share of disposable incomes fell correspondingly (Table 4.4). In other words, real disposable income in the market sector rose more slowly than output did. In the ten years between 1964 and 1973 the growth in volume terms of disposable income in the market sector was nonetheless four percent per year; however this growth was for the most part used to improve disposable labor income. Profits (in volume terms) could only rise slightly by keeping the labor force constant. Between 1974 and 1980 the public sector laid claim to more than the growth of output, so that disposable income in the market sector came under heavy

TABLE 4.4 Distribution of Value Added by the Market Sector

	1963	1973	1980	1964/1973	1974/1980
	As Percentage of Value Added by Market Sector			Average Percentage Rise Per Annum in Volume Terms	
(1) Value added by the market sector	100	100	100	6	1
(2) Payments and transfers from the market sector to the public sector	38.5	49.0	54.3	9	2
(3) Disposable income of the market sector (1-2)	61.5	51.0	45.7	4	−½
3(i) Labor income net result of:	50.1	42.5	41.3	4½	½
—disposable labor income per person				4½	1
—number of persons employed					−½
3(ii) Capital income	11.4	8.5	4.4	3	−8½

pressure. Labor nonetheless increased its purchasing power, so that profits fell sharply.

Beyond a critical level each fall in profits is a threat to the continuity of production and thus to the income of the public sector. The reality of this threat can be seen from the very low rate of growth in output in the last years. After all profits provide an important source of finance for essential investments and consequently for the growth in output and in employment.

Summary

The growth of the public sector has long been a topic of discussion and many different explanations have been put forward. This chapter looks at one specific explanation: the growth of the public sector as a result of developments in the market sector, which in turn is the result of the developments in the public sector, among other factors. To highlight this interaction between the public sector and the market sector the relevant data had to be compiled, regrouped, and subjected to statistical analyses. These processes form the main subject of this article. The results of the analyses show that for the Netherlands evidence can be found that this interaction has become the major explanatory factor for the growth of the public sector in the seventies. The passing on to industry of the increasing burden of taxation and social security contributions has, through a decline in profitability, negatively affected the propensity to invest. As a consequence, the employment situation in the market sector has deteriorated and an increasing number of persons have had to be financially supported by the government. This in return has led to a further rise in the burden of taxation and social insurance contributions.

NOTES

1. This is made up of central, local and state authorities and social security functions.

2. It should be noted that this is nothing more than a refinement of the better-known rule that the improvement in open income per worker should not exceed the growth in production per worker.

REFERENCES

KESSLER, G. A. (1979) "De publieke sector in de jaren tachtig," Economische Statistische Berichten, October.

De Nederlandsche Bank (1979, 1980) Annual Reports. The Hague.

Sociaal-Economische Raad (1979) "Advies inzake het sociaal-economishe beleid op middel-lange termijn," June.

———— (1978) "Advies inzake omvang en groei van de collectieve sector," September.

CHAPTER 5

THE GROWTH AND INFLUENCE
OF EXPENDITURE
The United Kingdom, 1961-1979

WALTER ELTIS

It is conventional to assess the possible influence of extra public expenditure and taxation by relating their levels and growth to the national product. Since the national product sums a country's outputs, this ought to provide at first sight the best indication of the resources the country can make available to the public sector.

Table 5.1 therefore sets out U.K. public expenditure, taxation, and the national product for the cyclical peak years of 1961, 1965, 1969, 1973, and 1979 and, in addition, 1976. It is well known that the ratio of public expenditure to the national product varies considerably in the cycle. Most public expenditure is based on long-term social programs, and these are maintained or expanded irrespective of whether the national product is rising or falling in particular years. Public expenditure therefore forms a higher fraction of the national product in recession than at cyclical peaks. Social security support for the unemployed is actually higher in recession, which accentuates the tendency for the public expenditure ratio to fluctuate counter-cyclically. For an estimation of the trend of the increase in public expenditure and taxation, it is obviously important to observe this in years that are strictly comparable. The cyclical peak years provide the best indication of the pressure of the public sector on real resources. However, 1976 has been added to the cyclical peak comparisons because that is the year government policy with regard to the public sector changed from Keynesian to a classical approach due to a new belief by British governments that extra public expenditure would crowd out private investment expenditures.[1] There is no doubt

TABLE 5.1   The Ratio of Taxation and Public Expenditure to the National
             Product (in million pounds sterling)

	1961	1965	1969	1973	1976	1979
(1)	27513	35859	47071	74204	125635	189991
(2)	2204	2882	3885	7012	13362	22163
(3)	25309	32977	43186	67192	112273	167828
(4)	9438	12861	18199	29179	56108	81574
(5)	8036	10961	17138	24098	44726	68085
(6)	849	1177	−290	3679	7889	12128
(7)	37.29%	39.00%	42.14%	43.43%	49.97%	48.61%
(8)	31.75%	33.24%	39.68%	35.86%	39.84%	40.57%
(9)	3.09%	3.28%	−0.67%	5.48%	7.03%	7.23%

NOTE: Data in this and the following tables are derived from *National Income and Expenditure* (1972, 1980). Please see the Appendix for amplification of 1 through 9 above.

that from 1976 onwards, both Mr. Callaghan's Labour government and Mrs. Thatcher's Conservative government have endeavored to halt the growth of public spending for reasons many Keynesians have found bewildering. The comparison between 1976 and 1979, which cuts across a cycle, also shows the first effects of the new public expenditure policies.

Table 5.1 measures public expenditure and the national product at market prices. In the case of Britain, market prices exceed factor cost by between ten and twenty percent, so a comparison between public expenditure at market prices and the national product at factor cost would exaggerate the public expenditure ratio by between one-tenth and one-fifth.[2] The table shows that the ratio of general government expenditure to the national product net of capital consumption increased by eleven percentage points from 37.29 to 48.61 percent in the four cycles, 1961-1965, 1965-1969, 1969-1973, and 1973-1979. Total taxation and social security contributions increased by 8.82 percentage points from 31.75 to 40.57 percent of the net national product in the same period. There are two obvious points to note here. First taxation and government expenditure do not increase at the same rate because budgets are not balanced. It is in fact possible for expenditure to increase and for taxation to fall quite significantly as occurred in Britain in the cycle from 1969 to 1973, which was dominated by Mr. Edward Heath's ultra-Keynesian dash for growth. The ratio of taxation was slashed from 39.68 percent in 1969 to 35.86 percent in 1973, while expenditure grew from 42.14 to 43.43 percent. In 1969 the Labour Chancellor, Mr. Roy Jenkins, actually ran a budget surplus and repaid a little debt, while in 1973 Mr. Heath's Chancellor, Mr. Anthony Barber, ran a budget deficit of 5.48 percent of the national product, enabling him to spend more than Mr. Jenkins while taxing substantially less. One needs information on both taxation and public expenditure to assess the influence of the rate of growth of the public sector. From information on taxation alone it could be surmised that the British public sector grew by less than one percentage point from 1969 to 1979. In this period, however, the public expenditure ratio grew by 6.47 percentage points. Almost the entire increase was financed by borrowing, so an examination of the weight of taxation alone would entirely overlook what was occurring.

Keynes was the first modern economist to argue that a failure to finance extra public expenditure by taxation was likely to lead to a faster rate of increase of the money supply and therefore to faster inflation, which would act as a tax on cash balances.[3] This certainly occurred from 1969 to 1973, so it would be misleading to believe that the total burden of taxation fell as Table 5.1 indicates. The table does not and cannot include the effect of inflation acting as a tax on cash balances. In consequence, attention should be focused on the public expenditure ratio and not the tax ratio on the argument that the extra expenditure must create a burden of some kind however it is financed. Focusing attention on expenditure rather than taxation emphasizes that its ratio to the national product increased in each cycle, but relatively slowly until 1973. It increased by 1.71 percentage points from 1961 to 1965 when Mr. Harold Macmillan's Conservative government was in power for most of the time. Mr. Harold Wilson's Labour government increased the public expenditure ratio almost twice as fast: by 3.14 percentage points from 1965 to 1969. It increased by only 1.29 percentage points from 1969 to 1973, mainly the years of Mr. Heath's Conservative government, and it increased by 5.18 percentage points from 1973 to 1979, a period dominated by the Labour Governments of Mr. Wilson and Mr. Callaghan. However, most of this increase occurred between 1973 and 1976. During these years the government expenditure ratio increased by 6.54 percentage points, although a considerable part of this increase is a result of comparing a recession with a boom ratio of public expenditure. In Mr. Callaghan's three years as prime minister (1976 to 1979) the public expenditure ratio actually fell by 1.36 percentage points.

A second point to note about Table 5.1 is that borrowing does not precisely equal expenditure minus taxation. Governments raise a little money by methods other than taxing and borrowing. General government receives some income from rents and so on, so there are slight statistical discrepancies that have no particular significance between total government expenditure and the sum of taxation and borrowing.

The pressure on the private sector of the economy from growth in public expenditure and taxation obviously depends partly on how fast output is growing. If output grows by 20 percent in a four-year cycle, and the public expenditure ratio grows by 2 percentage points from say 40 to 42 percent, the national product net of public expenditure will increase 16 percent. A 2 percentage point growth in public expenditure reduces the growth of real resources available to the private sector only from 20 to 16 percent in the four years. If output grows just 5 percent in the four-year cycle, growth in the government's share from 40 to 42 percent will reduce the growth of real resources available to the private sector from 5 to 1.5 percent. Table 5.2 shows how the real national product has increased in Britain over the four cycles, and how far the growth in public expenditure has influenced the growth of real resources available to the private sector. The table shows that over the whole eighteen-year period making up four complete cycles, the net national product increased 48 percent, that is, at an annual rate of 2.2 percent. In the same period real public expenditure increased 93 percent, that is, at an annual rate of 3.7 percent. That meant that what was available to the private sector net of public expenditure increased only 22 percent in eighteen years, that is, at an annual rate of only 1.1 percent. Public expenditure therefore increased over three times as fast as the part of the national product that remained after public expenditure.

That is the situation over the eighteen-year period as a whole. The final cycle from 1973 to 1979 was however far more damaging to the private sector than the three previous cycles, mainly because the rate of growth of the net national product fell from 3.1 percent in the three cycles from 1961 to 1973 to a mere 0.5 percent per annum from 1973 to 1979. Real government expenditure increased at a rate of 4.4 percent per annum from 1961 to 1973, but because output was growing at a reasonable rate, what remained after public expenditure increased at a rate of 2.2 percent. Public expenditure was, therefore, growing just twice as fast as the growth of real resources available to the rest of the economy. From 1973 to 1979 the growth of real government expenditure increased at only 2.6 percent against the previous 4.4 percent, but because output net of capital consumption was increasing by a mere 0.5 percent per annum, the real resources available net of public expenditure actually declined 1.1 percent per annum. Within the 1973-1979 cycle there is of course a sharp contrast between what occurred from 1973 to 1976 and 1976 to 1979, and this is influenced both by the change in public

TABLE 5.2   The Growth of the National Product Gross and Net of Public Expenditure and Taxation (real gross domestic product, 1975 = 100)

	1961	1965	1969	1973	1976	1979
(10)	72.1	82.0	90.5	105.0	104.3	111.0
(11)	66.3	75.4	83.0	95.1	93.2	98.1
(12)	24.7	29.4	35.0	41.3	46.6	47.7
(13)	21.1	25.1	32.9	34.1	37.1	39.8
(14)	41.6	46.0	48.0	53.8	46.6	50.4
(15)	45.2	50.3	50.1	61.0	56.1	58.3

NOTE: Please see the Appendix for an amplification of 10-15 above.

policy with regard to public expenditure in 1976 and the fact that 1973-1976 was a peak to recession period, while 1976-1979 was a recession to recovery period. In 1973-1976 real public expenditure increased at an annual rate of 4.1 percent, almost as fast as in the three previous complete cycles, while the net national product less public expenditure fell at an annual rate of 4.7 percent. From 1976 to 1979 , in contrast, real public expenditure increased at an annual rate of only 0.8 percent, which represents a complete contrast to any previous period; while the net national product less public expenditure increased at an annual rate of 2.6 percent. Thus for the first time, in this stage of the final cycle, the extra resources available to the private sector increased faster, indeed over three times as fast, as real public expenditure. Considering the whole period from 1961 to 1979, 1973 to 1976 stands out as the sole period in which there is a strong a priori possibility that public expenditure grew at a rate that risked the destabilization of the economy. In the three cycles prior to 1973, public expenditure grew at 4.4 percent, thus growing faster than the net national product, which grew at only 3.1 percent. However, that excess growth would be justified by an income elasticity of no more than 1.42, if it were hypothesized that public expenditure growth was entirely the result of an income elasticity of demand for more than one of the public services implemented by the political process. So what occurred in these three cycles may not be far from what would have occurred if resources had to be allocated to these items of expenditure through private spending decisions instead of by political processes. In these three cycles what remained for the private sector after public expenditure increased at an annual rate of 2.1 percent (about two-thirds as fast as the net national product) should, on a priori grounds, have allowed the private sector to expand private consumption and investment at acceptable long-term rates—indeed, at considerably faster rates than in almost all the decades of the previous century. The period from 1976 to 1979 was also a time when the private sector apparently obtained considerable extra real resources. The years 1973 to 1976 stand out as the one subperiod in which there was the extraordinary imbalance of 4.1 percent more per annum for the public sector, while the private sector was obtaining 5.3 percent per annum less. It is no wonder that there was a severe political reaction in 1976, assisted by pressure from the International Monetary Fund, which resulted in efforts to persuade the U.K. government to curb the growth of public expenditure, which, in fact, it was already in the process of doing.

Prior to 1973, however, there were difficulties associated with the growth of taxation and public expenditure despite the relative trends that appear to leave an ample rate of growth of real resources for both sectors. It is widely believed that the explanation of the wage explosion in 1969 lay in part in a tax revolt.[4] There was no significant monetary expansion prior to 1969 (when the chancellor was, as has been shown, actually repaying debt), but there was a very considerable increase in the average worker's tax deductions. The government deducted 16 percent of the average worker's earnings in 1963, 18 percent in 1964, 20 percent in 1965, 21 percent in 1966, 22 percent in 1967, 23 percent in 1968, and 24 percent in 1969.[5] Therefore, in this six-year period, while the real pretax earnings of the average worker increased 24.4 percent (that is, at an annual rate of 3.7 percent, which is a very high rate for Britain), net of tax real earnings increased only 8 percent, or at an annual rate of 1.2 percent. Money wages increased at an annual rate of 6.9 percent from 1963 to 1969, and then increased 10.4 percent from 1969 to 1970, 10.8 percent from 1970 to 1971, and 11.6 percent from 1971 to 1972. There may well have been an element of tax frustration in this acceleration of wage increase. Table 5.2 shows that from 1965 to 1969 the net national product net of all taxes actually fell. Net of public expenditure rose at an annual rate of 1.1 percent, but net of all taxes fell at an annual rate of 0.1 percent. Since Mr. Jenkins was shifting the budget from a borrowing requirement of 3.28 percent of the national income in 1965 to a repayment of debt of 0.67 percent in 1969, the shift to taxation in this period was greater than the increase in expenditure.

In contrast, the net national product net of all taxes actually increased from 1969 to 1973 by 21.8 percent (5 percent per annum), but this extraordinarily rapid increase in net of tax incomes was associated with a massive widening of the budget deficit. There was therefore a monetary explosion that produced the inflation tax on cash balances previously remarked upon. The monetary explosion and the widening of the budget deficit also had strong adverse effects on the balance of payments.

It appears from the data so far presented that the modest relative rate of growth of public expenditure in the cycles prior to 1973 may have had significant adverse effects on the economy from 1965 to 1969 and from 1969 to 1973. These are most directly attributable to huge swings in budgetary policy rather than to the rate of growth of public expenditure itself. Taxation rose massively from 1965 to 1969 because a budget deficit of three percent of the national product was turned into a surplus of almost one percent in this period, which raised taxation nineteen percent relative to the real national product in just four years. The increase in public expenditure in itself would have required an increase in taxation of only eight percent in relation to the national product, which would not have caused such strain over a four-year period. In the following cycle of 1969 to 1973, budgetary policy went to the opposite extreme and allowed a huge deficit to develop. If taxation had followed public expenditure upward, it would have had to rise three percent relative to the national product in four years, causing little strain. In fact it was cut ten percent in relation to the national income producing a huge budgetary swing that plausibly had a variety of adverse effects on the economy which had nothing at all to do with the underlying rate of growth of public expenditure.

The argument has so far been expressed in terms of conventional national income accounts. These are, however, not the ideal tools to use in an examination of the influence of growth in public expenditure on the development of the economy. Both the numerator and the denominator of the ratio public expenditure/national product contain items that should not ideally be included in an account of the relationship between the public and private sectors that attempts to estimate the influence of the resources taken by the public sector on the real resources still available to the private sector.

For this purpose the item public expenditure, as conventionally measured, suffers from the defect that £100 of public expenditure often results in purchases of goods and services with government financed incomes of very much less than £100. Insofar as the £100 consists of wages and salaries paid to workers employed by central and local government, they will pay taxes and save some of each £100 the receive. If, for instance, they pay direct taxes and social security contributions of £25, £100 of public expenditure will then entitle them to purchase £75 of the national product measured at market prices. The crude subtractions of Table 5.2 imply that an extra £100 of public expenditure reduces what is available to the private sector by £100. If £10 of the £75 is saved, the goods and services available to private sector workers and companies will in fact be reduced by £65 and not by £75. Purchases of capital goods or raw materials by general government will, in contrast, reduce the goods available to the two sectors together at a cyclical peak. Some items of public expenditure therefore deprive the private sector of more goods and marketed services than other items. In any case, the private sector will have to give up significantly less investment and consumption than the aggregate public expenditure statistics in Tables 5.1 and 5.2 imply.

Moreover, the denominator national product in the ratio public expenditure/national product exaggerates what is available. The national product as conventionally measured includes estimates of the output of unmarketed public services such as administration, defense, and state-funded education. If the objective is to discover the impact of the goods and services required by general government on the real resources available for investment and consumption by the companies and workers of the private sector, then the provision of unmarketed public services should be excluded from output because they can be neither invested nor privately consumed. If, however, the national product is measured net of the output of unmarketed public services, so that it is the economy's total *marketed* output, it will provide an accurate measure of the investable and the privately consumable goods and services available to the public and the private sectors taken together.

In algebraic terms, if total marketed output is Y(m), this will be available for investment and consumption by those who produce no marketed output, G(m), for consumption by those who produce marketed output in the market sector, C(m), for investment in the market sector, I(m), and for exports of marketed output, X(m). Since marketed output to meet the investment and consumption needs of the market sector and of those who live off nonmarket incomes can also be obtained through imports, M(m), the following relationship will hold, as with conventional national income accounts:

Domestic demand for marketed output = G(m) + C(m) + I(m)
Supply of marketed output available for domestic investment and con-
    sumption = Y(m) + M(m) − X(m)
so that: Y(m) = G(m) + C(m) + I(m) + (X(m) − M(m)),
that is, 1 = G(m)/Y(m) + C(m)/Y(m) + I(m)/Y(m) + X(m)−
    M(m)/Y(m)

G(m)/Y(m) is the proportion of marketed output absorbed by general government, which leaves (1 − G(m)/Y(m)) for market sector producers and for meeting the needs of international trade. If G(m)/Y(m) rises, (1 − G(m)/Y(m)) must fall equivalently, and this in turn must reduce either C(m)/Y(m) (the proportion of marketed output that is consumed by those who produce marketed output), or I(m)/Y(m) (the ratio of market sector investment to marketed output), or X(m) − M(m)/Y(m) (the marketed output available for the acquisition of overseas assets expressed as a ratio of marketed output).

If G(m) and Y(m) rise equally, there will be no increase in G(m)/Y(m) and no adverse pressures on the share of output available to the market sector where marketed output is produced. It is only where marketed output is at, or close to, its ceiling that an increase in G(m) is bound to raise the ratio G(m)/Y(m), thereby placing adverse pressures on the output available to the market sector. It is important, therefore, to focus attention on the growth of the ratio G(m)/Y(m) in the cyclical peak years of 1961, 1965, 1969, 1973, and 1979, since these estimates are most likely to indicate the degree of adverse pressure actually exerted by growth in the share of marketed output absorbed in the nonmarket sector on the availability of marketed output to those who produce it. For the reasons set out previously, G(m)/Y(m) is also estimated for 1976, the policy turning-point year.[6]

Marketed output itself, Y(m), is simple to estimate. Statisticians estimate the output of unmarketed public services such as public administration by summing the wages and salaries paid to provide this. Hence the total of net marketed output, Y(m), will equal the gross national product at market prices, less capital consumption in the market sector, and less the wage and salary bill of general government. These totals are set out in Table 5.3. The table shows that the ratio of marketed output to the national product has fallen from 89.6 percent in 1961 to 86.7 percent in 1979. The fall has therefore been a relatively modest one. Marketed output (i.e., what is actually

TABLE 5.3 The Relationship Between the National Product and Marketed Output (in million pounds sterling)

	1961	1965	1969	1973	1976	1979
(1)	27513	35859	47071	74204	125635	189991
(16)	2872	3821	5135	9026	17701	23925
(17)	24641	32035	41935	65178	107934	166066
(18)	1972	2613	3539	6374	12313	20558
(19)	22669	29425	38397	58804	95621	145508
(20)	0.896	0.892	0.889	0.875	0.852	0.867

NOTE: Please see the Appendix for an amplification of 1 and 16-20 above.

available for private consumption, investment, and exports) has, however, been 10 percent or more below the national product as conventionally measured throughout the period.

The economy's net marketed output has to provide C(m), consumption by those who produce it; I(m), investment by the firms, and so on, that produce it; X(m) − M(m), and G(m). The measurement of I(m) and X(m) − M(m) is entirely straightforward. I(m), total net investment in the market sector, is simply the total of investment in the market sector expressed in market prices and net of capital consumption. There are, however, two complications. The market sector is that part of the economy producing marketed outputs. It will therefore include not only the whole private sector that is financed entirely from the sale of marketed outputs, but also investment by public or nationalized corporations and housing investment by general government. Since public corporations and general government housing agencies finance a high fraction of their costs through the marketing of the goods and services they produce or provide, they are, economically speaking, in the market sector. Legally speaking they are, of course, in the public sector. In an economic argument their role is most clearly understood if they are aggregated with the private sector, which is also financed by charging prices rather through taxation or government borrowing.[7] There are no problems in the measurement of X(m) − M(m) since all exports and imports are marketed, so this will be the total of visible and invisible exports less imports (all measured at market prices). Exports will of course include the net property income received from overseas on current account.

G(m), the marketed outputs used up in the nonmarket sector, and C(m), the marketed outputs consumed by market sector producers, are far more difficult to estimate. G(m), total general government financed purchases of marketed output, comprises the following:

G(i) = nonhousing investment by general government.
G(q) = material purchases by general government for current use, for example, equipment for the armed services, hospitals, and schools.

G(w) = consumption from the wages and salaries paid to provide public services.

G(t) = consumption from social transfers arranged by general government.

G(d) = consumption from debt interest paid by general government less interest received by general government.

Thus $G(m) = G(i) + G(q) + G(w) + G(t) + G(d)$.

This total omits three categories of government expenditure included in the public expenditure total in Tables 5.1 and 5.2. First, investment by general government, which totaled £2,100 millions or 1.3 percent of the net national product in 1979, is now included in market sector investment for the reasons which have been outlined. Second, subsidies that totaled £4,306 millions or 2.6 percent of the net national product in 1979 are excluded, because these mostly go to the market sector and there is no satisfactory way of segregating out the small fraction that goes to the nonmarket sector. Third, net lending to the public corporations, and so on, which totaled £3,273 millions or 2.0 percent of the gross domestic product in 1979, is excluded because this is lending to firms in the economy's market sector. These three items of government expenditure (which came to 5.9 percent of the net national product in 1979), are excluded from G(m) because they are in fact purchases that are intended mainly to assist the market sector. The remaining items making up G(m), (G(i) + G(q) + G(w) + G(t) + G(d)) are all items of expenditure, which, at a given level of marketed output, reduce the amounts that those who produce marketed output can invest and consume.

Of these, G(i) and G(q) can be estimated straightforwardly; they are simply the statistical series for general government investment and current expenditures on materials. A first step toward the estimation of consumption from general government financed personal incomes, G(w), G(t) and G(d), is to make use of the identity:

$C(p) = C(m) + G(w) + G(t) + G(d)$

where C(p) is total personal consumption at market prices for which data are readily available; C(m) is market finances personal consumption; and G(w), G(t) and G(d) are the three categories of general government financed personal consumption. A simple assumption to make would be that each group consumes the same fraction of pretax personal incomes. Then if, for instance, C(p) were seventy percent of Y(p) (total personal incomes for which data are again readily available in the national income accounts of all advanced countries), it would be assumed that seventy percent of government-financed wages and salaries, seventy percent of social transfers, and seventy percent of debt interest were consumed. This assumption was made by Robert Bacon and myself in the second edition of *Britain's Economic Problem:*

Too Few Producers, but at about the same time Mr. Ralph Turvey made similar calculations from OECD accounts with the refinement that recipients of social transfers spend all that they receive.[8]

Between 1961 and 1979, social transfers that were mostly untaxed in Britain went mainly to those whose total incomes were well below the national average. It is therefore more accurate to follow Turvey's procedure and assume that $G(t) = Y(t)$ where $Y(t)$ is the total of social transfers received, or that consumption from social transfers at market prices equals the transfers themselves. Although there will be some saving from social transfers, and some taxes will be paid on state pensions by the minority of pensioners who have sufficient other income in retirement to bring their total incomes into the taxable range, consumption from transfers may fall short of the incomes received by a relatively slender margin. It is therefore more accurate to assume that the tax and savings ratio from these is the same as with personal incomes in general. Assuming that $G(t) = Y(t)$, it follows that

$$C(p) - G(t) = C(m) + G(w) + G(d) = c(Y(p) - Y(t))$$

where c is the proportion of nontransfer personal incomes consumed. Table 5.4 shows the U.K. estimates of c derived as above. During the four complete cycles from 1961 to 1979, the proportion of nontransfer personal incomes consumed fell from about 76 percent in 1961 to a little over sixty-four percent in 1979. This meant that the cost to the market sector of £100 paid to civil servants or teachers fell from about £76 in 1961 to about £64 in 1979. This occurred partly because the taxes paid by civil servants and teachers rose substantially throughout the period, and partly because the savings ratio from personal incomes also rose substantially. This estimate of the consumption ratio from personal income allows the actual consumption from personal incomes to be estimated quite straightforwardly. $G(w)$ is simply c times $Y(w)$, where $Y(w)$ is total government-financed wages and salaries received. $G(d)$ is equal to c times $Y(d)$. $C(m)$ (total personal consumption from market financed personal incomes) will equal $C(p)$ (total consumption from personal incomes) less $G(w) + G(d) + G(t)$. The estimates in Table 5.5 can then be set out for the cyclical peak years and 1976.

When Table 5.5 is compared with Table 5.1, it emerges that the ratio nonmarket purchases/net marketed output increased similarly to the ratio

TABLE 5.4 Consumption from United Kingdom Nontransfer Personal Incomes (in million pounds sterling)

	1961	1965	1969	1973	1976	1979
(21)	16127	20295	25296	39339	61990	93837
(22)	21181	27516	35305	57119	97906	145498
(23)	0.7614	0.7376	0.7165	0.6887	0.6332	0.6449

NOTE: Please see the Appendix for an amplification of 21-23 above.

TABLE 5.5   Where United Kingdom Marketed Output Went: 1961-79

percentages of net marketed output	*1961*	*1965*	*1969*	*1973*	*1976*	*1979*
(24)	·9.65	9.58	9.58	10.57	11.72	10.60
(25)	2.63	2.13	2.09	1.60	2.01	2.44
(26)	7.53	8.82	10.25	10.92	13.35	14.41
(27)	2.93	3.38	3.91	4.75	3.64	2.09
(28)	7.53	7.52	7.45	7.40	9.49	9.89
(29)	30.27	31.43	33.28	35.24	40.21	39.43
(30)	58.86	57.26	54.21	54.73	51.10	51.45
(31)	10.39	10.85	10.74	11.08	9.07	8.81
(32)	(3.03)	(2.32)	(2.36)	(1.36)	(1.06)	(1.39)
(33)	(2.19)	(2.94)	(3.13)	(3.02)	(3.18)	(2.08)
(34)	(3.77)	(4.30)	(3.76)	(4.29)	(3.96)	(3.45)
(35)	(1.40)	(1.34)	(1.49)	(2.46)	(0.90)	(1.90)
(36)	0.47	0.46	1.76	−1.06	−0.37	0.32

NOTE: Please see the Appendix for an amplification of 24-36 above.

government expenditure/net national product but was seven to nine percentage points lower. Thus the ratio of government expenditure to the national product increased from 37.29 to 48.61 percent in the four complete cycles from 1961 to 1979, while the ratio of nonmarket purchases to marketed output increased from 30.27 to 39.43 percent in the same period. The ratio of nonmarket purchases is lower, both because it excludes government investment in housing, subsidies, and lending to the nationalized industries predominantly in the market sector and because spending from government financed wages and salaries (included in nonmarket purchases) is lower than the salaries themselves (which are included in full in the government expenditure total). The lower nonmarket expenditure series should provide a better indication of the marketed output that growth of government spending actually takes from those who produce it.

The government expenditure ratio increased by 1.71, 3.14, 1.29, and 5.18 percentage points in the four successive cycles, amounting to 11.32 percentage points in all. The nonmarket purchases series increases by 1.16, 1.85, 1.96, and 4.19 percentage points in these cycles, amounting to 9.16 percentage points in all. Therefore, the differences amount to no more than 0.5 to 1.5 percentage points in each cycle.

It is of some interest to consider the actual components of government finance expenditures, which increased sharply from 1961 to 1979. By far the most significant increase is consumption from social transfers which increased from an estimated 7.53 percent of marketed output in 1961 to 14.41 percent in 1979. This increase accounts for 6.88 percentage points of the 9.16 overall increase in non-market purchases. However, market financed consumption fell by 7.41 percentage points from 58.86 to 51.45 percent of marketed output. This makes it tempting to conclude that the main change that occurred during this period was a fall in the ratio of personal consumption from market-financed incomes of around seven percentage points to finance a seven percentage-point increase in democratically determined social transfer levels. There is a strong element of truth in this broad generalization, but it misses one major development occurring simultaneously. In 1961, 9.65 percent of marketed output went to provide consumer goods for those receiving wages and salaries from general government and 58.86 to providing consumer goods for those in receipt of market financed incomes. If it had been known then that in the next eighteen years roughly seven percent of marketed output would be needed to provide extra social transfers, then an equal proportion could have been diverted from market-financed wages, salaries, dividends, and from government-financed wages and salaries. This would have taken six percentage points from the approximately sixty percent that was being consumed from market financed incomes, and one percentage point from the ten percent or so that was being consumed from government-financed wages and salaries. Instead of giving up one percentage point of marketed output to help provide for extra social transfers, the government employees consumed an extra percentage point in the eighteen years, which increased the burden on market-financed consumption by approximately two percentage points.

The reason for the increase in consumption from government-financed wages and salaries from 9.65 to 10.60 percent of marketed output when it should have fallen to around 8.60 percent to finance its proportional share of increased social transfers is clear enough. In 1961, 3,558,000 workers were employed by general government, while 21,499,000 worked in the market sector. By 1979 general-government employment had risen 51 percent to 5,389,000, while market sector employment had fallen 9 percent to 19,636,000[9] There was thus a 66 percent increase in general government employment relative to market sector employment. It is somewhat remarkable therefore that consumption from general government financed wages and salaries increased by only 1 percent of marketed output, and by only 26 percent relative to market financed consumption. A considerable fraction of the extra workers employed by general government were, in fact, part-timers and women. As a result, the government salary bill increased far less than the numbers employed.[10] This helps to explain the far smaller *relative* increase in consumption from general government wages than in the numbers employed. The small *absolute* increase—only 1 percent more of marketed output being needed to provide extra consumer goods for 51 percent more general government workers—is due to the fact that these workers saved and paid back in direct taxation a high fraction of the extra money they received.

It has been estimated that in 1961 they consumed 76.14 percent of their wages and salaries. If they had continued to consume 76.14 percent in 1979, they would have consumed 12.51 percent of marketed output. Instead, they were paying far higher tax rates and saving more, so it is estimated that they only increased their consumption from 9.65 to 10.60 percent of marketed output instead of to 12.51 percent. The enormous growth in general government employment thus placed far less strain on market sector consumption than appears at first sight. Moreover, in 1979 relative wages and salaries in the provision of public services had fallen a little behind those in the private sector. They rose sharply in the next two years. The 1979 data may therefore show a cost of public sector pay that was below trend.

The other item of nonmarket expenditure that rose was consumption from government-current material purchases, which increased from 7.53 percent of marketed output in 1961 to 9.89 percent in 1979. This increase of 2.36 percentage points reflects almost wholly the increase in total government current spending in relation to marketed output. In the case of government-financed wages and salaries, the increase in consumption from these was substantially less than the crude increase in government spending because these workers paid back to the government a growing fraction of what they received. In the case of the material purchases making up the remainder of current spending, there was no such offset. This item of nonmarket expenditure increased in line with current government spending in general, which led to the increase in its ratio of total marketed output from 7.53 to 9.89 percent in the eighteen-year period as a whole.

The remaining items in nonmarket expenditure, investment and consumption from debt interest, show no increase during the eighteen-year period. Nonhousing investment by general government increased sharply from 2.93 percent of marketed output in 1961 to 4.75 percent in 1973. It proved the easiest item to cut after the change of policy with regard to public expenditure in 1976, and it fell back to 2.09 percent of marketed output in 1979. Estimated consumption from debt interest fell from 2.63 percent of marketed output in 1961 to 1.60 percent in 1973. It then rose, largely as a result of the very large budget deficits that became endemic after 1972, to 2.44 percent of marketed output in 1979. Thus there was no trend increase but rather some fluctuation in estimated consumption from debt interest as government deficits were first eliminated and then allowed to increase massively. The figures for debt interest and consumption from debt interest would be much larger if the statistics were based solely on interest paid out by general government, but general government also receives substantial interest. Interest and dividends received have been netted from debt interest paid out to produce the quite modest figures for debt interest that are shown in all the tables. In 1979, for instance, the interest paid out by general government totaled £8829 million while general government received interest and dividends, and the like, of £3332 million. The tables are therefore based on the assumption that general government paid out £5497 million in interest in 1979. Even this figure exaggerates the burden that consumption from this interest places on the rest of the economy. This is because in a period of inflation the real value of the obligation to repay government debt falls each year by approximately the inflation rate times the debt that must be repaid. The Bank of England has estimated the effect of deducting the capital gains made by the government (through a fall in the real value of its obligations to repay debt) from the interest it pays out, and shown that when this is done, interest of government debt has recently had zero real cost to the government sector.[11] The statistics in the tables do not go to this extreme, but by netting out interest receipts from interest payments, they do show that despite massive borrowing, debt interest has not imposed a growing burden on the market sector during the period as a whole. The burdens that have mattered have been the huge increase in social transfers and to a lesser extent the increase in current expenditure by general government. This has squeezed the resources available to the market sector more through the extra materials purchased than through the payments of additional wages and salaries.

Table 5.6 shows that over the four complete cycles, real marketed output per worker increased at an annual rate of 2.5 percent. Nonmarket purchases of this output increased considerably faster, at a rate of 4.1 percent per annum on behalf of each market sector worker. What remained for the market sector itself increased more slowly at 1.7 percent per annum. These are not, however, discrepancies that must clearly be out of line with the income elasticity of demand for the services the public sector provides. The implicit income elasticity of demand for nonmarket expenditures such as health, education, and pension rights that would justify this faster rate of growth of nonmarket expenditures is 1.64, which is high but not impossibly high. The possibility that nonmarket expenditure may have grown in line with individ-

TABLE 5.6 The Growth of Real Resources Available to the Market Sector: 1961-1979 (real gross domestic product, 1975 = 100)

	1961	1965	1969	1973	1976	1979
(11)	66.3	75.4	83.0	95.1	93.2	98.1
(37)	59.4	67.3	73.8	83.2	79.4	85.1
(38)	109.1	107.9	104.0	101.9	98.6	99.6
(39)	54.45	62.37	70.96	81.65	80.53	85.4
(40)	16.48	19.60	23.62	28.77	32.38	33.6
(41)	37.97	42.77	47.34	52.88	48.15	51.7
(42)	32.05	35.71	38.47	44.69	41.15	43.9

NOTE: Please see the Appendix for an amplification of 11 and 37-42 above.

ual preferences appears greater if attention is focused on the three cycles from 1961 to 1973. In these twelve years marketed output per worker increased at an annual rate of 3.4 percent. Nonmarket purchases on behalf of each market sector worker increased at an annual rate of 4.8 percent, just 1.41 times as fast. That is by no means an implausibly high income elasticity of demand for health, education, and pension rights. Up to 1973, what remained for the market sector itself increased at 2.8 percent per annum, which is one of the fastest rates of increase in privately consumable and investable resources per worker that Britain has ever achieved.

The final cycle from 1973 to 1979 produced a far less satisfactory balance between the growth of resources to the market sector and the nonmarket sector. In these six years marketed output per worker increased by a mere 0.8 percent per annum. Nonmarket purchases on behalf of each worker increased at an annual rate of 2.7 percent, while what remained from the market sector itself fell at an annual rate of 0.4 percent. That cannot conceivably have corresponded to the actual preferences of the population for the services and pension rights that the nonmarket sector provides, and there was of course the change of policy in 1976. From 1976 to 1979 nonmarket purchases increased at an annual rate of 1.3 percent, while what remained for the market sector increased by 2.4 percent per annum, thereby helping to restore the balance between market and nonmarket expenditures.

Consumption per market sector worker followed much the same course as the output per worker that was available after nonmarket purchases. In the eighteen years as a whole it increased at an annual rate of 1.8 percent, against 1.7 percent for the residual after nonmarket expenditures. In the first cycle from 1961 to 1965 private consumption per market sector worker increased at an annual rate of 2.7 percent. Its rate of increase fell to 1.9 percent in the next cycle, 1965 to 1969, which was dominated by the Wilson government's personal tax increases. From 1969 to 1973, personal consumption increased at a record annual rate of 3.8 percent, but then ceased to grow after 1973. In the 1973-1979 cycle taken as a whole, personal consumption per worker fell at an annual rate of 0.4 percent, but it increased by 2.2 percent per annum from 1976 onwards. It is therefore only from 1973 to 1976, a three-year period that included a great deal of cyclical recession, that the growth of private consumption halted totally. In the three previous cycles, and from 1976 to 1979, the growth of personal consumption was quite substantial by British historical standards.

The statistics based on market sector accounts therefore tell a story not dissimilar to the one told in Tables 5.1 and 5.2, where the argument was confined to conventional national income accounts. Both sets of statistics show rapid growth in both private and public incomes from 1961 to 1973 and from 1976 to 1979. Both show a great discrepancy between the growth in public expenditures on behalf of each worker and the lack of growth of private sector incomes and expenditures from 1973 to 1976. The market sector accounts do, however, throw a rather different light on the period 1965 to 1969. In that time the net national product net of taxation ceased to grow, so it seemed extremely plausible that there was an element of tax revolt in the acceleration of wages after 1968. The market sector accounts, which show an increase in real private consumption per worker of 1.9 percent per annum from 1965 to 1969, throw doubt on this interpretation. The actual data for the growth of earnings net of tax show an increase of only 1.1 percent per annum for the average male worker from 1965 to 1969 (Bacon and Eltis, 1978: 212-213), but the personal savings ratio fell slightly from 8.5 to 7.9 percent. This explains part of the discrepancy between the 1.1 percent growth of male earnings net of tax and the 1.9 percent growth in consumption. An increase in the earnings of women relative to men could be one of the considerations that helps to explain the remaining discrepancy. There may certainly have been an element of tax revolt in this period, but the evidence in favor of this hypothesis is by no means clear cut.

In the following cycle, market-financed consumption increased from 54.21 percent of output in 1969 to 54.73 percent in 1973, and the government's share for the nonmarket sector increased by 1.96 percentage points at the same time. This combined increase in the share of personal consumption and of the nonmarket sector of 2.5 percentage points was bound to take 2.5 percentage points away from investment or the balance of payments. As it happened, market sector investment increased slightly and the current account of the balance of payments deteriorated by 2.82 percent of marketed output. This had serious repercussions on subsequent government policy, including the pursuit of highly deflationary policies over the next three years.

These policies contributed to the real decline of output that forced up the government expenditure ratio so markedly from 1973 to 1976. This severe balance of payments deterioration from 1969 to 1973 followed from the simultaneous increase in nonmarket expenditure and private consumption as a share of output. This is best explained by Table 5.1, which shows that in this cycle the ratio of taxation to the net national product was cut from 39.68 to 35.86 percent in a four-year period, while the public expenditure ratio was raised from 42.14 to 43.43 percent. It is this discrepancy between growth in the public expenditure ratio and a decline in the tax ratio that explains the increase in personal consumption at a time when the public expenditure ratio was also rising. Table 5.5 therefore sets out what happened to investment and consumption most accurately, but Table 5.1 shows why these moved in a way that made a balance of payments crisis entirely inevitable. The growth in public expenditure was not rapid from 1969 to 1973. The government could have financed this with extra taxation instead of borrowing, and still left ample growth in net of tax incomes for the private sector. The enormous budgetary swing into deficit resulting from the failure of Mr. Heath's government to finance extra government spending with taxation may well have been the prime cause of the severe financial and balance of payments difficulties after 1972, as well as the great acceleration of inflation that occurred. It was therefore not the growth of public expenditure but the way in which it was financed that may well have been a vital factor in the troubles that afflicted the British economy from then onward.

The statistics of Table 5.5 indicate that the ratio of total market sector investment in marketed output increased from 1961 to 1973. There was therefore no measured tendency for extra public expenditure to crowd out market sector investment. There was, however, a severe fall in net investment in manufacturing industry. This has caused much concern in Britain because the connection between growth in manufacturing output and overall growth in productivity is believed to be especially strong, given that economies of scale and the technological advances of the rest of the world are mainly exploitable through manufacturing, and not through the service sector or agriculture.[12] The connection between capital investment and the actual creation of jobs is also believed to be closer in manufacturing than in other economic activities. The decline of manufacturing investment is therefore widely seen as a significant factor in explaining both the great slow down of productivity growth and the very great increase in unemployment after 1973. There were only 575,000 unemployed in 1973, but this figure rose to 1,344,000 by the next cyclical peak of 1979 and to almost 2,500,000 in the cyclical depression year of 1981. It is perfectly plausible that this great increase in unemployment was partly due to the relative decline of employment in manufacturing industry, which fell from 8,356,000 in 1969 to 7,830,000 in 1973 and 7,155,000 in 1979 (*National Income and Expenditure*, 1980: Table 1.12). The fall in net investment in manufacturing that Table 5.5 indicates would explain a persistent tendency for investment in the creation of new jobs to fail to match the destruction of jobs that goes on all the time in manufacturing as a result of technical progress. Since 1969, Britain has almost certainly been investing too little in manufacturing to make good the loss of jobs that technical progress continuously imposes.

What connection may there be between the fall of manufacturing investment, which may well have been quite as damaging as the argument indicates, and the growth in public expenditure? At first sight there is no reason why there should be any particular connection. If investment falls specifically in manufacturing, there may well be particular reasons why resources shift away from manufacturing and into other sectors of the United Kingdom economy. In the 1970s the attractions of investment in North Sea oil exploration and extraction are an obvious explanation of a shift of investment away from manufacturing and into this more profitable economic activity. A given amount of investment unhappily provides far less employment in North Sea oil extraction than in manufacturing investment that has nothing to do with the growth of government expenditure. The further tendency of North Sea oil to improve the balance of payments and therefore to raise the real exchange rate is another factor behind the decline in manufacturing investment and employment, since British manufacturing is bound to be less competitive at a higher real exchange rate.[13]

A possible connection between the growth of public expenditure and the decline of manufacturing investment could run as follows. The tax squeeze on workers' consumption from 1965 to 1969 persuaded the British trade unions to become more militant and to choose more militant leaders. These forced up money earnings more rapidly after 1969. The government responded by seeking to halt inflation through price and wage controls after 1971, and these acted far more sharply on prices than on wages. They also acted more sharply in the manufacturing industries, where prices can be controlled more effectively, than in the service sector, where most prices are uncontrolled and uncontrollable. The severe price controls in 1972 and 1973 reduced the share of profits drastically in manufacturing but not in the remainder of the economy. This fall in the share of profits in manufacturing then led to the rapid loss of employment in manufacturing and to the decline in investment, as capital markets allocated finance to the more profitable sectors of the British economy.[14]

There are obviously other hypotheses that could explain the decline in manufacturing profitability and employment in the early 1970s. The most obvious alternative hypothesis is that British industry improved its products more slowly than its main competitors, with the result that it found it increasingly difficult to pass on cost increases in international competition with the manufactures of Japan, West Germany, France, and Italy. This together with the increase in competition resulting from entry into the EEC in 1972 then produced a continuing fall in employment, investment, and profits in manufacturing.[15] The influence of North Sea oil on the sterling exchange rate then reinforced these tendencies in the late 1970s and in the early 1980s. The explanation starting from worker frustration due to growing public expenditure and taxation from 1965 to 1969 therefore explains at most a part (and perhaps not a large part) of what occurred. Table 5.6 indicates in particular that there may have been less reason for worker frustration from 1965 to 1969 than Table 5.2 suggests. Whether there is a significant line of causation from growing public expenditure to deindustrialization is therefore controversial.

There is no controversy, however, about the deleterious effects of the explosion of government borrowing in 1969-1973 from which so many adverse effects, including the acceleration of inflation and the collapse of the balance of payments, undoubtedly followed. This led to the extremely disappointing cycle of 1973-1979. In this cycle real personal consumption per market sector worker actually fell, although it rose towards the end of the cycle when the growth of public expenditure was all but halted. There was also, as has been indicated, an increase in unemployment of around three quarters of a million between 1973 and 1979. Vacancy levels in the 1979 recovery were however about as great as at the peak of previous cyclical booms.[16] This led some commentators to argue that the economy's equilibrium unemployment rate, or natural rate as monetarists call it,[17] had risen by around three-quarters of a million from 1973 to 1979.

Thus the argument that growing tax deductions prevented a rise in living standards in terms of private consumption, thereby making the unions increasingly militant, may have had more force during the above cycle than during the wage explosion of 1969. The argument is that worker frustration led to more militant unions, which produced sharply accelerating inflation at unemployment rates where the labor market was formerly in equilibrium. The government then used deflationary policies to check the acceleration of inflation. These had to be applied at unemployment rates that were far higher than those at which deflationary policies were resorted to in previous cycles. The deflationary policies (assisted by a tough incomes policy in the public sector) arrested the acceleration of inflation, which fell to around ten percent in 1979, but inflation was only stabilized at an unemployment rate that was far higher than previously needed to achieve this purpose.

If this explanation of the rise in Britain's underlying unemployment rate is broadly correct (and it conflicts with the Cambridge theory that it is structural unemployment that has risen), the growth of public expenditure may have been most damaging of all in the cycle of 1973-1979. The deep worker frustration evident by 1975 could help to explain why Mr. Callaghan's government, and now Mrs. Thatcher's, attached high priority to reducing taxation, especially personal taxation. Moreover, because they also wished to bring borrowing and the growth of the money supply under control both governments have also attached high priority to efforts to halt the growth of government expenditure.

Appendix:
The Derivation of the Tables

The data in tables are derived from *National Income and Expenditure*, which provides the most detailed statements available of United Kingdom national income accounts. The data for 1969, 1973, 1976, and 1979 are derived from the 1980 edition, and the data for 1961 and 1965 from the 1972 edition. In the explanation below, reference will be made in each case to the table number from which information is derived in the 1980 edition. The 1961 and 1965 data are derived from the corresponding table, which is numbered differently in the 1972 edition.

(1) Gross national product at market prices. Table 1.1.
(2) Capital consumption. Table 1.1.
(3) Net national product. $1 - 2$.
(4) General government expenditure. The expenditure total in Table 9.1, which includes debt interest paid out, less the receipts item, interest and dividends, and so on, which is also in Table 9.1.
(5) Taxation and social security contributions. The sum of taxes on income, taxes on expenditure, national insurance, etc. Contributions and taxes on capital and other capital receipts from Table 9.1.
(6) Borrowing. Borrowing requirement from Table 9.1.
(7) General government expenditure/net national product. 4/3.
(8) Taxation/net national product. 5/3.
(9) Borrowing/net national product. 6/3.
(10) Real gross national product.
(11) Real net national product. $10 \times 3/1$.
(12) Government expenditure. $7 \times 10/1$.
(13) Taxation. $8 \times 10/1$
(14) NNP—Government expenditure. $11 - 12$.
(15) NNP—taxation. $11 - 13$.
(16) General government wages and salaries. The income from employment paid by central government and local authorities in Table 1.10.
(17) Gross marketed output. $1 - 16$.
(18) Market sector capital consumption. Total capital consumption less the non-dwellings capital consumption of central government and local authorities from Table 11.9.
(19) Net marketed output. $17 - 18$.
(20) Net marketed output/net national product. 19/3.
(21) Personal consumption less social transfers. Consumers expenditure at market prices from Table 1.1 less national insurance benefits and other grants from central government from Table 4.1.
(22) Personal incomes less social transfers. Total personal income from Table 4.1 less national insurance benefits and other grants from central government from Table 4.1.
(23) Ratio of nontransfer personal income consumed. 21/22.
(24) Consumption from general government wages $(G(w)/Y(m))$. $23 \times 16/19$.
(25) Consumption from debt interest $(G(d)/Y(m))$. Debt interest paid less interest and dividends, etc., received by general government from Table 9.1, times 23 divided by 19.
(26) Consumption from social transfers $(G(t)/Y(m))$. National insurance benefits and other grants from central government, from Table 4.1 divided by 19.
(27) Government nonhousing investment $(G(i)/Y(m))$. General government

gross domestic capital formation less dwellings from Table 10.1, divided by 19.

(28) Consumption from government material purchases $(G(q)/Y(m))$. General government final consumption at market prices from Table 1.1, less general government wages and salaries 16, divided by 19.

(29) Nonmarket total $(G(c)/Y(m))$. $24 + 25 + 26 + 27 + 28$.

(30) Market financed consumption $(C(m)/Y(m))$. Consumers expenditure at market prices from Table 1.1 divided by 19 minus the nonmarket personal consumption ratios found in 24, 25 and 26.

(31) Market financed investment $(I(m)/Y(m))$. Gross domestic fixed capital formation plus value of physical increase in stocks and work in progress at market prices from Table 1.1 divided by 19 less the government nonhousing investment ratio found in 27.

(32) Fixed investment in manufacturing. Net domestic fixed capital formation in manufacturing at current prices from Table 11.7 divided by 19.

(33) Investment in housing. Net domestic fixed capital formation in dwellings at current prices from Table 11.10 divided by 19.

(34) Other market financed fixed investment. Total net domestic fixed capital formation at current prices from Table 11.10, divided by 19, less the ratios for investment in manufacturing and housing found in 32 and 33.

(35) Investment in inventories. Value of physical increase in stocks and work in progress at current prices from Table 1.1 divided by 19.

(36) Exports less imports including property income $X(m) - M(m)/Y(m)$. Export of goods and services less imports of goods and services at current prices plus net property income from abroad, from Table 1.1 divided by 19.

(37) Real marketed output. 11×20.

(38) Market sector employment (1975 = 100). The sum of employment in the private sector and the public corporations in Table 1.12 for the year in question divided by this total for 1975. The figure for 1965 is derived from *National Income and Expenditure* 1965-1975.

(39) Real marketed output per worker. 37/38.

(40) Nonmarket purchases per market sector worker. 39×29.

(41) Remains for market sector per market sector worker. $39 - 40$.

(42) Real private consumption per market sector worker. 39×30.

NOTES

1. This is made extremely clear in *Public Expenditure to 1979-80* (1976).

2. It is not an uncommon error to measure public expenditure in market prices (i.e., what the government actually spends) and the national product at factor cost (i.e., the real resources available to provide it). When a pensioner receives £100, those £100 will actually be spent at market prices, so the goods and services needed to provide his or her pension are £100 at market prices. Hence the comparison between the resources needed to meet a pension and the pension itself will be potentially accurate if both are measured at market prices. They could equally both be measured at factor cost, but in practice that involves far more intricate statistical calculation, and renders international comparison more difficult since many countries only provide detailed

national accounts statistics in market prices. The ratio of nonmarket expenditure ratio as conventionally measured (see the argument that follows), was estimated at factor cost by Robert Bacon and Walter Eltis (1979) with results quite similar to those set out in this article. The method of estimation used in this article can, however, be applied to the published statistics of virtually all developed economies.

3. See J. M. Keynes (1924).

4. This was argued in Robert Bacon and Walter Eltis (1978). It was also argued by Dudley Jackson et al. (1972: ch. 3), while S. G. B. Henry et al. (1976) tested the hypothesis that trade unions pass on taxations.

5. See the statistical series set out in Bacon and Eltis (1978: 212-213).

6. The detailed algebraic interconnections between marketed output and its various uses are set out fully in Bacon and Eltis (1978: ch. 7).

7. Strictly speaking, the public corporations are in the nonmarket sector in so far as they make losses, and the implications of this are set out and developed in Eltis (1979).

8. Mr. Turvey sent his calculations to the present author and to Mr. Robert Bacon 1977.

9. These statistics are set out each year in *National Income and Expenditure*. Market sector employment is the sum of employment in the private sector and the public corporations.

10. See, for instance, A. R. Thatcher (1979).

11. The statistics for debt interest, allowing for the influence of inflation, are derived and set out in C. T. Taylor and A. R. Threadgold (1980).

12. This line of argument was initiated by N. Kaldor (1966) and developed especially by John Cornwall (1977).

13. See, for instance, W. M. Corden (1981) for a careful account of the interconnection between North Sea oil and profitability in the economy's tradeable sector which is mainly manufacturing industry.

14. This line of argument is set out most fully and carefully in Robert Bacon and Walter Eltis (1979).

15. This is the New Cambridge explanation of deindustrialization in Britain, which is set out in various versions in the successive editions of the University of Cambridge Department of Applied Economics' *Economic Policy Review*, published each February or March since 1975. See also A. Thirlwall (1978).

16. Vacancies reached peaks of 280,000 in the second quarter of 1966 (when unemployment was 314,000), of 203,000 in the second quarter of 1969 (when unemployment was 567,000), of 361,000 in the fourth quarter of 1973 (when unemployment was 525,000) and of 252,000 in the second quarter of 1979 (when unemployment was 1,304,000). If vacancies (and not unemployment) are the true indication of the degree of tightness of the labor market, then it was not that much less tight in 1979 than in 1973, and it was tighter than in 1969.

17. The concept of the "natural rate of unemployment" was originated by Milton Friedman (1968).

REFERENCES

BACON, R. and W. ELTIS, (1979) "The measurement of the growth of the nonmarket sector and its influence: a reply to Hadjimatheou and Skouras." Economic Journal (June).
——————— (1978) Britain's Economic Problem: Too Few Producers. London: Macmillan.
CORDEN, W. M. (1981) "The exchange rate, monetary policy and North Sea oil: the economic theory of the squeeze on tradeables," in W. A. Eltis and P. J. N. Sinclair (eds.) The Money Supply and the Exchange Rate. London: Oxford University Press.
CORNWALL, J. (1977) Modern Capitalism. London: Martin Robertson.
Economic Policy Review (1975 to present).

ELTIS, W. (1979) "The true deficits of the public corporations." Lloyds Bank Review (January).

FRIEDMAN, M. (1968) "The role of monetary policy." American Economic Review (March).

HENRY, S. G. B., M. C. SAWYER, and P. SMITH (1976) "Models of inflation in the United Kingdom: an evaluation." National Institute Economic Review 1: 216-230.

JACKSON, D., H. A. TURNER, and F. WILKINSON (1972) Do Trade Unions Cause Inflation? Cambridge: Cambridge University Press.

KALDOR, N. (1966) Causes of the Slow Rate of Growth of the United Kingdom. Inaugural lecture, Cambridge.

KEYNES, J. M. (1924) "Inflation as a method of taxation," ch. 2 in A Tract on Monetary Reform. London: Duckworth.

National Income and Expenditure (yearly). London: Her Majesty's Stationery Office.

Public Expenditure to 1979-80, Command 6393 (1976). London: Her Majesty's Stationery Office.

TAYLOR, C. T. and A. R. THREADGOLD (1980) "Real" National Saving and Its Sectoral Composition. Bank of England Discussion Paper 6. London: Bank of England.

THATCHER A. R. (1979) "Labour supply and employment trends," in F. Blackaby (ed.) De-Industrialization. London: Heinemann.

THIRLWALL, A. (1978) "The UK's economic problem: a balance of payments constraint?" National Westminster Bank Quarterly Review (February): 23-25.

CHAPTER 6

THE USSR AND EASTERN EUROPE, I

GERTRUDE E. SCHROEDER
JOHN S. PITZER

The meaning of the government or public sector is not easy to delineate in the centrally planned economies of the USSR and its East European neighbors, where the government owns nearly all of the means of production and where, in a sense, nearly everyone works for the government. The public sector in these countries might be defined broadly to include all final expenditures except the personal consumption expenditures of households, or the definition might be limited to cover only government final consumption expenditures. Similarly, public sector employment could be defined to include all workers providing the public services making up the bulk of government final consumption outlays or, alternatively, only those workers whose wages are directly financed from the state budget.

Whatever the definition chosen for government, the difficulties encountered in measuring its size and growth in centrally planned economies are formidable. National product, employment, and budgetary data published by these countries use radically different conceptual frameworks and classification systems from those used in Western countries. Moreover, the definitions employed are often obscure and data series are revised without explanation.

In general the conceptual and statistical frameworks used in the USSR and Eastern Europe are not couched in terms of a government sector, as opposed to a private sector. Rather, the distinction, following Marx, is between productive and nonproductive activity. Productive activity includes

AUTHORS' NOTE: This chapter reflects the personal views of the authors only and does not necessarily represent the view of the Central Intelligence Agency or any other component of the U.S. Government.

the production of goods and the associated transportation and distribution services. Nonproductive activity includes all other services. The government sector as usually defined in the West is considered nonproductive. Many other services are also considered nonproductive, however, and Soviet and East European statistics do not readily distinguish between types of nonproductive services.

A second important distinction in centrally planned economies is between institutions, which are largely, but not entirely, financed from state budgets, and enterprises, which operate on a system of economic accountability, labeled *khozraschet* in the USSR. The latter produce and sell goods or services, are expected to cover costs from revenues and make a profit, are responsible for their material assets, and are subject to financial controls by the banks.[1] Budget institutions are concentrated in defense, administration, education, health, research and development (R&D), and other sectors normally associated with the government; but a substantial number also are in nongovernment sectors as defined in the West.

In order to improve administrative control and economic performance, there has been a persistent trend toward shifting budgetary institutions to a khozraschet basis, especially in public housing and R&D.[2] For this reason the distinction between khozraschet enterprises and budget institutions has become less useful in determining the boundary between the production sector and final government expenditures. Finally, state budgets finance a variety of activities besides the upkeep of institutions, notably a large share of investment and many subsidies affecting khozraschet enterprises. Both factors seriously impair the usefulness of definitions of the public sector based on state budget expenditures.

National product statistics are published within the framework of productive and nonproductive activity. Net Material Product (NMP), the Marxian analogue of the Gross National Product, measures the net value added in the production of goods. As such it excludes much of what would be considered government expenditures in the West, because it omits personnel services in the nonproductive sectors of the economy (Becker, 1972; Central Intelligence Agency, 1978a). Thus only material outlays for defense, administration, health, education, and similar government services are counted in NMP. Moreover, these outlays are not shown separately but are mingled with the material outlays of the other nonproductive services, such as passenger transportation, personal communications, housing, and recreation.

Employment data also are published within the construct of productive and nonproductive sectors. The groupings in which data are published make it difficult to delineate accurately those that might be defined as employed in government services. For example, the single figure published for housing and municipal services employment is rarely disaggregated, and the numbers employed in defense and police activities are not published at all, except occasionally in obscure forms in periodic censuses.

Western scholars have approached the problem of defining and measuring the government sector in centrally planned economies in several ways. Frederick Pryor used budget data to compare selected public consumption expenditures among countries, mainly for the 1950s (Pryor, 1968).[3] Stephen Rapawy compared government employment in detail in the United States and the USSR (Rapawy, 1972). Gross national product accounts for the USSR and Eastern Europe, periodically published in compendia issued by the Joint Economic Committee of the U.S. Congress, attempt to measure various categories of government final consumption expenditures on a basis comparable with those published for Western countries (Greenslade, 1976; Alton, 1977). In this chapter we shall discuss the problems involved in defining and measuring the size and growth of government in terms of (1) GNP accounts and (2) employment data. Both the USSR and Eastern Europe will be considered, although the USSR is the primary subject of investigation. An approach based on budget expenditure data is presented in the chapter by Donna Bahry in this volume.

Government Final Consumption Expenditures

The determination of government final consumption expenditures[4] in the Soviet Union or Eastern Europe is impeded by several conceptual problems. A major obstacle stems from the NMP system of national income accounting used by the Soviet Union and East European nations. The differences between the NMP and GNP systems have been discussed elsewhere and need be reviewed only briefly here (Becker, 1972). The NMP system concentrates on the division between material and nonmaterial products. In addition to expenditures on the final goods and services included in private consumption and the growth of capital stock, NMP includes material expenditures by khozraschet enterprises and also by budget institutions that produce nonproductive services. The GNP system does not distinguish between material and nonmaterial products but, in distribution by end-use, does distinguish between private consumption, investment, and government expenditures.

Within the GNP system, however, two ways to define the government sector are in common use: one based on institutional arrangements and the other on functional purposes. The system proposed by the United Nations and used by most noncommunist nations, the System of National Accounts (SNA), is based on institutional distinctions. The SNA defines the government sector as including

> all bodies, departments and establishments of government—central, state or provincial, district or county, municipal, town or village—which engage in a

wide range of activities, for example, administration, defense and regulation of the public order; health, educational, cultural, recreational and other social services; and promotion of economic growth and welfare and technological development [United Nations, 1968: 75].

This classification divides expenditures between the private and government sectors purely on the basis of what entities perform the services. For example, one nation may have a largely private health system, while another nation may have a completely public system. Most health expenditures would be part of personal consumption expenditures in the former, and all of them part of government expenditures in the latter. In contrast, in order to facilitate international comparisons of the size and structure of GNP, the United Nations International Comparison Project (ICP) defines government on a functional basis:

> "Government" is viewed as comprising those final products which most societies, regardless of economic and social system, have found can best be provided through public organizations and financed by tax revenues. These final products take the form largely of services that provide citizens with physical, social, and national security. They include the making of laws, the administration of justice, and the establishment and maintenance of standards where necessary to promote the public welfare, as in foods and drugs, medical practice, and education [Kravis et al., 1975: 28].

Unlike the SNA system, the ICP system tends to include social organizations and expenditures by nonprofit institutions for research within the government sector but treats government current outlays for housing, health, education, recreation, and culture as part of personal consumption expenditures.

A third definition of government often employed attempts to measure the gross influence of the government sector on the economy by relating all government budgetary expenditures to total GNP or to national income. In the West, this concept includes—in addition to direct consumption outlays —all benefits, investment outlays on government account, and subsidies. In centrally planned economies, budget-financed investment by khozraschet enterprises would also have to be included.

There are several problems in measuring government expenditures in the Soviet Union and Eastern Europe using any of the three definitions just discussed. Although khozraschet enterprises mainly produce nongovernment goods and services and budget institutions produce most of the government services, this distinction is not a reliable guide. These countries distinguish between khozraschet and budget financing as a matter of administrative convenience, so that the scope of government activity may expand or contract over time for administrative reasons rather than as a result of changes in the supply of and demand for government services. The functional definition used by the ICP, however, lends itself reasonably well to statistical measurement. Activities falling within the ICP definition of government can be treated in the same manner in the Soviet Union and Eastern Europe, regardless of who actually performs the services.[5]

The ICP system considers all current health and education expenditures to be part of personal consumption, but many countries have largely state-financed health and education systems that would be treated as part of government activity in the SNA system. In the Soviet Union and East European nations virtually all such services are provided as government services without charge. To provide comparability with both SNA and ICP data, we present our expenditure data here with and without health and education expenditures.

Other problems relate to defense, R&D and investment expenditures. Although defense is clearly part of the government sector, it is often separated from the civilian government component for analytical purposes, and Western governments usually publish the relevant data. In the case of the Soviet Union, the total amount of defense expenditures and its distribution by type of good or service purchased are not published statistics. They must be estimated from a large variety of evidence and using diverse methodologies.[6] The results differ; those presented in this chapter, although not precise, are thought to be of the correct order of magnitude.

In most Western economies a large share of R&D activity is carried out and financed by private organizations—with its cost included in the final sales of goods and services. Thus much R&D is treated as intermediate product. Only R&D that is either funded or conducted directly by the government is included in government expenditures and therefore in GNP as a final outlay. In the Soviet Union virtually all R&D programs are centrally directed and managed, although not all are financed from the state budget. For this reason and also because a large share is believed to be defense related, it was decided to declare all R&D expenditures to be final product in the Soviet GNP accounts. This procedure may somewhat overstate the size and growth of government relative to other countries, as R&D has been one of the most dynamic sectors in the economy.

In the ICP and SNA accounting systems, government investment expenditures are included in investment. Such government expenditure can be quite large, most notably those for education facilities and public highways. About two percent of American GNP in 1979, for example, represented government investment expenditures. Data on investment expenditures in the Soviet Union and Eastern Europe are not sufficiently disaggregated to separate that part of investment which is for the government sector from the total. Moreover, in the case of the USSR an unknown but possibly sizable share of investment may consist of common-use durables used for military purposes.[7] The outlays for such items as military trucks, transport aircraft, and forklifts would be treated as a part of defense expenditures in the West, but may be part of investment in the USSR.

The GNP accounting framework. GNP accounts for the Soviet Union in recent years have been constructed by the Office of Economic Research of the Central Intelligence Agency, although in much less detail than given by the GNP accounts of the United States and other Western countries (Central Intelligence Agency, 1975). Similar accounts have been constructed for the East European nations by the Research Project on National Income in East Central Europe (Alton and Associates, 1977). This section describes the structure of the GNP accounts for the Soviet Union and considers how the government sector might be defined.

The American and Soviet GNP accounts both consist of a set of balanced income and outlay accounts for a number of sectors. The American economy is divided into the personal, business, government, and rest-of-the-world sectors. The relevant incomes and expenditures from each account are consolidated into the total GNP account. Compared with the American GNP accounts, those constructed for the USSR differ in two main ways. First, the amount of detail is much less because of severe limitations of available data. Second, the Soviet accounts do not attempt to differentiate between the production and government sectors, primarily because there are insufficient data to disaggregate the payments between the sectors.

As a result the Soviet GNP accounts consist of one account showing the incomes and outlays of the household sector and a second account showing the incomes and outlays of the combined public sector. Household incomes include wages, agricultural income-in-kind, earnings from private services, and transfer receipts. Household outlays include purchases of goods and services from state enterprises, consumption-in-kind, purchases of private services, net savings, taxes, and transfer payments. Total household expenditures for goods and services in 1970 are estimated to have been 192 billion rubles or fifty percent of total GNP.

Public sector incomes include profits, taxes, foreign trade revenues, depreciation, social insurance contributions, transfer receipts, and miscellaneous special revenues. Public sector outlays include communal services, investment, government administrative services, R&D, net exports, transfer payments, and a large residual consisting mainly of defense outlays. Of primary interest here are government administrative services, communal services, R&D, and defense expenditures. The government administrative services category is defined to include general agricultural programs, state administration and social organizations, and R&D expenditures.

General agricultural programs include organizations providing general services to agriculture and financed largely if not entirely from the state budget; types of services are plant and animal disease control, general veterinary services and inspection, erosion control and land improvement, management of land tenure procedures, and a variety of others. *Forestry* encompasses enterprises and organizations engaged in the management and protection of state forests and parks, including reforestation services; it is financed largely from the state budget.

State administration and social organizations include the activities of state administrative bodies at all levels (ministries, state committees, and the like), legislative and judicial organs, and administrative organs of state security and defense. The activity is financed mainly from state budget funds, but also in part from charges to enterprise costs. This category also includes the administrative organs of the All-Union Society of Consumer Cooperatives, the Communist Party and Komsomol, the trade unions and professional unions, and a number of other groups (the Red Cross, civil defense, nature societies, and the like). *Culture* is accounted for mainly by public libraries, museums, parks, zoos, clubs, and children's camps. *Municipal services* consist mainly of the upkeep of city streets and municipal facilities, garbage and trash collection, sewage disposal, fire protection, and the like. The category of *police* is an estimate intended to account for the costs of civilian police protection. *Communal consumption* includes current outlays for health and education.

R&D expenditures reflect current outlays for these activities, both civilian and military. *Defense expenditures* are not directly estimated in the Soviet GNP accounts because the single budget expenditure figure published by the USSR clearly is not complete; other outlays for defense are included in investment, R&D, and other expenditure categories and cannot be separately identified with accuracy. For example, we believe that published investment expenditures may include defense common-use durables and that data on administration may include the administrative expenditures of the Ministry of Defense. The GNP accounts do, however, include a residual labeled "outlays n.e.c.," which is defined as total public sector incomes less all identified public sector outlays. Although this residual includes a few small civilian categories, such as increases in state grain reserves, it consists primarily of the defense expenditures not included in other end-use categories. In 1970 outlays n.e.c. amounted to 27 billion rubles, or seven percent of GNP.

In most nations GNP is computed using market prices. Most Soviet prices, however, are established by administrative decision rather than by market forces. The basic methodology used by the Soviets to construct a price is to sum average unit costs for materials, wages, depreciation allowances, social insurance contributions, and other direct outlays and to add an arbitrary surcharge for profits. Soviet established prices often include the so-called turnover tax, a large excise tax applied to selected (mostly consumer) products at widely varying rates. These prices also reflect subsidies, which have been mainly on agricultural products since the mid-1960s, notably meat, and also on housing. The agricultural subsidy is now over 25 billion rubles per year and the rent subsidy about six billion.

Because Soviet prices are administratively established, are heavily and unevenly influenced by taxes and subsidies, and do not reflect the rate of return on capital, they are seriously flawed for purposes of measuring changes in Soviet production potential over time or resource allocation patterns. As an alternative, Professor Abram Bergson (1961: 25-41) devised his adjusted factor cost standard. In essence he proposed calculating average cost prices by eliminating turnover taxes and subsidies and replacing profits with an imputed charge based on an equal return to the capital stock of each sector. For the most part the data presented here are in factor-cost prices. First, a set of established-price GNP accounts was constructed for 1970 by sector of origin and by end-use. The sector-of-origin data were then adjusted in accordance with Bergson's standard. Finally, the end-use data were converted to factor-cost prices using the revised sector-of-origin data and a Soviet input-output table. The impact of these price adjustments falls primarily on consumer goods and services, but the value of government expenditures is raised somewhat. The East European accounts are compiled in established prices for various recent years; no factor cost adjustment affecting government services has been made.

Measuring the growth of the government sector. The growth of all sectors of the economy, including the government sector, is measured by constructing constant-price activity indexes for each end-use and each sector of origin of GNP. Expenditure values in factor-cost prices (for the USSR) are then used as weights to compute the growth of total GNP and its components. As discussed above, the relevant end-use sectors for the government sector are government administrative services, health, education, R&D, and defense.

The index used for each component of the government administrative services sector for the USSR is total man hour employment.[8] To the extent that productivity advance has occurred, such a measure understates the growth of the real output produced by this group of services. The alternative procedure—to deflate current expenditures on these activities by appropriate price indexes—cannot be used because there is little information on nonwage outlays for the sector and suitable price deflators are not available. The procedure used in the American accounts is to deflate general government expenditures largely by input (wage) price indexes. Thus the procedure adopted for the USSR is similar to that used in the United States.

The indexes of health and education expenditures are weighted indexes of personnel services and material expenditures. The personnel service indexes are man hour employment measures. The material expenditure indexes are deflated current-price measures. The current-price data are extracted from periodic Soviet budget handbooks and the annual statistical handbook. The deflator used for both the health and education indexes is an implicit price index derived from Soviet data on retail sales in current prices and an independently derived index of consumer retail purchases in constant prices. The index shows a gradual, but steady increase in prices, which accords with available evidence. The Soviet published index of retail prices shows virtually no change in recent years.

The index for R&D activity is a weighted index of personnel services and material purchases, the latter a large and rapidly growing component relative to the former. The index of personnel services is man hour employment, and the index of material purchases is a deflated current-price series. The deflator is a weighted average of wholesale price indexes, all but one of which are published in the annual Soviet statistical handbook. The one exception is for machinery. The Soviet published machinery price index shows a steady decline, while all available evidence indicates a steady increase in the level of machinery prices. We have, therefore, substituted our own price index. It is constructed in a fairly arbitrary manner but is believed more accurately to reflect the real changes in Soviet machinery prices. For the reasons previ-

TABLE 6.1   USSR: Average Annual Rates of Growth of Government Expenditures, 1950-1980.

	1951-1955	1956-1960	1961-1965	1966-1970	1971-1975	1976-1980
Total nondefense government services	1.2	3.5	5.5	4.9	3.6	2.7
Total less education and health	−2.0	2.8	5.3	5.9	5.0	3.1
Apparat and police	−6.0	−4.1	2.2	4.9	3.5	2.5
Municipal services	2.7	1.4	3.4	5.3	4.5	3.3
General agricultural programs	−4.5	9.7	−1.3	4.8	4.8	5.4
Forestry	−2.8	−4.0	1.3	1.7	0.9	0.3
Culture	3.5	1.6	5.5	8.4	5.0	3.6
R&D	7.5	12.5	9.0	6.7	6.0	3.2
Education	3.3	3.3	6.8	4.0	2.4	2.6
Health	6.1	5.3	3.6	4.2	2.4	2.1
GNP	5.5	5.9	5.0	5.2	3.7	2.7

Sources: Growth rates were calculated from indexes of GNP in 1970 factor cost prices as compiled by the Central Intelligence Agency. A full description and documentation of these indexes is scheduled to be published by the Joint Economic Committee of the U.S. Congress.

ously noted, a separate index of defense expenditures has not been calculated within the framework of the GNP accounts.

Government final consumption expenditures in the USSR. Table 6.1 gives average annual rates of growth computed from indexes for the various components of the government sector in the Soviet GNP accounts. Since 1960 most of the government administrative services have grown at rates similar to GNP itself, except for forestry, which has shown little growth. R&D has consistently grown more rapidly but has slowed in the past five years to a rate similar to the other components of government. Education and health services have increased steadily but nearly always more slowly than GNP.

Table 6.2 shows the percentage shares of the various government services in total real GNP, measured at factor cost. Since 1960 nondefense government expenditures have maintained a steady thirteen percent of real GNP. The drop in their shares in the 1950s resulted from a concerted effort, following the death of Stalin in 1953, to pare the Communist party, state, and police bureaucracies. The shares of government administrative services and R&D have increased slightly, and the share of health and education services has decreased by about the same amount. Also shown in Table 6.2 are some estimates for defense. As noted above, it is believed that substantial amounts of defense expenditures are contained in other identified components of GNP. Within the government sector as considered here, most of R&D proba-

TABLE 6.2   USSR: Government Expenditures as a Percentage of GNP, 1950-1980 (1970 factor cost prices)

	1950	1955	1960	1965	1970	1975	1980
Total nondefense government services	17.9	14.5	13.0	13.2	13.0	13.0	13.0
Total less health and education	9.4	6.5	5.7	5.7	5.9	6.3	6.4
Apparat	4.5	2.5	1.5	1.3	1.3	1.3	1.3
Police	1.4	0.8	0.5	0.4	0.4	0.4	0.4
Municipal services	0.4	0.3	0.2	0.2	0.2	0.2	0.2
General agricultural programs	0.5	0.3	0.4	0.3	0.3	0.3	0.3
Forestry	0.6	0.4	0.2	0.2	0.2	0.1	0.1
Culture	0.5	0.4	0.3	0.3	0.4	0.4	0.5
R&D	1.6	1.8	2.4	2.9	3.1	3.5	3.6
Education	5.5	5.0	4.4	4.8	4.5	4.2	4.2
Health	2.9	3.0	2.9	2.7	2.6	2.4	2.4
Defense n.e.c.				8-11	8-11	8-11	8-11
Total (including defense) government services				21-24	21-24	21-24	21-24

Sources: Soviet GNP accounts in factor cost prices as compiled by the Central Intelligence Agency. Defense estimates are the authors' estimates as described in the text. See source notes to Table 6.1.

bly is defense oriented and small amounts of defense outlays also are included in administrative services, health, and education. Other estimates indicate that about eleven to thirteen percent of GNP has been allocated to defense since 1965 (U.S. Congress, Joint Economic Committee, 1981: 109). If it is assumed that two or three percent of GNP represents defense expenditures contained in other government categories (primarily R&D), then eight to eleven percentage points need to be added to obtain the total share of the GNP allocated to all government purposes. This adjustment is shown in Table 6.2. The addition of defense raises the share of GNP allocated to government to over twenty percent.

Table 6.3 assesses the effect of changing prices on the share of government expenditures in GNP. It shows the percentage shares of the components of the government sector for 1960 and 1976 in current prices and in 1970 prices, based on comparable sets of national accounts constructed for those years. The results show that the shares of government expenditures tend to increase when measured in the prices of a later year. Similar results have been obtained for Western economies. This effect probably results from the lack of labor productivity growth, by definition, in government services.

Finally, Table 6.4 compares the shares of GNP allocated to the government sector in the USSR in 1960, 1970, and 1976 with similar data for selected OECD nations; the shares are based on data in current prices. The table gives three versions for the Soviet Union: version I is the share of government administrative services plus R&D; version II adds health and education; version III adds, for 1970 only, all of defense expenditures not already covered in the other services. Since the OECD data include all final consumption expenditures of the governments, including defense, version III for the USSR is most nearly comparable. By this definition the USSR,

TABLE 6.3   USSR: The Nondefense Government Sector as a Percentage of GNP in 1960 and 1976 in Current and Constant Prices (established prices)

	1960		1976	
	1960 Prices	*1970 Prices*	*1970 Prices*	*1976 Prices*
Total nondefense government services	10.0	11.2	10.7	11.1
Government administrative services	2.1	2.8	2.3	2.5
R & D	2.2	2.1	2.9	2.9
Education	3.3	3.7	3.4	3.6
Health	2.4	2.6	2.0	2.1

Sources: Shares were calculated from sets of national accounts and indexes compiled by the Central Intelligence Agency. See source notes to Table 6.1.

**TABLE 6.4   USSR and Selected OECD Countries: Comparison of
Government Expenditures as a Percentage of GNP, 1960,
1970, 1976***

	1960	1970	1976
USSR (version I)	4	5	5
USSR (version II)	10	11	11
USSR (version III)	n.a.	20	n.a.
United States	17	19	19
Federal Republic of Germany	13	16	20
France	13	13	15
Japan	9	7	10
Italy	13	14	15
Canada	14	19	20
Belgium	12	13	16
Denmark	12	20	24
Spain	9	9	10
United Kingdom	17	18	22

Sources: The OECD data are from OECD (1981). The USSR data are from the GNP accounts in established prices constructed by the Central Intelligence Agency as described in the text. See source notes for Table 6.1.

*The percentages are derived from expenditure data in current market prices for OECD countries and from data in established prices for the USSR.

with a per capita GNP about half that of the United States, allocates a somewhat larger share of its GNP to government activities than most OECD countries do, and the share evidently has been rising, as it has elsewhere. It appears that, under this definition, the shares of nondefense government services are relatively small compared with Western countries, while the share of defense is quite large. This is true despite the fact that nearly all education and health services are state provided in the USSR.[9]

Government final consumption expenditures in Eastern Europe. As noted earlier, the countries of Eastern Europe follow the Soviet practice in adopting the net material product system of national income accounts. Recent Western research has produced a set of gross national product accounts by end-use for five East European countries covering the years 1965 to 1978 (Alton and Associates, 1981). Although these accounts and indexes are much more aggregated than comparable ones for the USSR, they do provide useful data for assessing the size and growth of selected government services in Eastern Europe. The services include health and social welfare, education and culture, defense, and administration and internal security. Definitions of the several groups are believed to be roughly comparable among the countries.

Table 6.5 provides data on average annual rates of growth of these groups of services in real terms, together with their respective shares of total GNP in

TABLE 6.5   Eastern Europe: Indicators of the Size and Growth of Government Final Consumption Expenditures

(A) Average Annual Rates of Real Growth of Government Outlays on Selected Services, 1965-1980* (percentage per year)

	Education and Culture	Health and Social Welfare	Administration, Justice, and Internal Security	Total GNP
Bulgaria	3.4	5.1	1.3	3.0
Czechoslovakia	2.5	3.6	2.1	2.7
East Germany	2.7	2.5	0.6	2.8
Hungary	2.3	3.6	2.2	2.7
Poland	2.7	3.9	−0.4	4.0

*Calculated from indexes in constant 1967, 1968 or 1969 prices.

(B) Percentage Shares of Government Outlays on Selected Services in GNP, Current Prices

	Education and Culture	Health and Social Welfare	Administration, Justice, and Internal Security	Defense[3]	Total
Bulgaria					
1968	3.42	2.96	1.23	2.3	9.9
1975	5.45	2.96	1.42	3.0	12.8
Czechoslovakia					
1967	3.79	3.04	1.77	3.8	12.4
1977	4.29	3.24	1.89	3.1	12.5
East Germany					
1968	4.66	4.25	4.69[1]	3.9	—
1975	4.98	4.07	2.11	4.0	15.2
Hungary					
1969	3.16	3.04	2.11	2.3	10.6
1976	2.32	3.48	2.11	2.1	10.0
Poland					
1969	3.21	3.02	1.82	3.8	11.9
1977	2.74	2.96	1.72[2]	2.7	10.1

1. Includes "other services."
2. Omits "internal security."
3. Based on budget data.
Sources: Alton (1979, 1981).

current prices. As a group these government services increased less rapidly than total GNP from 1965 to 1980. All five countries had low rates of growth for administrative services, but there was considerable diversity among the countries in the expansion of education and health services. The data do not permit the measurement of defense in real terms. Government services make up ten to fifteen percent of total GNP in both years for which comparisons could be made. Although the shares of social and administrative services in the GNPs of Eastern Europe are similar to those for the USSR, the shares of defense are far smaller. East European defense expenditures used here probably are understated, however, because they are based mainly on announced budget expenditures. The shares of government services as a whole, and for education and health in particular, appear to be smaller than those in Western countries, even though virtually all of these services are provided by the government in Eastern Europe.

Measuring Government Employment

Soviet Union. In its annual statistical handbooks the Soviet government publishes only a single number purporting to represent employment in government; the category is labeled "apparatus of organs of state and economic administration and administrative organs of cooperative and social organizations." Essentially this category includes persons employed in legislative and judicial organs and in the upper echelons of ministries and other state administrative units. It excludes most employment in such typical government functions as police and fire protection, municipal services, public libraries, agricultural and forestry services, defense logistics, and R&D. Employment in these latter services is included in various other statistical categories and is seldom separately identified. The "apparat" category also excludes most of the full-time salaried employees of the Communist Party, who are largely engaged in administrative functions, and employees of the health, welfare, education, and culture sectors. Many of these employees would be considered part of the government sector in the West.[10]

Judging from statistics relating to the Soviet category apparat, one would have to conclude that government employment in the USSR is very small and that it has declined as a share of total nonagriculture employment. Thus in 1950 apparat employment was 1.8 million, or 4.9 percent of the nonagricultural labor force; corresponding figures for 1979 are 2.4 million and 2.4 percent; the increase during the period was a mere one-third. If this measure truly reflected total employment in the Soviet government bureaucracy, one would be compelled to agree heartily with Gur Ofer's finding that a large "public administration gap" existed in the USSR as compared with other countries at comparable levels of development (Ofer, 1973: 157-159).

A more comprehensive measure of government employment in the USSR can be obtained by adding to apparat the reported or estimated employment in the additional services enumerated above, most of which are financed mainly from the state budget and most of which are regularly performed by governments in Western countries. The added services are health and welfare, education, culture, municipal services, police, forestry, general agricultural programs, and R&D. This measure, here called Total Government Services, is a rough indicator of the employment associated with the GNP category government final consumption expenditures (excluding most of defense) in Western accounting practice. This measure, along with apparat em-

ployment, is shown in Table 6.6 for 1960 to 1979. Omitted for lack of data
are most civilian employees of the Ministry of Defense and most paid employees of the Communist Party. Also omitted are employees providing public housing services. As a guess, the inclusion of these three groups would
add perhaps three million persons (and three percent of nonagricultural employment) to the total in 1979.

The more comprehensive measure of total government services shown in
Table 6.6 gives quite a different picture of the size of government employment in the USSR from that given by apparat employment alone. Employment in total government services was 12.2 million in 1960 and 24.1 million
in 1979, roughly ten times the size of apparat. Employment in the health and

TABLE 6.6   USSR: Indicators of Employment in Government, 1960-1979
(thousands)

	Employment (thousands)				
	General Administration (apparat) (1)	General Government Services (2)	Health (3)	Education (4)	Total Government Services (5)
1960	1,245	4,373	3,461	3,598	12,232
1965	1,460	5,435	4,277	6,044	15,756
1970	1,838	6,759	5,080	7,246	19,085
1975	2,188	7,897	5,769	8,135	21,801
1979	2,411	9,014	6,197	8,893	24,054
	Shares of Nonagricultural Employment (percentages)				
1960	2.3	7.9	6.2	8.0	22.1
1965	2.1	8.0	6.3	8.9	23.6
1970	2.1	8.4	6.3	9.0	23.6
1975	2.4	8.6	6.3	8.9	23.8
1979	2.4	9.1	6.2	9.0	24.2

Column (1): Apparat of organs of state and economic administration, and administrative organs of cooperative and social organizations, including a part of total paid employment of the Communist party.

Column (2): Column (1) plus employment in general agricultural programs, forestry, municipal services,
police, culture, and R & D. The latter is calculated as the product of reported total employment in "science
and scientific services" and the share of total expenditures on "science" financed by the state budget.

Column (3): Employment in health, physical culture, and welfare.

Column (4): Employment in kindergartens, general education schools, vocational schools of all kinds, and
colleges.

Column (5): The sum of columns (2), (3), and (4).

Sources: The data are given in or estimated on the basis of employment data reported in *Narodnoe khoziaistvo SSSR v 1970 godu* (pp. 510-11); and *Narodnoe khoziaistvo SSSR v 1979 godu* (pp. 387-88). Employment in municipal services and police is not reported directly. The estimates used for 1960 and 1965 were
taken from Rapawy (1962: 17, 24). The estimate of employment in municipal services given there for 1969
was extended to 1970, 1975, and 1979 on the assumption of an unchanged share in total employment in the
Soviet category "Housing-Communal Economy." The estimate of police employment given by Rapawy for
1969 was extended to later years by using the growth rates reported for "other branches of material production," where the bulk of police are believed to be included under the label of "interdepartmental guards." Data
on total nonagricultural employment are taken from Rapawy (1976: 40). A comparable figure for 1979 was
provided by the author.

education sectors made up more than three-fifths of the total throughout the period. Total government services has been absorbing a slowly rising share of both total employment and nonagricultural employment.

Although comparisons are tenuous, the share of government employment in nonagricultural employment in the USSR under this relatively narrow definition seems to be smaller than the shares in the United States and most of Western Europe. Also, these shares have risen more slowly in the USSR during the 1970s than in the United States or Western Europe. These findings accord with other evidence indicating that the USSR is moving toward a modern, services-oriented economy at a snail's pace.

Stephen Rapawy has undertaken a more meticulous comparison of civilian employment in government in the USSR and the United States for the years 1950 to 1969 (Rapawy, 1972). His comparisons use, alternatively, the apparat category and the definition of government employment used in the United States (number of persons on federal, state, and local payrolls). The latter is broader than the definition of employment in total government services used in Table 6.6, since it adds estimated employment in the postal service, defense logistics, local transit, gas, and electric utilities, and some other enterprise activities that are carried out by government bodies in the United States. Using the Soviet apparat definition, Rapawy found that the USSR employed twenty-four percent more persons in that sector in 1969 than did the United States. Using the American definition he found that the USSR employed seventy-six percent more persons than did the United States. We have attempted a rough extension of Rapawy's estimates based on the American definition. During the 1970s the growth of total government employment slowed in both countries, but much more markedly in the United States than in the USSR. Our rough estimates indicate that in 1979 under this very broad definition, the USSR employed nearly twice as many persons in publicly provided services as did the United States, and that these services absorbed about twenty-eight percent of the nonagricultural labor force in the USSR and about sixteen percent in the United States.

Eastern Europe. Although for the most part the East European countries have adopted the Soviet approach to employment statistics, the countries differ considerably in the kinds of detail that are published (Elias, 1970: 217-219). The many problems with the data preclude assembly of a comparable and consistent set of data on government employment for these countries. To provide an idea of its likely size and trend, however, we present in Table 6.7 data on employment in community, social, and personal services. These data, submitted to the International Labour Office by the individual countries, are supposed to be generally comparable in definition to those submitted by Western countries. The category includes, for all countries, mainly activities that are largely budget-financed—education, health, cultural and

TABLE 6.7   Eastern Europe: Indicators of Employment in Government, 1965-1979

	Government Employment (thousands)			
	1965	1970	1975	1979
Bulgaria	403	513	637	652
Czechoslovakia	1,073	1,272	1,403	1,474
East Germany	1,328	1,493	1,715	1,837
Hungary	734	764	872	943
Poland	1,733	2,343	2,776	2,908
Romania	885	1,012	1,170	1,271
Total	6,156	7,397	8,573	9,085
	Share of Nonagricultural Labor Force (percentages)			
	1965	1970	1975	1979
Bulgaria	17.2	17.6	19.5	18.6
Czechoslovakia	20.2	22.2	22.3	22.7
East Germany	19.0	20.0	22.0	22.8
Hungary	21.9	20.4	21.1	22.4
Poland	19.6	22.2	22.8	22.1
Romania	20.5	18.4	17.3	16.6
Total	19.8	20.6	21.2	20.9

NOTE: Data represent employment in "Community, Social and Personal Services." The data for all countries except Czechoslovakia and Poland include financial services, such as banking and insurance, a very small number.

Sources: Data on employment in "Community, Social and Personal Services" are taken from International Labour Office, *Yearbook of Labour Statistics* (1975, 1979, 1980). The figure for Poland in 1965 is derived from data in Andrew Elias (1970: 222). Data on nonagricultural employment are taken from Central Intelligence Agency (1980: 49).

communal services, and public administration. Judging from the information available, health, education, and administration make up the bulk of the total in each country.

According to the data shown in Table 6.7, employment in these largely government-provided services rose steadily during 1965-1979 in all countries. In 1979, they absorbed sixteen to twenty-three percent of the nonagricultural labor force and, except in Romania, the shares had risen somewhat since 1965. The low share in Romania and its declining trend cast doubt on the reliability of those data. These findings are in line with the results of an earlier study, which found that employment in these services 1950 to 1967 rose considerably faster in each country than total civilian employment, thus absorbing relatively larger shares of total employment (Elias, 1970: 167). These general trends are in accord with those in the Soviet Union. The shares of these services in total nonagricultural employment in Eastern Europe, however, were quite a bit lower and their growth slower than in Western Europe, where they generally absorbed twenty-five to thirty-five percent of the nonagricultural labor force in 1979, and where levels of economic development, as measured by per capita

GNPs, also were substantially higher.[11] Not all of such services, of course, were provided by the government either in Eastern or Western Europe. The relatively low shares and slow growth of the labor force in government services in the countries of Eastern Europe follow the Soviet pattern of halting progress toward modern, services-oriented economies.

NOTES

1. For a detailed treatment of these concepts in the Soviet context see Gallik et al. (1968: 35-44).

2. For a discussion of the complexities involved in defining government expenditures on research and development in the USSR, see Nolting (1973).

3. The public expenditure categories considered by Pryor are those generally classified as government expenditures in Western national income accounting. Pryor also considered transfer payments to individuals.

4. The term "government final consumption expenditures" is used here as in national income accounts compiled for Western countries and regularly published by the OECD. It includes all purchases of final goods and services on current account by the government, however the government is defined. Excluded are government investment outlays and transfer payments.

5. This procedure may overstate the size of the government sector somewhat when compared with Western economies, because some government-type services are sometimes treated as intermediate rather than final consumption in the West. For example, many private corporations have their own health dispensaries. Expenditures for those services would be intermediate consumption in the West and final government consumption in a centrally planned economy.

6. For some estimates of Soviet defense expenditures see Central Intelligence Agency (1978b); Lee (1977); and Cohn (1978).

7. In general, the NMP system treats some purchases of fixed assests for military purposes as part of investment, while the SNA system treats the same purchases as part of government final consumption expenditures. The Soviet practice in this regard is not known. For a discussion of this issue, see United Nations (1977: 33).

8. For the East European countries indexes of employment are used to measure the growth of all government administrative and social services. Indexes of R&D and defense activities have not been computed for these countries.

9. The United Nation's ICP study found that in 1970, developed Western countries allocated eight to eleven percent of their GNPs to education and health services, both publicly and privately provided. The share in the USSR was six percent.

10. For a more detailed discussion of these Soviet data relating to employment and expenditures on public administration, see Schroeder (1976: 23-44).

11. These conclusions are drawn from relevant employment data given in International Labour Office (1980) and from per capita GNPs in 1979 given in Central Intelligence Agency (1980: 10-11).

REFERENCES

ALTON, T. P. (1977) "Comparative structure and growth of economic activity in Eastern Europe," pp. 199-266 in U.S. Congress, Joint Economic Committee, Eastern European Economies, Post-Helsinki. Washington, DC: Government Printing Office.

_____ and Associates (1981) Eastern Europe: Domestic Final Uses of Gross Product: Selected Years, 1965, 1970, and 1976-1980. Research Project on National Income in East Central Europe, Occasional Paper 66. New York: L. W. International Financial Research.

_____ (1979) Expenditures on Gross Domestic Product in East European Countries, 1975. Research Project on National Income in East Central Europe, Occasional Paper 52. New York: L. W. International Financial Research.

BECKER, A. S. (1972) "National Income accounting in the USSR," pp. 69-119 in Vladimir G. Treml and John P. Hardt (eds.) Soviet Economic Statistics. Durham, NC: Duke University Press.

BERGSON, A. (1961) The Real National Income of Soviet Russia Since 1928. Cambridge, MA: Harvard University Press.

Central Intelligence Agency (1980) Handbook of Economic Statistics 1980. ER 80-10452 (October). Langley, VA: CIA.

_____ (1978a) USSR: Toward a Reconciliation of Marxist and Western Measures of National Income. ER 78-10505 (November). Langley, VA: CIA.

_____ (1978b) Estimated Soviet Defense Spending in Rubles: Recent Trends and Prospects. SR 78-10121U (June). Langley, VA: CIA.

_____ (1975) USSR: Gross National Product Accounts, 1970. A(ER) 75-76 (November). Langley, VA: CIA.

COHN, S. (1978) Estimation of Military Durables Procurement Expenditures from Machinery Production and Sales Data. Informal Note SSC-IN-78-13 (September). Washington, DC: SRI International, Strategic Studies Center.

ELIAS, S. (1970) "Magnitudes and distribution of the labor force in Eastern Europe," in U.S. Congress, Joint Economic Committee, Economic Development in Countries of Eastern Europe. Washington, DC: Government Printing Office.

GALLIK, D., C. JESINA, and S. RAPAWY (1968) The Soviet Financial System, U.S. Bureau of the Census, International Statistics Reports. Series P-90, 23. Washington, DC: Government Printing Office.

GREENSLADE, R. V. (1976) "The real Gross National Product of the USSR, 1950-1975," pp. 269-300 in U.S. Congress, Joint Economic Committee, Soviet Economy in a New Perspective. Washington, DC: Government Printing Office.

International Labour Office (1975, 1979, 1980) Yearbook of Labour Statistics. Geneva: ILO.

KRAVIS, I. B. et al. (1975) A System of International Comparisons of Gross National Product and Purchasing Power. Baltimore and London: Johns Hopkins University Press.

LEE, W. T. (1977) The Estimation of Soviet Defense Expenditures, 1955-1975: An Unconventional Approach. New York: Praeger.

NOLTING, L. E. (1973) Sources of Financing the Stages of the Research, Development and Innovation Cycle in the USSR. U.S. Department of Commerce, Bureau of Economic Analysis. Foreign Economic Reports 3 (September). Washington, DC: Government Printing Office.

OFER, G. (1973) The Service Sector in Soviet Economic Growth: A Comparative Study. Cambridge, MA: Harvard University Press.

Organization for Economic Cooperation and Development (1981) National Accounts of OECD Countries, 1950-1979 (vol. 1). Paris: OECD.

PRYOR, F. L. (1968) Public Expenditures in Communist and Capitalist Nations. London: George Allen & Unwin.

RAPAWY, S. (1976) Estimate and Projections of the Labor Force and Civilian Employment in the USSR, 1950 to 1990. U.S. Department of Commerce, Bureau of Economic Analysis, Foreign Economic Report 10, (September). Washington, DC: Government Printing Office.

_____ (1972) Comparison of U.S. and USSR Employment in Government, 1950-1969. U.S.

Department of Commerce, Bureau of Economic Analysis. International Publication Reports. Series P-95, 69 (April). Washington, DC: Government Printing Office.

SCHROEDER, G. E. (1976) "A critique of official statistics on public administration in the USSR." ACES Bulletin 18 (Spring): 11-34.

United Nations (1977) Comparisons of the System of National Accounts and the System of Balances of the National Economy, Part I: Conceptual Relationships. New York: UN.

——— (1968) A System of National Accounts. Series F, 2, Rev. 2. New York: UN.

U.S. Congress, Joint Economic Committee (1981) Allocation of Resources in the Soviet Union and China—1980. Washington, DC: Government Printing Office.

CHAPTER 7

THE USSR AND EASTERN EUROPE, II

DONNA BAHRY

No matter what their form of political organization or level of economic development, most capitalist countries have succumbed to an "iron law of public sector growth" (Tarschys, 1975; Cameron, 1978; Meltzer and Richard, 1978; Peltzman, 1980). Virtually all of them have experienced an upward (if irregular) trend toward increasing government intervention in economic life. Whatever the yardstick one uses to measure government intervention—from tax yields and government expenditures and employment to regulatory output—the evidence points to expansion of the public sector. Ironically, the limited evidence that is available for communist bloc countries points to relative *contraction* of direct government intervention. Frederic Pryor (1968) has shown, for example, that government spending declined relative to national income in the USSR and the six East European bloc states between 1950 and 1962. Public expenditures for the standard functions of government (health, education, welfare, defense, public safety, and administration) lagged behind the growth of GNP in all seven nations (Pryor, 1968: 63). However, the 1950s were an unusual period in communist economic life, covering as they did the end of the Stalin era and the subsequent rush to de-stalinize (and decentralize). A full assessment of trends in communist states should thus extend well before and after the ferment of de-stalinization. This chapter provides such an assessment by updating and expanding Pryor's analysis of public spending under communism. It focuses

AUTHOR'S NOTE: I would like to thank the National Academy of Sciences, and the Department of Politics and Faculty of Arts and Sciences at New York University, for supporting the research on which this chapter is based. I would also like to thank Gertrude Schroeder Greenslade for her comments on an earlier version of this chapter.

primarily on the USSR, the model for fiscal systems in the socialist com-
monwealth. The available data suggest that Soviet client states have pursued
many of the same budgetary strategies and reforms, with comparable trends
in public spending.[1]

In any study that relies on government expenditures to measure the
growth of the public sector, some caveats are in order. Clearly public spending and tax yields understate other forms of government intervention such as
public enterprise, regulatory activities, and tax expenditures.[2] By definition,
the understatement is more extreme in a centrally planned economy, where
the government determines wages, prices, and aggregate investment and
owns virtually all land and productive capital.[3] Thus budgetary expenditures
in the USSR—as in the West—reveal just one aspect of government involvement in the economy. However, they represent the most centralized form of
involvement, since they are the means by which the state can directly control
consumption. Allan Meltzer and Scott Richard (1978: 111) make the same
case in analyzing American public spending: The growth of the budget, they
argue, represents a concentration of power. Moreover, in the Soviet case,
while the government budget is just one mechanism for allocating resources,
the choice of mechanism itself determines who will benefit from government
largesse. Reliance on budgetary or nonbudgetary channels has important
distributive consequences, and the consequences—as Musgrave and Brennan and Pincus stress—should be our chief concern in analyzing public sector growth.[4]

In the sections that follow, I outline the countervailing pressures on the
USSR to increase and to decrease government expenditures relative to national income, trace changes in the Soviet budget from 1920 onward, and
update Pryor's analysis of spending on the standard functions of government.
As with other data from communist countries, there are multiple gaps and
ambiguities in published budget and national income statistics. The problems they create and the sources used here are discussed in the appendices.

The Pressure for Change

Clearly some of the same hypotheses about expenditure growth apply to
both East and West. Economic development is just as likely (perhaps more
so) to stimulate increases in government services in communist as in capitalist systems. In fact, rapid development, Soviet style, intensifies all the disruptions normally created by urbanization and industrialization, with corresponding demands for state provision of public services. Sustained
economic growth requires an educated and able work force—a stimulus to
state investment in human capital. The resulting increases in government

spending should actually be greater in communist states than in the West, since central planners are in theory better able to consider externalities when they plan public services (Pryor, 1965). They are also under fewer political restraints in increasing revenues; in addition to their greater coercive powers, they collect only a small percentage of state revenue through direct taxes on individuals (see Appendix A.1), which permits the maintenance of a "money illusion" about the real cost of public services (Holzman, 1955).

These factors are especially important in the early stages of rapid development. Later stages create other pressures for raising government spending. Advancing technology requires more complex plans and these take time, money, and manpower. Old planning strategies actually grow more costly with time; imbalances created by traditional "buffer sector" planning—rapid development in a few key sectors and relative underdevelopment in others— give rise to serious bottlenecks that drag growth rates downward. Early successes created through "extensive development" (investing huge amounts of capital) give way to diminishing returns, as reflected in lagging labor productivity since the middle 1950s and in the negative marginal productivity of capital during the same period (Greenslade, 1976: 279). One solution to these problems, as some critics argue, is greater centralization to permit more careful fine tuning in every sector of the economy. In a sense this suggests a parallel with the crisis hypothesis for public sector growth under capitalism; the role of the state expands to cushion the effects of adverse economic conditions. This is not to argue that increased centralization will necessarily succeed, but simply to note that economic debates still include recommendations for greater central control.

On the other hand, technical progress and success in absorbing innovations—crucial for raising productivity—require a managerial environment free of the interference from above that is a hallmark of central planning (Montias, 1970). Economic growth, so the argument goes, demands a streamlining of the planning system, and this creates pressures to reduce both direct budgetary financing of production and spending for administration. In the Soviet case the pressures have been most intense since 1965, when plans for devolution (the so-called Liberman reforms) went into effect.

Lagging productivity can also lead to a shift in emphasis from public to private consumption goods. Whatever the social benefits of public goods, they are less effective than private ones as incentives to produce. As Richard Musgrave notes,

> Only goods which satisfy private wants permit the placing of unequal weights (in whatever pattern of inequality the planner desires) on individual consumption units. Only private goods can be used for purposes of differentiation, be it for incentive, political, or other reasons [Musgrave, 1969: 13].

As the growth rate drops, political and economic pressures mount to devote a smaller share of total consumption to collective goods.

In fact, budgetary growth has taken several directions. There were rapid increases in the early years of Soviet development and during World War II; Pryor has shown a relative decline in expenditures in the aftermath of Stalin's death. However, more recent trends—if there are any—are less easily predicted. It is clear, though, that many of the pressures for change will affect individual budget components differently. Clearly, it is only by disaggregating the concept of the public sector, as Richard Rose emphasizes, that we can explain growth or decline in the whole.[5] Thus the next section traces the growth of total expenditures and of the separate components of the government budget. The components are disaggregated two ways: first, in the standard Soviet categories and then in categories and with adjustments that Pryor used.[6]

Trends are measured in terms of implied elasticities, that is, the ratio of changes in spending by all levels of government to changes in GNP in current established prices (prices that prevail in the USSR). There are three potential problems with this choice of data. First, government expenditures include transfer payments that, by definition, are not counted in GNP. Strictly speaking, then, the expenditure/income ratios should exclude transfers. However, stipends, grants, and other forms of assistance are one of the key elements in public sector growth in industrialized societies, and excluding them could understate what we want to measure. This can be handled easily enough by calculating elasticities two ways: including and excluding transfers.

Second, the use of GNP to measure the size of the economy as a whole means that we will be inflating the value of national income by including depreciation. However, the effect appears to be negligible. The rates of change in GNP and NNP are virtually identical, at least since 1950 (see Appendix A.2). Soviet-defined net material product (the value of output in what are labeled productive sectors) has also grown at almost exactly the same rate (see Appendix A.2). For my purposes here—the comparison of growth rates—the three measures are interchangeable.

Third, there are contrasting arguments for the use of current established prices to measure expenditures and national income. On one hand, they can create a "price effect." Since productivity normally grows more slowly in government than in other sectors, current prices can exaggerate the rate of change in the government budget relative to national income. On the other hand, this also means that government programs become more costly compared to other economic activity and the state must preempt more resources in order to provide the same goods and services. This is precisely what we want to know, and thus it is appropriate to measure elasticities in current prices.

Directions of Budgetary Growth:
Soviet Categories

Table 7.1 presents income elasticities for Soviet budgetary expenditures measured in standard Soviet budget categories. As expected, total government spending mushroomed during the early years of Soviet rapid development. Between the financing of investment and the training of a new industrial labor force, budget expenditures registered an elevenfold increase between 1928 and 1937 (and had been on the rise during the 1920s as well).[7] However, the pace slackened during the mid-1930s. The inefficiencies of extreme centralization during the early years of industrialization prompted a drive to substitute self-financing of production for budget grants, which was a way of tying funding more closely to enterprise performance (Davies, 1958: 244-245). Later, as international tensions grew, social expenditures were cut back in order to economize during the conversion to a wartime economy (Davies, 1958: 252). The war itself revived the upward trend in the expenditure/income ratio, but this was the last instance of dramatic budgetary growth. Demobilization brought a sharp drop in government spending relative to national income. Subsequent changes in the ratio have been modest, with an upward swing only during the last five-year interval (which is somewhat exaggerated by a poor harvest and thus a low rate of growth of national income in 1975).

Much the same pattern emerges when transfer payments are subtracted from government spending (see Table 7.2). The ratio dips during the mid-1950s and rises again only during 1970 to 1975. Two differences are worth noting, however. One is a significant expansion in transfer payments during 1940 to 1950, to cover the social dislocations of the war. The second is another increase in transfers, this time during 1965 to 1970, when new pension provisions for collective farmers boosted social security payments and new prices for farm products boosted food subsidies.[8]

Still, the postwar Soviet budget shows little sign of the expansion prevalent in the West. The OECD calculates, for example, that the average expenditure/income elasticity among member countries for 1960 to 1976 was 1.21, with Sweden and Denmark at the high end of the scale (both had a value of 1.38) and France and New Zealand at the low end (with values of 1.09 and 1.02, respectively; OECD, 1978: 8-9). The Soviet ratio for the same period was 1.06.[9] The archetypal welfare state has had one of the very lowest rates of expenditure growth in the industrialized world since 1950.

However, the component parts of the Soviet budget have changed at very different rates. Some of them, such as administration and defense, have been the favorite targets for budget-cutting campaigns. For instance, administra-

TABLE 7.1 Income Elasticity of Soviet Budgetary Expenditures*

Years	Total Expenditures	Economy	Social-Cultural	Administration	Defense
1928-1937	1.37	1.34	1.35	1.0	2.21
1937-1940	1.06	.86	.85	1.0	2.10
1940-1944	1.48	.90	1.20	1.06	2.35
1944-1950	.77	1.44	1.13	.93	.30
1950-1955	1.01	1.14	.97	.69	1.0
1955-1960	.92	.99	1.15	.59	.59
1960-1965	.99	.94	1.09	.84	.98
1965-1970	1.01	1.11	.98	.87	.93
1970-1975	1.14	1.22	1.13	.97	.80

*Calculated as the ratio of the increase (or decrease) in expenditures to the increase in GNP.
Sources: See Appendix A.

TABLE 7.2   Income Elasticity of Soviet Budgetary Expenditures, Excluding Transfers and Subsidies to Households*

Years	Total Expenditures	Total Minus Transfers and Subsidies
1940-1950	1.13	1.07
1950-1955	1.01	1.0
1955-1960	.92	.87
1960-1965	.99	.96
1965-1970	1.01	.92
1970-1975	1.14	1.11

*Calculated as the ratio of the increase (or decrease) in expenditures to the increase in GNP.
Sources: See Appendix A.

tive expenditures just kept pace with national income up through World War II (see Table 7.1). They have grown more slowly ever since. This trend fits well with the prediction that the state apparatus will decline in importance as society advances toward communism, and in part, it does represent a real effort to trim administrative costs after Stalin's death. It also represents a move apparently begun in the 1950s to charge more of the expenses of economic planning and management to enterprise costs (Gallik et al., 1968: 40-41). Part of the cutback in spending, therefore, is simply attributable to a redefinition of budget categories.

Reported budgetary expenditures for defense have been more erratic. Spending tripled with preparations for the war and dropped at the war's end. Since then, reported defense spending has fluctuated, but the increases have never exceeded the growth of national income. The symbolic advantages of a low defense budget are obvious. What the official statistics in Table 7.1 omit, however, are expenditures for the most rapidly expanding military-related programs: research and development (R&D), stockpiling of reserves, military aid, space exploration, and nuclear energy development, among others. These apparently fall into other budgetary categories (such as economic appropriations and residual expenditures), so the total budget does include most if not all defense spending. As the continuing Western debate on this issue demonstrates, the size of the omitted items is in dispute (Lee, 1977; Holzman, 1976; Becker, 1979). However, a rough estimate of their magnitude and their impact on the government budget will be discussed in more detail.

In contrast to administration and defense, the two remaining budget categories have on the average outpaced national income. Expenditures for the economy, which include capital grants and subsidies to productive and service enterprises, grew rapidly during the initial phase of Soviet industrialization, during postwar reconstruction, and during the years 1965 to 1975. (Since agriculture subsidies are included in this item, their rapid expansion helps to explain part of the jump after 1965.)[10] Social welfare or social-cultural expenditures (including health, education, welfare, culture, and science) have been more consistent, outstripping the GNP during virtually every five-year interval since the war. The aftermath of the war, and post-Stalin campaigns to upgrade the standard of living and to revitalize science, all combined to keep spending on the increase. Still, the changes have been small in comparison with the early years of Soviet power, keeping total budgetary growth relatively modest.

Directions of Budgetary Growth:
Pryor's Categories

The same pattern of limited growth emerges when budgetary categories are reworked along the lines of Pryor's study. His data on public consumption expenditures (government budget expenditures minus capital investment) for standard government functions are updated in Table 7.3, with some modifications in his approach to estimating spending on three categories: defense, administration, and internal security or police. The modifications, and the derivation of the data, are described in Appendix B. As with the standard Soviet budgetary categories analyzed in Table 7.1, there have been gradual changes in aggregate spending. However, there have been more extensive shifts in individual items (see Table 7.3). The most dramatic have been in science, defense, and welfare; Soviet leaders have bought both guns *and* butter. They have also pushed for a scientific-technical revolution (especially in the management of the economy), which gave rise to a sevenfold expansion of the scientific establishment between 1950 and 1975.[11] A preoccupation with defense is also behind this increase, though the share of military research and development funds in the science budget is not altogether clear.

Explanations for the growth of defense spending are legion: the worsening of the Sino-Soviet split, the loss of prestige over the Cuban Missile Crisis, the Soviet military's dissatisfaction with Khrushchev and their subsequent demands on his successors, and the pressure of increases in American defense outlays. The reasons for increasing welfare spending are not unfamiliar: a gradual aging of the population, coupled with major reforms in 1956 and 1964 to upgrade benefits and widen eligibility.[12] Spending for education and health care, however, just barely kept pace with the growth of national income between 1950 and 1975. One reason may be a perception of relative saturation with these services. For example, critics have complained of underutilized hospitals and of overproduction of doctors.[13] In addition, the secular decline in the birthrate has meant relatively fewer students and the closing of schools in some parts of the country.

Finally, expenditures for police and for administration registered substantial declines during 1950 to 1975. The changes in the administration

TABLE 7.3 Income Elasticity of Soviet Public Consumption Expenditures*

Years	Health	Welfare	Education	Science	Police	Administration	Defense
1950-1955	1.13	.88	.95	1.18	.62	.69	na
1955-1960	1.03	1.36	.82	1.97	.67	.60	.78
1960-1965	.97	1.06	1.12	1.28	.90	.84	1.16
1965-1970	.87	1.02	.87	1.02	.93	.87	1.18
1970-1975	1.03	1.20	1.09	1.01	na	.99	1.27

*Calculated as the ratio of the increase (or decrease) in expenditures to the increase in GNP. Expenditures are net of capital investment, and the categories (except for police, administration, and defense) follow the conventions that Pryor used. For definitions and the derivation of these figures, see Appendix B.
Sources: See Appendix B.

category, as I noted above, involved both cutbacks in the state bureaucracy and some statistical sleight of hand in reformulating the category itself. It may be that the same developments explain the drop in spending on the police between 1950 and 1960, when there was apparently a genuine cutback of some thirty-five percent of police personnel (Rapawy, 1972: 24). However, there may also have been some shift in definitions. For example, security personnel connected with economic institutions may have been transferred from security to production in state statistics. Since 1960 the trend has been reversed: The number of police personnel has grown. Even so, the increase has lagged behind the growth of total employment, and expenditures on police services have increased slightly less than national income.[14]

Altogether, expenditures have roughly paralleled the growth of GNP, at least up until 1970 to 1975. All of the data—whether defined in Soviet or in Pryor's terms—point to relatively minor increases in government spending. The advocates of greater centralization apparently have been unsuccessful in the budgetary realm. In fact, there has been more decentralization than is evident from the size of the budget alone. Ever since 1950 items that were once funded through budget appropriations have been transferred to other institutions for support. An increasing share of funds for health, education, and welfare, for example, has come from outside the government budget. State enterprises, farms, trade unions, and other institutions contribute money, labor, and materials to supplement budgetary expenditures, and their contributions are growing steadily. Since an enterprise with its own day care center or with a good medical staff has an edge in attracting and keeping an adequate supply of labor, access to such fringe benefits is viewed as an incentive to productivity. In turn, the more successful the enterprise, the more funds become available for benefits to workers. Some of the funds, of course, may go toward the welfare of the community as a whole, but for the most part they are allotted first to the enterprise workers and their families. The growth of these extrabudgetary contributions is indicated in Table 7.4. For social welfare or social-cultural measures as a whole, outside funds actually doubled in importance between 1950 and 1975, and the change was especially pronounced in education. Extrabudgetary support for health care has grown less rapidly, but nonetheless it accounts for over a fifth of all the funds spent on health. All told, then, the level of funding for social welfare has been higher than is indicated strictly from budget data alone. Even so, the direction of change in social welfare spending, and the conclusions about individual expenditure items, remain the same.

The important point is that the role of the budget in financing collective consumption has declined. In one sense this may seem to be a distinction without a difference. Money may be spent from budgetary or from enterprise funds, but both are instruments of the state and both are controlled by the same set of planners. Undoubtedly this is true insofar as planners in Mos-

TABLE 7.4   The State Budget as a Share of Total Soviet Public Expenditures*

Year	Social-Cultural	Education	Health
1950	90.7	87.9	83.3
1955	89.1	85.5	84.6
1960	88.2	81.8	81.7
1965	84.3	78.1	84.8
1970	80.1	70.5	78.8
1975	78.9	65.7	78.8

*Budgetary expenditures expressed as a percentage of all spending by all public agencies.

Sources: *Narodnoe khoziaistvo SSSR v 1958 g.,* (M., Statistika, 1959): 899-905; hereafter listed as *Narkhoz; Narkhoz* (1960: 846-49; 1965: 783; 1977: 561-562).

cow determine the relative *shares* of budgetary and nonbudgetary funds to be allotted. Yet there is a crucial difference between the two; the more the funding from enterprises, farms, trade unions, and the like, the more the probable inequality in the distribution of social goods. Benefits and services are more clearly differentiated to reward production units, and with them, productive workers. Thus the distribution of such public goods should increasingly come to reflect job stratification.[15] In fact, the inequality is readily apparent in the frequent complaints by local officials that local factories take care of their own workers but contribute little to the rest of the community. The diminished role of the budget suggests a trend away from collective consumption and a closer connection between work and reward. To reiterate Musgrave's conclusion, collective, budget-financed goods simply do not work well as incentives for individual effort. It would be stretching the point to argue that the relative decline in collective consumption in any way represents a shift from public to private decision making. However, there *is* a measurable change within the public sector toward a distribution of goods that more closely aligns benefits with productivity.

A similar trend away from budget financing has characterized other types of expenditures as well, though the implications are less clear. As illustrated in Table 7.5, a smaller share of the funding for capital investment in productive sectors has come from the government budget since 1950. Economic units have come to rely more on financing from their own revenues (and, to a limited extent, from bank credit). The rationale, especially after the 1965 economic reforms, was to strengthen economic accountability and, in part, to shift some of the responsibility for decision (especially for replacement capital and for repairs) closer to production units. In financing for science the budget also has been downplayed. Research institutions reportedly received less than half their funding from the budget in 1974 and this share had been on the decline at least since 1960 (Arkhangel'skii, 1976: 92). Research is now supposed to rely more heavily on contracts—again an effort to

TABLE 7.5   Budget Grants as a Share of Soviet Capital Investment

Year	Percentage of Investment Financed from Budget
1945	77.8
1950	79.9
1955	71.1
1965	66
1971	44
1976	40.8

Sources: N. Kaplan (1951); Allakhverdian (1958: 32); S. Sitarian (1968: 12-20); Kazankova et al. (1971: 6); Aiushiev and Ivanitskii (1978: 37).

strengthen accountability, and also an effort to tie research more closely to the needs of producers.

Whether all of these maneuvers have had the expected results is debatable. It is interesting to note that the decline in budgetary financing of investment has been matched by an increase in complaints about the dispersion (*raspylenie*) of funds. Too many projects are begun, controls over planning are ineffective, and resources are spread too thin. In fact, the complaints have recently spurred a new move to recentralize control over dispersed investments, and that could well mean an increase in the share of funds channeled through the budget.

Conclusion

Despite its presumably greater ability to consider externalities in planning public goods, and despite the normal pressures for increased spending that pump up government budget elsewhere, the USSR has not experienced any upward spiral in government expenditures since World War II. This is partly a product of countervailing trends in individual expenditure categories and partly the result of devolution in financing public programs. The effect of devolution, at least in social welfare, is to deemphasize the equal provision of social goods and to intensify differences in their distribution. While all of this takes place within the public sector, it means that social consumption goods have become less public, less available to individuals outside the factory or farm that puts up money to finance them. Not all goods are likely to be equally limited; apparently the state budget continues to fund very basic items such as primary and secondary education and public clinics. Other benefits and services—including day care and some medical care—are more closely tied to employment. That hardly qualifies as the advent of a private sector in the USSR. However, it does signal an important change in public decision making, with serious implications for who gets what from government.

APPENDIX A.1
Direct Taxes on Individuals
As a Percentage of Total Soviet Budget Revenue*

Year	Direct taxes–Total Revenue
1940	12
1950	16
1955	15
1960	9
1965	8
1970	8
1975	9

*Direct taxes include levies on personal income, private plots, bachelors, and families with few or no children, and subscriptions to government bond issues (which, although nominally voluntary, were in effect a form of tax until they were discontinued in 1957). Profit payments into the budget from state enterprises can also be considered a form of direct taxation (analogous to a corporate income tax), but they are treated as a distributive share in the USSR. Profit payments, along with an excise or turnover tax, constitute the major sources of budgetary revenue. All data here include all levels of government.

Sources: *Gosudarstvennyi biudzhet SSSR i biudzhety soiuznykh respublik, 1956-1960 gg.* (M., Statistika, 1962: 7-9); *Gosudarstvennyi biudzhet SSSR i biudzhety soiuznykh respublik, 1961-1965 gg.* (M., Statistika, 1966: 10-11); *Gosudarstvennyi biudzhet SSSR i biudzhety soiuznykh respublik, 1966-1970 gg.*, (M., Statistika, 1972: 11-12); and *Gosudarstvennyi biudzhet SSSR i biudzhety soiuznykh respublik, 1971-1975 gg.* (M., Statistika, 1976: 8-9). Hereafter, these volumes are referred to as *Gosbiudzhet*.

(appendix continues on page 130)

Soviet Budget Expenditures and GNP, Selected Years
(in billions of current rubles)[1]

Year	Total[2]	Economy[3]	Social-Cultural[4]	Administration	Defense	GNP
1928[5]	.9	.4	.3	.1	.1	3.2
1937	10.6	4.3	3.1	.4	1.8	28.1
1940	17.4	5.8	4.1	.7	5.7	43.5
1944	26.4	5.4	5.1	.7	13.8	44.9
1950	41.3	15.8	11.7	1.4	8.3	91.2
1955	54.0	23.3	14.7	1.2	10.7	118.4
1960	73.1	34.1	24.9	1.1	9.3	174.0
1965	101.6	44.9	38.2	1.3	12.8	244.1
1970	154.6	74.6	55.9	1.7	17.9	365.6
1975	214.5	110.7	77.0	2.0	17.4	446.4[6]

1. 1960 decimal.

2. This total also includes an unexplained residual, which apparently covers appropriations for the KGB, grants to state banks, and various payments to state enterprises not originally included in the annual plan. The residual may also include foreign aid or trade subsidies. On this point see CIA (1977: 18).

3. Capital grants and subsidies to sectors on independent financial accounting (*khozraschet*), including industry, construction, agriculture, trade, transport, communications, housing, and municipal services.

4. Investment and operating expenses for budget-financed programs, including health care, education, welfare, culture, and science.

5. Budget data are for fiscal year 1928/9 (which ran from harvest-to-harvest, October to October).

6. Estimated following a procedure set out by Campbell (1972).

Sources: *Gosbiudzhet* (1962: 18-19); *Gosbiudzhet* (1966: 20, 53); *Gosbiudzhet* (1972: 25); *Gosbiudzhet* (1976: 22-23); K. N. Plotnikov, *Ocherki istorii biudzheta sovetskoi gosudarstva* (M., Gosfinizdat, 1954: passim); Bergson (1961); Campbell (1972: 34). The GNP data for 1975 were estimated following the procedure laid out by Campbell, with data taken from *Narodnoe khoziaistvo SSSR v 1977 g.* (M., Statistika, 1978: 378, 386, 404, 541, and 558).

APPENDIX A.3
Rates of Change in Soviet GNP, NMP, and NNP

Years	GNP	NMP	NNP
1950-1955	1.30	1.33	
1955-1960	1.47	1.47	
1960-1965	1.40	1.33	1.36
1965-1970	1.50	1.50	1.49
1970-1975	1.22	1.25	1.17

Sources: For GNP and NNP, as listed in Table 7.2; for NMP, Peshekhonov et al. (1978: 52).

APPENDIX A.4
Estimated Transfers and Subsidies to Households[1]

Year	Transfer Payments[2]	Housing and Food Subsidies[3]
1940	.95	.1
1950	4.2	.6[4]
1955	5.2	1.1[4]
1960	10.4	1.6[4]
1965	14.9	4.4
1970	23.1	18.2
1975	35.0	25.5

1. In billions of current rubles, 1960 decimal. The data do not include all subsidies and transfers: No data were available on budget grants for other consumer services (such as personal transportation) or for producers, and none were available to indicate interest and repayment of loans to the population.

2. Transfers here include pensions and grants through the state social security system (including budget payments through the collective farm pension system), grants to mothers, social insurance, and educational stipends. Of these, the latter include some (unspecified) contributions from nonbudgetary sources.

3. The housing subsidy includes payments to cover operating deficits in public housing units. Part of the total may include contributions from sources other than the state budget. The food subsidy includes payments to agricultural procurement agencies and to food processing enterprises to cover the deficit between the prices paid to farmers and the artificially low retail prices on basic food items.

4. Interpolated.

Sources: *Gosbiudzhet* (1962: 18-19); *Gosbiudzhet* (1966: 20-21); *Gosbiudzhet* (1972: 25); *Gosbiudzhet* (1976: 22-23); *Narodnoe khoziaistvo SSSR v 1970 g.* p. 537; *Narodnoe khoziaistvo SSSR v 1972 g.*, (1972: 535); *Narodnoe khoziaistvo SSSR v 1979 g.*, (1979: 409); and Treml (1978: 8).

APPENDIX B
Soviet Public Consumption Expenditures
(in billions of current rubles)[1]

Year	Education[2]	Health[3]	Welfare[4]	Science[5]	Administration[6]	Police[7]	Defense[8]
1950	3.8	1.9	4.9	.4	1.3	.8	na
1955	4.6	2.8	5.6	.6	1.2	.7	14.0
1960	5.6	4.2	11.1	1.8	1.0	.6	16.0
1965	8.8	5.9	16.6	3.2	1.2	.8	26.0
1970	11.4	8.3	25.4	4.9	1.5	1.1	46.0
1975	15.2	10.4	37.2	6.0	1.9	na	71.5[9]

1. Government budgetary expenditures excluding capital investment and modified as indicated in the following notes to correspond to Frederic Pryor's (1968: Appendix A-12) formulation. The data here are expressed with a post-1960 decimal. As a check on reliability, I reestimated data for some of the same years that Pryor analyzed (1950, 1955, and 1960), and discovered that the absolute amount given for each category did not always match (mainly because of different methods and assumptions in estimating and removing capital expenditures). However, the elasticities in the two sets of data were virtually identical, so the two are interchangeable for purposes of assessing trends in government spending.

2. Education represents the bill for general primary and secondary, secondary specialized, and higher education, excluding capital investment. Other items that are normally part of the Soviet education budget—preschool facilities, children's homes, and extracurricular activities—have been excluded from this estimate and are counted instead under welfare here. Capital investment data are reported in official publications for most years in the table (from 1960 on); where these data were incomplete I estimated capital expenditures for each component of the education budget from corresponding figures on the union republics.

3. Health expenditures include funds for hospitals, dispensaries, clinics, and other medical facilities. Spending for nursery schools, normally included in the Soviet budget under health care, is excluded from this item and listed instead under welfare. Capital expenditures have been excluded; when the data were incomplete, I followed the estimation procedure described in Note 2 above.

4. Welfare includes social security and social insurance payments, grants to single mothers and to those with large families, grants to the national pension fund for collective farmers, and expenses for preschools and children's homes, minus capital investment. Pryor (1968: 381) also included military pensions and excluded social insurance payments related to health care, for example, to finance trips to sanatoria.

5. Science expenditures include funding for scientific-research institutions, minus capital investment, with investment estimated as described in Note 2 above.

6. Administration includes expenditures for organs of state power and for the courts. No data are available on capital investment in this category; Pryor (1968: 376) estimated that investment is approximately three percent of the total, and I have done the same. Pryor also attempted to remove expenditures on the courts from this category and list them instead under internal security/police. But the data are too fragmentary to do this accurately, so I have made no attempt to separate spending on the judiciary from other administrative expenditures.

7. Police represents the bill for the regular *militsiia* and security guards in state agencies, estimated from data on employment, wages, and social security payments (there is no separate budget category for internal security in Soviet publications). (Pryor estimated this item by assuming that the number of personnel remained the same from 1955 on, and that wages therefore rose at the same rate as in the rest of the economy. However, more recent data challenge this assumption.)

8. Defense includes purchases of equipment and supplies for the military (including nuclear weapons and space hardware), operating and personnel costs, R&D, and military construction. The latter is normally considered to represent capital investment and should be omitted for the sake of comparability with other items in the table, but no data were available to separate construction costs from other defense-related items. The numbers in the table are derived from a range of estimates, and I have presented the midpoint of the range for each year.

9. This figure represents a projection to 1975 and may overstate total defense spending.

Sources: For education, health, science, and administration—*Gosbiudzhet* (1962: passim); *Gosbiudzhet* (1966: passim); *Gosbiudzhet* (1972: passim); and *Gosbiudzhet* (1976: passim). For police, Stephen Rapaway (1972: 24); and *Narodnoe khoziaistvo SSSR v 1972 g.*, (M., Statistika, 1973: 516-517). For defense, William T. Lee (1977: 65-67).

NOTES

1. Actually, the same strategies—such as a reduction in the role of the government budget—have been implemented in varying degrees, at different times, and in different ways in Eastern Europe, which complicates the task of collecting equivalent data. The common penchant in bloc states for changing the definitions and coverage of government statistics makes it difficult to distinguish real changes in government policy from simple reclassification of data. I describe some of the problems in an earlier work (Bahry, 1980).

2. An overview of the omissions and their implications is provided by B. Guy Peters and Martin Heisler in this volume.

3. According to official statistics, most productive assets in the USSR have been socialized since the mid-1930s; as of 1975, all assets reportedly belonged to the socialized sector (including private plots and livestock raised on them). In Eastern Europe the picture is the same except for Poland, where some fifteen percent of productive assets in 1975 were privately owned—apparently all in agriculture. See *Statisticheskii ezhegodnik stran-chlenov Soveta Ekonomicheskoi Vzaimopomoschi, 1977* (1977: 38).

4. See the chapters by Richard Musgrave and Geoffrey Brennan and Jonathan Pincus in this volume.

5. See the chapter by Richard Rose in this volume.

6. A third breakdown of expenditure data is also normally presented, with spending divided into consumption, transfers and subsidies, and investment. However, the USSR does not publish the relevant line items that would allow this kind of disaggregation over the period examined here.

7. For the years prior to 1928, R. W. Davies presents data that allow us to compare the elasticities of expenditures and Soviet net material product:

Years	Ratio: Change in Budget ÷ Change in NMP
1924/5-1925/6	1.03
1925/6-1926/7	1.27
1926/7-1927/8	1.13
1927/8-1928/9	1.03

The years are designated with a slash to indicate the old-style fiscal year, and the data are measured in current rubles (Davies, 1958: 107).

8. Food subsidies appear in the budget as grants to deficit-ridden agricultural procurement agencies and processing industries. However, they are normally considered to be the equivalent of a subsidy to consumers.

9. The data and sources used to calculate the ratio are presented in Appendix A.

10. Elasticities for so-called economic expenditures minus agricultural subsidies equaled .93 for 1965-1970, and 1.23 for 1970-75. Data and sources are listed in Appendix A.

11. Employment in science jumped from 162,500 to 1,223,400 between 1950 and 1975 (*Narodnoe khoziaistvo SSSR v 1975 g.,* 1976: 165).

12. The proportion of the population aged 60 or older has risen from 6.8 percent in 1939 to 11.8 percent in 1970; see data presented Peshekhonov et al. (1978: 57).

13. See, for example, Malov and Churakov (1981: 88-91) and Peshekhonov et al. (1978: 141).

14. The number of police personnel increased by thirty-four percent between 1960 and 1969, (Rapawy, 1972); total employment in the state sector increased by 42 percent during the same period (*Narodnoe khoziaistvo SSSR v 1975 q.,* 1976: 531).

15. That, in fact, is precisely what some Soviet authors recommend. See, for example, Bus'ko (1981: 20) and Peshekhonov (1978: 64-65).

134   *Using Aggregate Data*

REFERENCES

AIUSHIEV, A. D. and V. P. IVANITSKII (1978) "Istochniki finansirovaniia kapitalovlozhe-niia." Finansy SSSR 6: 37.
ALLAKHVERDIAN, D. A. (1958) Ekonomicheskoe soderzhanie raskhodov sovetskogo biudzheta. Moscow: Gosfinizdat.
ARKHANGEL'SKII, V. N. (1976) Planirovanie i finansirovanie nauchnykh issledovanii. Moscow: Finansy.
BAHRY, D. (1980) "Measuring communist priorities: budgets, investments, and the problem of equivalence." Comparative Political Studies 13 (October): 267-292.
BECKER, A. (1979) "The meaning and measure of Soviet military expenditure." pp. 352–368 in U.S. Congress, Joint Economic Committee, Soviet Economy in a Time of Change, vol. 1. Washington, DC: Government Printing Office.
BERGSON, A. (1961) The Real National Income of Soviet Russia Since 1928. Cambridge, MA: Harvard University Press.
BUS'KO, V. N. (1981) "Nuzhen edinyi istochnik." Finansy SSSR 5.
CAMERON, D. (1978) "The expansion of the public economy." American Political Science Review 72 (December): 1243-1261.
CAMPBELL, R. (1972) "A shortcut method for estimating Soviet GNP." ACES Bulletin 14 (Fall): 34.
_____ (1966) Soviet Economic Power. New York: Houghton Mifflin.
Central Intelligence Agency (1977) The Soviet State Budget Since 1965. Research Paper ER 77-10529 (December). Langley, VA: CIA.
DAVIES, R. W. (1958) The Development of the Soviet Budgetary System. Cambridge: Cambridge University Press.
GALLIK, D., C. JESINA, and S. RAPAWY (1968) The Soviet Financial System. U.S. Department of Commerce, International Population Statistics Reports. Series P-90, 23. Washington, DC: Government Printing Office.
GOLDMAN, M. (1967) "Economic growth and institutional change in the Soviet Union," pp. 61-82 in P. Juviler and H. Moton (eds.) Soviet Policy-Making. New York: Praeger.
GREENSLADE, R. V. (1976) "The real Gross National Product of the USSR, 1950-1975," pp. 269–300 in U.S. Congress, Joint Economic Committee, Soviet Economy in a New Perspective. Washington, DC: Government Printing Office.
HOLZMAN, F. D. (1976) Financial Checks on Soviet Defense Expenditures. Lexington, MA: D. C. Heath.
_____ (1955) Soviet Taxation. Cambridge, MA: Harvard University Press.
JOHNSON, C. (1970) "Comparing communist nations," in C. Johnson (ed.) Change in Communist Systems. Stanford, CA: Stanford University Press.
KAPLAN, N. (1951) Capital Investments in the Soviet Union, 1924-1951. RM-735, Santa Monica, CA: Rand Corporation.
KAZANKOVA, K. A. et al. (1971) Finansy ministerstv i ob'edineniia v novykh usloviiakh khoziaistvovaniia. Moscow: Finansy.
LEE, W. T. (1977) The Estimation of Soviet Defense Expenditures: An Unconventional Approach. New York: Praeger.
MALOV, N. and V. CHURAKOV (1981) "Voprosy meditsinskogo obsluzhivaniia naseleniia." Planovoe khoziaistvo 1.
MELTZER, A. and S. RICHARD (1978) "Why government grows (and grows) in a democracy." Public Interest 52 (Summer): 111-118.
MONTIAS, J. M. (1970) "Types of communist economic systems," pp. 117-34 in C. Johnson (ed.) Change in Communist Systems. Stanford, CA: Stanford University Press.

MUSGRAVE, R. (1969) Fiscal Systems. New Haven, CT: Yale University Press.

Narodnoe khoziaistvo SSSR v 1975 g. (1976) M., Statistika.

Organization of Economic Cooperation and Development (1978) Public Expenditure Trends. Studies in Resource Allocation, 5. Paris: OECD.

PELTZMAN, S. (1980) "The growth of government." Journal of Law and Economics 23 (October): 209-287.

PESHEKHONOV, V. et al. (1978) Razvitie i finansirovanie obshchestvennykh fondov potrebleniia. Moscow: Finansy.

PRYOR, F. (1968) Public Expenditures in Communist and Capitalist Nations. Homewood, IL: Dorsey.

———— (1965) "East and West German governmental expenditures." Public Finance 20 (3-4): 300-357.

RAPAWY, S. (1972) Comparison of U.S. and USSR Civilian Employment in Government: 1950-1969. U.S. Department of Commerce, International Population Reports, Series P-95, 69 (April). Washington, DC: Government Printing Office.

SCHROEDER, G. (1979) "The Soviet economy on a treadmill of reforms," pp. 312–340 in U.S. Congress, Joint Economic Committee, Soviet Economy in a Time of Change (vol. 1). Washington, DC: Government Printing Office.

SITARIAN, S. (1968) Khoziaistvennaia reforma i biudzhet. Moscow: Finansy.

Statisticheskii ezhegodnik stran-chlenov Soveta Ekonomicheskoi Vzaimopomoshchi (1977) Moscow: Statistika.

TARSCHYS, D. (1975) "The growth of public expenditures: nine modes of explanation." Scandinavian Political Studies 10: 9-42.

TREML, V. (1978) Agricultural Subsidies in the Soviet Union. U.S. Bureau of the Census, Foreign Economic Reports, 15. Washington, DC: Government Printing Office.

WRIGHT, A. W. (1980) "Soviet economic planning and performance," pp. 122-123 in Stephen F. Cohen et al., The Soviet Union Since Stalin. Bloomington: Indiana University Press.

CHAPTER 8

PROBLEMS IN USING
PUBLIC EMPLOYMENT DATA

RICHARD C. EICHENBERG

Recent research in comparative public policy points to a revival of interest in public bureaucracies, both as a phenomenon to be explained and as a major causal factor in the origin and reform of government programs. However, relatively few studies include quantitative measures of bureaucracy in models of policy change or government growth. Although research has clearly pointed to the important role of bureaucracy in comparative studies, major progress has been hindered by the lack of a broad, comparative data base.

This is not to suggest that interest in the public sector has been lacking among social scientists. Rather, interest in bureaucracy and public employment (and thus in data collection) seems to have waned as other measures of government growth have gained the attention of scholars. Whereas bureaucracy and public employment formed the major focus in the work of the earliest policy analysts (Sharp, 1931, 1933; White, 1935; Rivet, 1932; Kupper, 1929; Friedrich and Cole, 1932), more recent work has been concentrated on the taxing and spending policies of the state (Pryor, 1968; Cameron, 1978; Kohl, 1979, 1981), the differentiation of government agencies (Rose, 1976), the centralization of governmental authority (Pryor, 1968), and the expansion of the regulatory authority of the state (Andrain, 1980).

Bureaucracy in the HIWED Project

This chapter presents new data on public employment for twelve West European democracies. Although the full data collection includes figures for both total and central government employment, we focus in this report on problems in measuring total government employment.[1] In addition to employment totals, the data collection includes a functional breakdown of employees in administration, education, post, transport, and industrial activities. The data cover the period 1870-1970, although earlier figures are available for some countries.

This chapter describes the problems encountered in collecting the data and the solutions sought to preserve reliability and comparability. Before turning to these technical issues, however, it is useful to review the theoretical context of the data collection. Public employment was only one of a number of topics investigated in a broader project on the modernization of the West European democracies and the development of the welfare state (the HIWED project—Historical Indicators of the West European Democracies).[2] The project included studies on demographic change, national product, income distribution, public revenues and expenditures, social insurance, electoral behavior, and labor unions and strikes. A brief review of the theoretical approach employed in the HIWED project will clarify the wider context of our data collection and the types of information that were sought (see also Flora and Alber, 1981).

The changing nature of state activity, especially welfare policy, is conceived in the project as one response to the problems arising from modernization, by which we mean the transformation of societies from predominantly rural/agricultural to urban/industrial. We hypothesize that government response will to some extent be related to the socioeconomic problems created during the modernization process. This hypothesis rests on the assumption that modernization produces similar societal problems, especially in terms of the security demands resulting from dependence on an industrial labor market. However, this prediction says little about potentially different forms of policy response, and it provides few supplementary hypotheses should social change variables prove weak in predicting even the fact of policy response. Thus we ask, What additional factors are likely to affect the timing and perhaps the form of governments' response to modernization? (For empirical analyses of these questions, see Flora and Alber, 1981; and Alber, 1978, 1979.)

The HIWED project sought answers to these questions in the historical experience of the countries under study, following quite closely the typology of variables and relationships developed by Stein Rokkan. Rokkan placed heavy emphasis on the major task of elites during the process of state and nation building: territorial and cultural unification and the maintenance of external security. We use the variables specified by Rokkan to describe these "historical problem complexes" in formulating hypotheses concerning the later policy responses of governments (Rokkan, 1970, 1975).

Bureaucracy provides a useful example of the theoretical linkage between historical experience and the later development of governmental pol-

icy. As governments begin to experience the problem pressures of modernization, the likelihood and perhaps the form of policy response will depend
to some extent on the bureaucracy's ability to monitor social conditions, raise
necessary revenues, and implement complex legislation. This administrative
capacity cannot be created overnight, but rather exists as a result of previous
historical experience, such as participation in international power competition (including war), the presence of competitors in defining the national
culture, or early socioeconomic development. By analyzing this historical
experience, we hoped both to improve our understanding of bureaucratization and to refine our analyses of the origin and growth of the welfare state.

It is clear from this brief review that the HIWED project's theoretical
interest in policy initiation, extension, and reform directed our data collection toward the administrative or policy-making part of the public sector. We
were most interested in those employees of the state engaged in the collection and evaluation of information, the advising of political decision makers,
and the implementation of programs.

To this primary interest was added a secondary goal: the publication of an
historical data handbook on the West European democracies (Flora et al., in
press). One purpose of the handbook is to measure the growth of government, including the expansion of government authority into areas previously
reserved to markets or private associations. This latter focus required that
data collection on the public sector go beyond the traditional administrative
areas dictated by our theoretical interest in policy development. Thus we
collected data for three areas in which governmental authority has played a
crucial role: education, communication, and transportation. Personnel in
industrial enterprises owned and operated directly by the government were
collected when available. As discussed below in more detail, three types of
government activity are only partially covered in the data. Health, welfare,
and nationalized industries are in large part missing. The reasons for this
exclusion are practical rather than theoretical; data for these categories are
simply not available for any length of time.

Problems of Definition and Data Collection

Between the two world wars, growing interest in public administration
was accompanied by attempts to ascertain the number of persons employed
by governments. Often to the surprise of the searchers, the attempts met with
a uniform response from statisticians and budget officials in government
ministries: The information was not available (Sharp, 1931, 1933; White,
1935; Rivet, 1932; Friedrich and Cole, 1932). Lacking official payroll or
staff statistics, scholars turned to the next best source: the occupational enumerations of the population censuses. These sources offered several advan-

tages. First, they provided historical coverage; most governments began relatively sophisticated occupational censuses sometime between 1860 and 1880. Second, the census occurs at regular historical intervals; for most countries, it is possible to collect data for ten- to fifteen- year data points. Finally, government employment, at least in the traditional administrative sectors, has historically been among the five or six major economic sectors enumerated in the censuses.

The census became a logical source for our attempt to update and expand earlier collections. Unfortunately, occupational enumerations are beset with a number of difficulties and must be supplemented by other sources in many instances. Since it is crucial to an interpretation of our own data, we discuss these problems serially before turning to a description of the data themselves.

Availability. Original, detailed census publications are rarely available in one central location. Summary reports in statistical yearbooks are too general for purposes of isolating the public sector. Our solution to this problem was to retrieve the original census volumes and to photocopy the detailed listing of occupational categories and subcategories. This task was the most difficult and time-consuming part of the research. Over a period of several years, visits were made to libraries and government offices in several of the countries under study.

Definition of employment. Occupational censuses often include a broader definition of the activity employed than would normally apply. Whereas "full time, actively in service" comes closest to an operationalization of working civil servant, census data cover both full- and part-time workers and the temporarily unemployed without distinction (Bairoch, 1968).

The inclusion of part-time workers obviously introduces some overestimation. It is particularly likely that we overestimate the number engaged in policy formation or administration since part-time workers are likely to be concentrated among support personnel. Finally, the extent of overestimation is likely to grow over time since the ratio of support personnel to administrators probably increases as policy and administration become more complex. (This assumption is controversial; see Nolan, 1979.) Unfortunately, we have no way of specifying precisely the magnitude of overestimation short of conducting an additional study of part-time government employment. We assume that cross-national comparisons are not made impossible by this difficulty, however, since they are included in the censuses of almost all countries. This assumes, of course, that the ratio of part-time to full-time is approximately equal across countries.

The inclusion of the temporarily unemployed introduces a second upward bias in the data. Data for the Great Depression, however, suggest that actual discharge from employment is captured by the census takers. We have confidence that our data measure the number of persons hired by government, even if these are temporarily laid off.

Problems of functional classification. Although all national censuses include some variant of a public administration category, the uniformity ends here. Specific problems of comparability and our solutions are as follows:

- *Education personnel* are sometimes listed as part of administration. We have taken them from this category and listed them separately.
- *Military personnel* are also sometimes listed as part of public administration. Whenever possible, our solution was to delete them. Our major interest was in civil administration and policy making. Moreover, census data on military personnel usually exclude conscripts. Finally, total military personnel are available from other projects that are better able to deal with the complexities of these data (Correlates of War Project, 1971).
- Definitions for *police and court personnel* vary. Fireman are often included with policemen or both are included with employees of the justice system. Users should check Eichenberg (1979) for the specific determination applied for each country.
- Some *health personnel* are excluded. Census tables include only employment in health functions that developed as part of administrative responsibility (e.g., public health offices or sanitary inspection), but their employees are few in number when compared to those in public hospitals. The latter are usually listed outside the government sector in a combined category with private health professions. We have no way of separating the two and have omitted them.
- *Personnel in welfare institutions* are also often excluded. Employees in direct, governmental agencies (e.g., public assistance offices, unemployment bureaus, or social ministries) tend to be given, but employees outside the normal administrative stream (e.g., homes for children or the elderly) tend to be listed under services or as part of the profession to which they belong. A breakdown between private and public is rarely available. Hence, they are omitted.
- *Semipublic agencies' employees* are omitted. In the United States and the United Kingdom, social insurance institutions are fully consolidated in the government apparatus, but in most European states, social benefits are administered by semipublic agencies. Although these agencies are created by public statute and much of their work is determined by legislation, their staffs are not always government employees and do not appear as such in the censuses.
- *Education personnel* for some countries are not distinguished in terms of private versus public. Alternative sources were consulted, but in some cases it has been necessary to report combined totals with some estimate of the overreporting that this entails.
- *Employment in postal, telephone, and telegraph services* is relatively straightforward in census returns. Insofar as other sources are used, the ministry of post and telephone has been added to ensure comparability with census sources.
- *Employment in transportation* often does not include data for local transport, unfortunately. Insofar as other sources are used, the ministry of transport has been added to insure comparability with census sources.

- *Employment in industry*, as noted above, is generally excluded, but data for public utilities and other industrial enterprises owned and operated by the government were collected when easily available from sources in our possession. They are included in the longer report.

The Data:
Summary Description

As this list of difficulties makes clear, the final data collection was the result of setbacks, compromises, and estimates; therefore, the data represent the lowest common denominator of available public employment data. This denominator can be summarized as the following standard definition:

> full-time and part-time civilian employees of government at all levels, including those temporarily unemployed.

The working definitions of the five functional categories are as follows:

- *Administration*—civilian employees in public administration, excluding employees in institutions and quasi-public agencies.
- *Education*—public education, including clergy employed by government, where applicable.
- *Post*—employment in post, telephone, and telegraph, including appropriate ministry, where applicable.
- *Transportation*—employment in public transportation (rail and local), including appropriate ministry.
- *Industrial*—employment in miscellaneous industrial enterprises and public utilities, excluding nationalized industries.

These definitions reveal an immediate weakness in the data collection. We clearly have not measured the entire range of public sector activities in which government employees are engaged. Generally, more modern governmental activities and services—health, welfare, and nationalized industries—are ignored.

It would be useful to estimate the exact amount of undercounting implied by our limited definition of the public sector, but such an effort is difficult without additional historical studies to use as reference points. However, a more limited check on data for recent years can be conducted using unpublished figures collected by the Organization for Economic Cooperation and Development (OECD, 1980). Table 8.1 compares total public employment as a percentage of the active labor force using our own data and those of the OECD. As expected, given our limited definition of the public sector, the HIWED data are generally lower than the OECD data. The twelve-country average differs by 1.9 percent of the labor force in 1960 and by 3.0 percent in 1970.

**TABLE 8.1   Comparison of HIWED Total Public Employment Data with
OECD Data Collection (percentage of labor force)**

	1960			1970		
	OECD	*HIWED*	*Difference*	*OECD*	*HIWED*	*Difference*
Austria	10.8	10.7	.1	14.1	12.5	1.6
Belgium	12.2	8.6	3.6	13.9	9.3	4.6
Denmark	na	(8.0)		16.9	9.0	7.9
Finland	na	(7.3)		12.0	8.8	3.2
France	12.3	11.1	1.2	12.4	12.9	−.5
Germany	8.0	9.2	−1.2	11.2	10.9	.3
Italy	8.1	7.7	.4	10.9	12.0	−1.1
Netherlands	11.7	7.7	4.0	12.1	8.9	3.2
Norway	12.7	8.2	4.5	16.4	10.1	6.3
Sweden	12.8	8.0	4.8	20.6	9.8	10.8
Switzerland	6.3	7.3	−1.0	7.9	8.3	−.4
Average	10.6	8.7		12.4	9.4	

TABLE 8.2   Administrative Employment per One Thousand Population

	1880	*1890*	*1900*	*1920*	*1930*	*1950*	*1960*	*1970*
Austria	5.9	5.5	6.4	11.1	9.9	16.5	16.7	20.9
Belgium	5.3	6.0	6.2	9.6	9.4	11.6	15.2	18.3
Denmark	5.9	5.8	4.3	3.5	4.1	9.1	10.2	14.2
Finland	1.7	2.2	3.1	3.7	4.9	7.9	10.0	15.9
France	6.7	6.6	7.9	12.0	9.9	21.1	24.3	27.9
Germany	5.0	5.4	6.3	13.9	16.6	20.4	22.0	24.5
Italy	11.8	12.0	12.2	15.3	12.2	17.0	19.0	22.6
Netherlands	4.9	4.9	5.1	7.1	6.2	16.7	11.6	18.8
Norway	2.1	2.2	2.6	4.5	4.3	8.4	10.4	11.1
Sweden	1.0	2.5	2.4	4.1	4.2	8.3	9.3	14.6
Switzerland	3.8	3.2	3.9	6.7	6.2	9.1	9.4	12.2
Great Britain	4.4	6.2	8.0	16.7	17.4	27.6	24.4	26.8
Twelve-Country Average	4.9	5.2	5.7	9.0	8.8	14.5	15.2	19.0
Change in average from previous decade		.3	.5	3.3	−.2	5.7	.7	3.8
Standard deviation	2.7	2.6	2.1	4.5	4.5	6.1	5.7	5.4

What is the source of disparity? Nationalized industries do not appear to
be the source; those countries with large nationalized sectors, such as
France, Italy, and Germany, do not show large discrepancies. Instead, the
largest differences are for the Scandinavian countries. These differences
appear to come from the absence of health and welfare professionals in the
HIWED data. The Scandinavian countries are exceptional in the degree to

which they offer public services directly rather than through cash transfers to individuals (Kohl, 1981). Since direct provision requires more personnel, this is likely to be the cause of the difference.

This gap in coverage is obviously a weakness for purposes of developing a comprehensive measure of the scope of the public sector, but it could be a virtue in other research contexts. By eliminating employees in a variety of service tasks at the periphery of the welfare state, our data probably yield a cleaner measure of the purely administrative component of government. Administrative capability plays an important role in larger theoretical questions of interest to students of bureaucracy and public policy. Moreover, it can be argued that it is administrative personnel who are the focus of debates about bloated government.

Table 8.2 provides data on administrative personnel for a number of decades since 1880. Administrative capabilities have grown dramatically. Among the twelve countries shown in the table, there was an average growth from five bureaucrats per 1000 population to almost twenty between 1880 and 1970. However, the European average masks considerable variation.

The early levels of administrative development do not lend support for an hypothesis linking the development of the state to industrialization or urbanization (Eliasberg and Abramovitz, 1957; Cullity, 1964). Indeed, the most industrialized state in 1880, Great Britain, is near the bottom of the list of administrative personnel. Some of the higher scores are among the least developed countries. Conclusions must be preliminary at this point, but the data suggest that the pressure of development is not a particularly useful explanation for the growth of administrative employment.

Table 8.2 reveals interesting patterns of change. Between 1880 and 1910 the employment levels changed only slowly. During the world wars, however, it grew rapidly in a way not matched until the 1960s. From 1880 to 1900 the standard deviation from the average was decreasing, suggesting that the European countries were becoming more similar in levels of administrative development. This pattern was broken by World War I and, after a period of stability between the wars, there was further differentiation as a result of World War II. Since 1950 the countries are moving together once again. One interpretation of this is that similar pressures operating within countries lead to similar responses in the form of administrative development, but that the process of convergence is interrupted by the differential impact of war.

The impact of war is further highlighted when we examine time trends in public employment. Figure 8.1 displays both administrative and total employment as a percentage of total population.[3] Most striking is the extreme stability of administrative employment until 1910; only in France and Austria is there evidence of even a mild increase. In spite of industrialization and democratization, total public employment did not grow, and the growth of

(text continues on page 148)

Percent of Total Employment

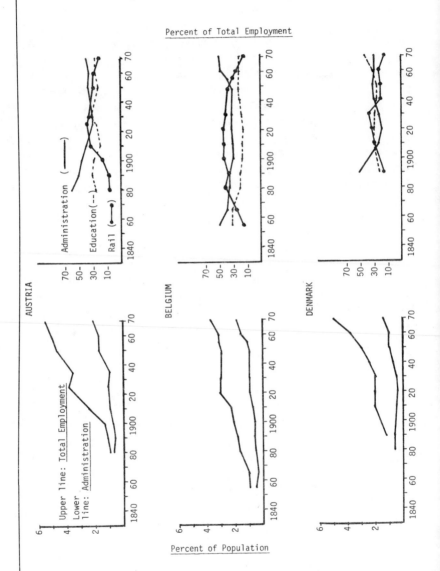

Percent of Population

144

Percent of Total Employment

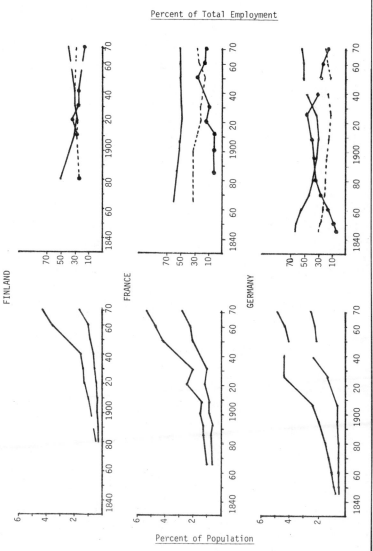

FINLAND

FRANCE

GERMANY

Percent of Population

(continued)

FIGURE 8.1: Trends in Public Employment as a Percentage of Population and in Types of Public Employment as a Share of Total Employment

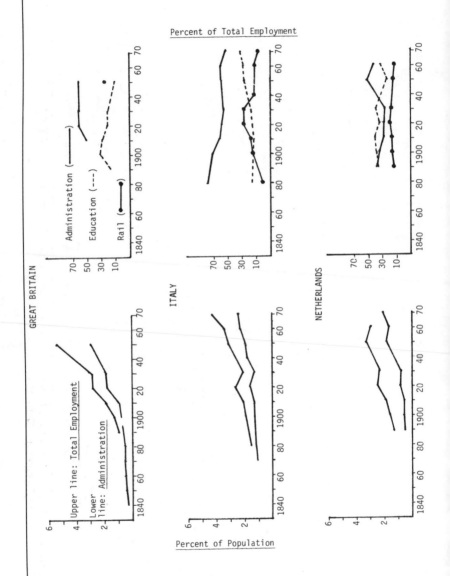

GREAT BRITAIN

Percent of Total Employment

Administration (——)

Education (---)

Rail (●——●)

Upper line: Total Employment

Lower line: Administration

ITALY

NETHERLANDS

Percent of Population

146

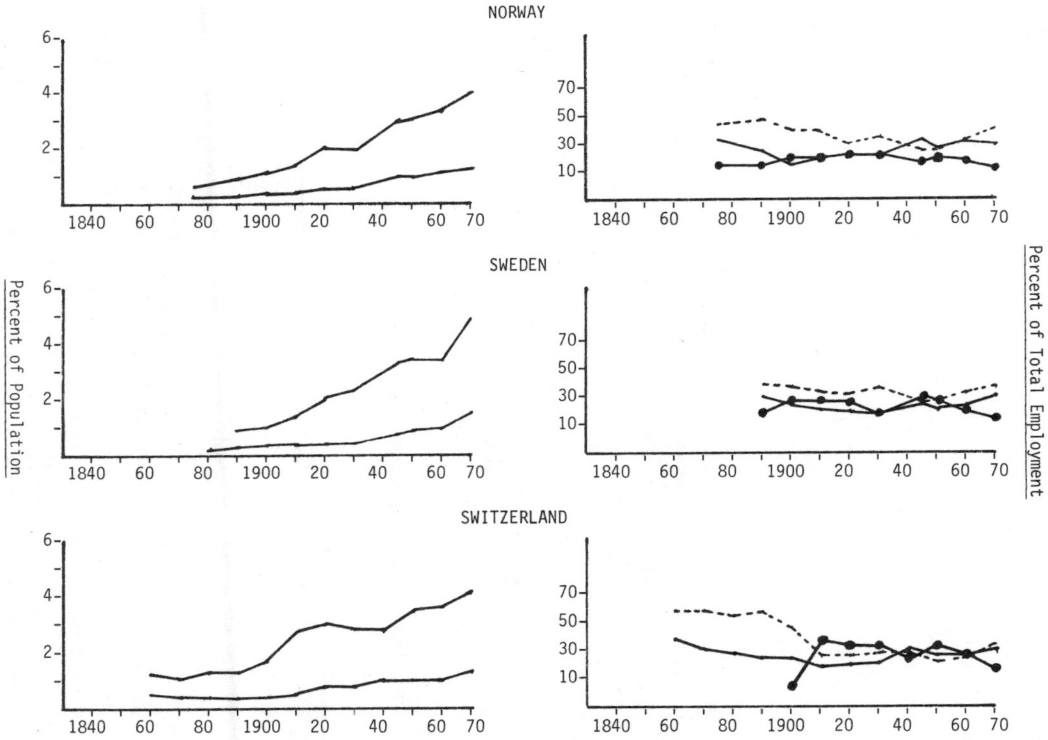
NORWAY
SWEDEN
SWITZERLAND
Percent of Population
Percent of Total Employment
6
4
2
70
50
30
10
1840
60
80
1900
20
40
60
70

FIGURE 8.1 (Continued)

the public sector took place outside the traditional administrative competencies normally associated with bureaucracy. Administrative personnel shows a sharp increase in most countries, especially among the belligerents, after World War I. They return to a stable pattern during the Depression and show further increases after World War II. In fact, only in the 1960s is there significant growth without war.

These patterns do not provide a conclusive test of hypotheses related to government growth, but they do offer some curiosities that need to be explained. Perhaps most interesting is the fact that growth in administrative employment appears almost totally the result of turbulence caused by war. For most of the nineteenth and early twentieth centuries, there was little or no growth in the bureaucracy relative to the general population. This casts some doubt upon the notion of inevitable expansion and upon theories relating growth in the administrative apparatus to long-term societal developments in the social, economic, and political spheres. Equally fascinating is the growth of the bureaucracy during the 1960s. It is possible that this growth is related to political factors such as those suggested by scholars to explain growth in the public spending of this period, a possibility indicated by large increases in the Scandinavian countries (Hibbs, 1977; Cameron, 1978).

Finally, we can note that total government employment has been increasing faster than total population in almost all the countries since the end of the nineteenth century. Coupled with the stability of administrative employment, this implies that the composition of government employment has changed over time, a point confirmed by an examination of the shares of employment shown in the right hand side of Figure 8.1. These shares reveal three distinct periods. From 1880 to 1910, increases in rail (and in some cases, education) employment were balanced by a decline in the share of employees in administration. Beginning in 1910 or 1920 and lasting until 1960, there was little change in the shares of employment. From 1960 administrative employment began to increase once again in relation to other types of government employment.

Before comparing public employment indicators to other measures of public sector activity, it is useful to ask if the patterns described above would be substantially different were our data to include more of the peripheral or semipublic agencies associated with the modern welfare state. We think not. As Alber (1979) has demonstrated, growth of the welfare state was halting until well after World War I, reaching its period of rapid growth only after World War II. Thus it is unlikely that our measure of administrative employment has missed much in the way of welfare employment in the period before World War II. As we have seen, addition of these employees after that war would reinforce trends already evident in our data, that is, large increases in administrative employment in the 1960s.

Comparing Measures of the Public Sector

The most serious problem in measuring the public sector is the unavailability of data. Only two or three studies existed before the present effort and our own investment has yielded data for only twelve countries. More important, our experience in the HIWED project reveals a number of problems with the data. Perhaps most serious is the fact that the data do not always correspond to theoretical or accounting definitions of the public sector, so that resulting measures may somewhat underestimate the extension of governmental activity into areas previously left to market or societal forces. They do not capture the complex range of modern service administrations that have developed to administer welfare programs. The latter point was underscored by our comparatively small ratios for Scandinavian administrative personnel.

Of course, the negative should not be exaggerated. We have succeeded in describing important historical trends in administrative and total government employment, quantities that play important roles in social science theory. Nonetheless, difficulties in public employment data raise the question of more efficient measurement strategies. Is it possible that other measures of the public sector will yield similar insights at lower cost?

In fact, some work in the comparative policy area seems to proceed from the assumption that the public sector represents a coherent dimension of activities; the expansion of public finances, authority, personnel, and centralization are often treated interchangeably, or at least are not differentiated explicitly. Eliasberg and Abramovitz go so far as to argue that "there is a powerful tendency for administrative and financial responsibility to run together" (1957: 84), and they suggest that there are important reasons why the expansion of administration and financial authority of governments will also result in increasing centralization. This line of reasoning would suggest that different indicators of public sector activity are indeed equivalent, if not for purposes of social accounting, then at least for purposes of comparing trends in the growth of government or for comparing the effect of the size of the public sector on policy development and political processes. If so, a more efficient measurement strategy would be to concentrate on those indicators that are more accessible or more easily compared. The obvious alternative would be public spending figures that are regularly published by national and international agencies and by individual scholars.

Research on the public sector is faced with a dilemma: to forge on with the difficult task of collecting data on different aspects of governmental activity, or to withdraw to the more practical but less satisfying position of using more easily available summary measures. Of course the solution to this dilemma will ultimately be found in the theoretical development of the field and in the empirical testing of the assumption that the public sector is a coherent cluster of related activities.

Given the slow pace of theory development, however, it may be more useful to investigate the empirical relationship among alternative measures of public sector activity. Is it true that expansion of public authority leads to equivalent growth in public spending and public employment? Because we have personnel data for only twelve countries, our analysis of this question is necessarily limited, but such exploratory analyses may provide a useful guide for further research.

The question to be addressed is the extent to which the state's tendency to extract and spend a larger share of the national product is related to a tendency toward bureaucratization, as measured by our two indicators of public employment. Table 8.3 shows the simple Pearsonian correlation coefficients among four measures of the extent of public sector involvement in society and the market place: administrative personnel, total personnel, total public spending as a percentage of GNP, and transfer spending as a percentage of GNP. In each case one might plausibly hypothesize a strong positive correlation. A large share of government spending in the national product, for example, presumably reflects an extension of government authority, and it should increase the need for personnel to administer programs and provide services. Further, increases in transfer spending—the core of the welfare state—are often associated with the growth of state power and by implication with the increasing bureaucratization of society.

As the correlations make clear, however, there appear to be no overwhelming relationships among different measures of government activity. In both 1960 and 1970, for example, the correlation between administrative

TABLE 8.3 Simple Bivariate Correlation Between Different Measures of Public Sector Activity

	Administrative Personnel[1]	Total Personnel[2]	Expenditures/GNP[3]
1960			
Total personnel	.58		
Expenditures	.28	.14	
Transfers/GNP[4]	.56	.36	.48
1970			
Total personnel	.43		
Expenditures	.06	−.08	
Transfers/GNP	.13	.49	−.06

1. Per thousand population.
2. Per thousand population.
3. Expenditures by all levels of government, from Kohl (1981).
4. Social transfers by all levels of government, from Kohl (1981).

employment and total government employment was moderate at best, suggesting that the size of public payrolls is not a unidimensional phenomenon affecting all types of employment. Bureaucratization, the administrative personnel measure, is also weakly related to public spending, showing almost no relationship in 1970 and only a moderate association to transfer spending in 1960. Total employment also shows weak correlations with the spending measures.

These simple analyses suggest that an easy solution to the measurement dilemma is unlikely to emerge. As in the conceptual arguments of Rose and Peters and Heisler in this volume, it appears that government and public sector are multidimensional phenomena that must be disaggregated if meaningful results are to emerge from research.

Summary

This chapter has presented a description of the public employment data collection of the HIWED project and examined some of the measurement difficulties associated with that effort. In spite of considerable difficulties, we think that the data provide a rich mine for historical analysis of the growth of the state. Since many theories of public sector growth are by their nature historical, we think there is no substitute for this kind of data. Our description of the data point to a number of interesting avenues of inquiry on the subject of public employment and bureaucracy. Unquestionably, the importance of war to the growth of the state remains an issue of considerable interest. Much as earlier studies of public spending growth (Peacock and Wiseman, 1967) and more recent analyses of welfare spending (Kaufman, 1981) and state building (Tilly, 1975), our data suggest that war is one of the primary stimuli for public sector expansion and cross-national differentiation. Of course, it remains unclear exactly what causal mechanism underlies this displacement effect, but the data point to a pattern in which war interrupts an otherwise slow and incremental increase in the state's role.

Interest in data on the public sector goes beyond describing and explaining the growth of government. Indicators of administrative capability could play a significant role in studies of policy innovation and political protest. Some topics outside the mainstream of political science might even be treated using these or similar data. This report has only touched on some of these possibilities and there is a potential for much broader analysis of the data.

NOTES

1. Readers are urged to consult the more detailed documentation of the data found in Eichenberg (1979).

2. The HIWED project was funded by a grant from the Volkswagen Foundation to Professor Peter Flora at the University of Cologne. I am grateful to Professor Flora for his invitation to join the HIWED staff and to Jens Alber for advice and encouragement during the research.

3. Population is chosen as the denominator for two reasons. First, labor force data, the usual denominator, is not available for a large number of countries in historical series. Second, we wish to measure the weight of bureaucracy in society at large, and this measure is best carried out by using total population.

REFERENCES

ALBER, J. (1979) "Modernisierung und die Entwicklung der Sozialversicherung in West-europa." Ph.D. dissertation, University of Mannheim.
——— (1978) "Regierungen, Arbeitslosigkeit und Arbeitslosenschutz: die Entwicklung der Arbeitslosenversicherung in Westeurop." Koelner Zeitschrift fuer Soziologie, 30 (December): 726-760.
ANDRAIN, C. (1980) Politics and Economic Policy in Western Democracies. Belmont, CA: Duxbury Press.
BAIROCH, R. (1968) La Population Active et sa Structure. Brussels: Editions de l'Institut de Sociologie.
CAMERON, D. (1978) "The expansion of the public economy: a comparative analysis." American Political Science Review 72,4: 1243-1261.
Correlates of War Project (1971) Instructions for Collecting and Coding Military Personnel Data. Mental Health Research Institute, University of Michigan.
CULLITY, J. (1964) "The Growth of Government Employment in Germany." Ph.D. dissertation, Department of Economics, Columbia University.
DAALDER, H. (1966) "Parties, elites and political developments in Western Europe," in J. LaPalombara and M. Weiner (eds.) Political Parties and Political Development. Princeton, NJ: Princeton University Press.
EICHENBERG, R. (1979) Bureaucracy and Public Employment: Historical Data for the West European Democracies. Cologne: HIWED Report 10. (under revision)
——— (1978) "The growth of public employment in five European countries." Prepared for delivery at the Annual Meeting of the American Political Science Association, New York.
ELIASBERG, V. and M. ABRAMOVITZ (1957) The Growth of Public Employment in Great Britain. Princeton, NJ: Princeton University Press.
FABRICANT, S. (1949) The Rising Trend of Government Employment. New York: National Bureau of Economic Research.
FLORA, P. et al. (in press) State, Economy and Society in Western Europe. New York and Frankfurt: Campus Books.
FLORA, P. and J. ALBER (1981) "Modernization, democratization, and the development of welfare states in Western Europe," in P. Flora and A. Heidenheimer (eds.) The Development of Welfare States in Europe and America. New Brunswick, NJ: Transaction Press.
FLORA, P. and A. HEIDENHEIMER (eds.) (1981) The Development of Welfare States in Europe and America. New Brunswick, NJ: Transaction Press.
FRIEDRICH, C. and T. COLE (1932) Responsible Bureaucracy: The Swiss Civil Service. Cambridge, MA: Harvard University Press.
HECLO, H. (1974) Modern Social Politics in Britain and Sweden. New Haven, CT: Yale University Press.
HEIDENHEIMER, A. (1973) "The politics of health, education and welfare in the USA and Western Europe: how growth and reform potential have differed." British Journal of Political Science 3,3: 315-340.

HIBBS, D. A., Jr. (1977) "Political parties and macroeconomic policy." American Political Science Review 71: 467-487.

INGRAHAM, P. (1979) "Patterns of social welfare policies in Western societies." Ph.D. dissertation, State University of New York at Binghamton.

KAUFMAN, J. P. (1983) "The social consequences of war." Armed Forces and Society 9 (Winter): 245–264.

KOHL, J. (1981) "Trends and problems in postwar public expenditure development in North America and Western Europe," in P. Flora and A. Heidenheimer (eds.) The Development of Welfare States in Europe and America. New Brunswick, NJ: Transaction Press.

——— (1979) "Die Entwicklung der Staatsausgaben in Westeurop." Ph.D. dissertation, University of Mannheim.

KUPPER, E. (1929) "Die Besoldungspolitik des Bundes seit 1848." Ph.D. dissertation, University of Zurich.

LAPALOMBARA, J. and M. WEINER (eds.) (1966) Political Parties and Political Development. Princeton, NJ: Princeton University Press.

NOLAN, P. (1979) "Size and administrative intensity in nations." American Sociological Review 44: 110-125.

Organization for Economic Cooperation and Development (1980) Working Party on Employment: Public Sector Employment Trends. Paris: OECD.

PEACOCK, A. T. and J. WISEMAN (1961) The Growth of Public Expenditures in the United Kingdom. Princeton, NJ: Princeton University Press.

PETERS, B. G. (1972) "Economic and political effects on the development of social expenditures in France, Sweden, and the United Kingdom." Midwest Journal of Political Science 16,2: 225-238.

PRYOR, F. (1968) Public Expenditure in Communist and Capitalist Countries. Homewood, IL: Irwin.

RIVET, R. (1932) "Statistique des fonctionnaires en France et en divers pays." Statistique Generale de la France: 95-140.

ROKKAN, S. (1975) "Dimensions of state formation and nation building," pp. 562–600 in C. Tilly (ed.) The Formation of National States in Western Europe. Princeton, NJ: Princeton University Press.

———(1970) Citizens, Elections, Parties. New York: McKay.

ROSE, R. (1976) "On the priorities of government: a developmental analysis of public policies." European Journal of Political Research 4, 3: 321-350.

SCHNEIDER, R. (forthcoming) On the Development of Education in Western Europe. Cologne: HIWED Report 9.

SHARP, W. R. (1933) "Public employment," pp. 628-637 in Encyclopedia of the Social Sciences (vol. 12). New York: Macmillan.

——— (1931) The French Civil Service. New York: Macmillan.

TILLY, C. [ed.] (1975) The Formation of National States in Western Europe. Princeton, NJ: Princeton University Press.

VERBA, S. (1971) "Sequences and development," in Leonard Binder, et al., Crises and Sequences in Political Development. Princeton, NJ: Princeton University Press.

WHITE, L. D. (1935) The Civil Service Abroad. New York: McGraw-Hill.

WILENSKY, H. (1976) The New Corporatism, Centralization, and the Welfare State. Beverly Hills, CA: Sage.

——— (1975) The Welfare State and Equality. Berkeley: University of California Press.

PART IV

Other Indicators of
Public Sector Size
and Growth

CHAPTER 9

DISAGGREGATING
THE CONCEPT OF GOVERNMENT

RICHARD ROSE

Abstraction is a necessary condition for creating the concepts that are the building blocks of social science theory; operationally, abstraction implies the aggregation of many different phenomena under a single conceptual label. However, differentiation is also a necessary condition of constructing theories: only if we can differentiate our interests into a number of related concepts can we begin to create models involving cause and effect relationships. To speak of a single undifferentiated concept, such as the state or the political system is to risk speaking of everything and, therefore, of nothing. Operationally, differentiation implies the need to disaggregate varied phenomena into a variety of concepts.

Conceptualization comes before quantification. If we do not have some idea of what we are interested in measuring, then any set of numbers will do (cf. Sartori, 1970). Readily available government statistics can be suitable as indicators for some properties of government. However, there are biases, both historical and political, in what government does and does not report as statistics. Furthermore, only by comparing available statistics with an a priori model of what government is can we know in what ways and to what extent available data provide adequate indicators of the properties of government, thus realizing the implications of data that can be called missing only if we have a prior idea of what is needed to provide a complete picture of government.

Catching your dependent variable is a precondition for explanation. Theories of the growth of government are all very well, but before they can be tested, we must know What grows when government grows. Conceptualiz-

ing the dependent variable is necessary in any attempt to theorize successfully about what government is, how it changes, and what consequences this
has for society past, present, or future. Confronting problems of measurement can guide theory as well as theory guiding measurement; the two are
not alternatives or even separate stages in research, but rather should be
performed *gleichzeitig*.

The first object of this chapter is to define government as a disaggregated
complex construct. The second object is to review briefly the different parts
into which government is disaggregated, with particular attention paid to
properties that make measures of individual parts incommensurable in relation to each other. The third section draws together implications of viewing
government as a complex entity, and reviews alternative research strategies—from global to nation-specific studies—for making further advances.

Government as a Complex Phenomenon

Q. In what respect can government be considered a simple entity?
A. Only at very high level of abstraction.

Operationally, it is very important to consider whether government is a
simple entity, for only if it is can it then be reduced to a single indicator. At
the simplest level of analysis, we may be able to agree on a definition and a
single indicator that can answer the question: Does or does not a government
exist in society? However, this measure will be of interest only to historically
oriented anthropologists, for almost all political scientists start by studying a
society where the existence of a government is taken for granted.

In the world of pure philosophy or pure theory, simple entities may be
considered desirable; they are certainly common. However, an undifferentiated concept of government is limited in what it can tell us about the real world
and historical governments. For example, writings about the state usually
present it as a monolith whether it is a singular tool of other interests or an
autonomous actor. Yet empirical research in international relations, where
states are in international law undifferentiated units, emphasizes subdivisions
of institutions, individuals, and interests that can be found, each claiming to
speak in the name of a single undifferentiated national interest (Allison,
1971). The behavioral revolution in political science went a step further, frag-
menting the idea of the state into a number of different functional categories;
yet it put in its place a holistic idea of the political system. While this approach
has had many positive advantages, it is hardly acceptable to deal with the
problem of identifying government by broadening the scope of an undifferentiated concept from the state to the whole of a system. Moreover, when the

concept of a political system is disaggregated, far more emphasis is given to nongovernmental concerns: the politics side of politics and government.

A simple concept of government implies that a single indicator should be acceptable for purposes of analysis. Identifying government can be extremely difficult, whether it be called the Crown, as in the United Kingdom, the Bundesrepublik Deutschland, or the government of the United States of America. *The World Handbook of Political and Social Indicators* addressed this issue and concludes, as Queen Victoria did, that government is plural. Three alternative definitions are offered: year of independence, year of current constitution, and period of the consolidation of modernizing leadership (Taylor and Hudson, 1972: Table 2.1). In everyday English-language discussions of party politics, a change of government can be taken to mean one party replacing another in the chief elective offices or even one prime minister or president replacing another. Such a definition emphasizes transitory personalities and changeable combinations of politicians at the expense of that which persists. To identify government with a constitutionally defined regime is to emphasize permanence at the expense of change, to imply that basically nothing has changed in the government of the United States since 1789, and nothing has changed in the government of England since time immemorial. Analyzing regime structure does identify one very meaningful variable in twentieth-century Germany and France—but not the only variable.

Granting the existence of a sovereign authority (which not all behavioralists would do) does not mean that there is a single institutional locus that constitutes government. Federalism presents an obvious complication for reducing American or German government to a single unitary concept. However, the Crown represents the unity of the United Kingdom only because it is a legal fiction; the agents of the Crown's authority are multiplex, being differentiated territorially as well as functionally throughout the United Kingdom. What government is differs between England, Scotland, and Wales—as well as within England (Rose, 1982). To say that government is everywhere is, at one level, reasonable, but at another it implies that it is nowhere in particular. Pervasive attributes of systems are not to be confused with specific institutions.

Government is not a multiattribute concept, but a *multiconcept* abstraction. It is better considered a family of concepts or the label given a model that consists of a number of distinctive concepts. This is especially evident when we think in terms of what government does, as well as what it is. Constitutionally, government may have a single formally unified set of institutions. In policy terms, however, a government is not a unified actor, with a single homogeneous stream of undifferentiated resources and outputs, but a conglomerate or holding company whose multiple institutions produce heterogeneous outputs, not the undifferentiated pure utility of welfare economics.

To analyze contemporary government, we must disaggregate the concept into a number of different terms. In effect this means that we must think of government as a more or less complex *system* or subsystem rather than as a simple entity. One distinguishing characteristic of a system is that it has a number of different parts. Another is that these parts are interrelated. To treat government in this way is not to deny the theoretical importance of high-level abstractions such as the political system or the state, but simply to complement these terms with concepts that begin to differentiate among the complexities of empirical reality.

A model of government should have at least the following characteristics. First of all, the terms in the model should be generic, so that the model is in principle capable of application to more than one country. Second, the terms should be defined with sufficient clarity so that it is in principle possible to conceive of empirical referents and indicators for each term. Third, the number of terms should be limited in order to gain clarity and concentrate upon matters deemed important. Finally, the separate terms should be linked by explicitly stated relationships; aggregation and disaggregation are analytically complementary.

Disaggregating government into several parts makes it possible to combine distinctive and different concerns of classic theories of government as institutions and contemporary theories of governing as an activity. The model proposed here joins two complementary and necessary properties: what government is (institutions) and what government does (the activities that produce policies from resources). To define government in these terms is to concentrate attention more narrowly than in political systems analysis, yet it also breaks away from the single-attribute approach that characterizes institutionalists and those reductionist political economists who regard public expenditure as the sole measure of public policy.

The model of government proposed here is a simple input-output model; therefore, it must have at least three elements.

(1) *Inputs*: The principal resources of government today are laws, public revenues, and public employees.

(2) *Processors*: A plurality of organizations mobilize and process the resources of government. Organizations play an active role in the governing process; they are not passive instruments responding to demands.

(3) *Outputs*: Programs comprise statutory powers, personnel, and money as the primary outputs of government organizations (see Figure 9.1).

The model discussed here is not the only model that would meet the criteria specified above. It would be easy to see how additional terms could be inserted in the model. One of the strengths of this model is that additional terms can be added by further disaggregation. A variety of societal condi-

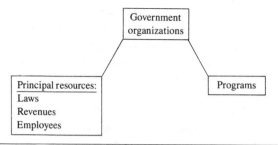

FIGURE 9.1:   A Simple Model of Government in the Policy Process

tions can be added to expand the model for purposes of program evaluation, and feedback loops can also be added thus making it a model of government in society (cf. Deutsch, 1963).

The Different Parts of Government

When government is disaggregated, questions of the size or rate of growth of government depend upon two factors. The first is the selection of the term of the model to be examined; the second is the size and rate of growth of that term. In other words, the particular term that the analyst chooses to let stand for the whole of government can prejudge conclusions. A brief review of each of the terms of the model is sufficient to call attention to many features that differentiate each term from others and therefore show the insubstitutability of one measure for another in an analysis of the growth of government.

(1) Laws. Laws are a *unique* resource of government. Whereas government usually claims less than half a country's gross national product and about one-quarter of its labor force, it enacts one hundred percent of the laws of a society. Government originated as a law-making body, and its size is based upon laws establishing the scope of government's policies. While there is room for discretion within a given matrix of laws, there is less scope than within a matrix of institutions. For example, a conservative administration cannot decide to ignore welfare state legislation, nor can a left-of-center administration carry out its wishes without first writing down what it seeks in legislation and gaining for its intentions the force of law.

Laws are far less amenable to quantitative measurement than are other major resources of government. Whereas money is fungible and public employees in the same grade or with the same function can be interchangeable, laws are not. Each statute is unique in terms of its specific content, and the specific properties of laws are much more important than the specific properties of civil servants or particular sums of money. Moreover, laws differ greatly from each other in terms of their impact upon other resources of government. For example, a single social security law can make a far more sizable claim on public revenue than a thousand other acts added together. Similarly, a single law establishing a national health service increases public employment far more than hundreds of other laws. To add up laws, except for strictly limited purposes, is to risk adding incommensurables.

Existing methods for quantifying laws, a necessary step in measuring their size and growth, show that some simple tabulations are possible. For example, it is possible to count the number of acts passed each year; doing this is likely to emphasize continuities in legislation, for in any one year only a very small number of new laws will likely be added to the statute book. It is also possible to count the number of pages added to the statute book each year as an indicator of the growth in the volume of legislation, a more precise measure than the number of acts enacted. This runs into trouble in comparative analysis, for the average length of a statute differs very greatly from country to country. Such measures tell us something, but not all that much. They assume that the length of a law is more important than its content, an assumption that few in government would make. The political content of legislation—that is, the extent to which it reveals parliamentary differences—is measurable. In the supposedly adversary system of parliamentary government in Britain, seventy-eight percent of government bills are enacted without the opposition party voting against them in principle (Rose, 1980a: 80; cf. di Palma, 1977: 58ff).

The significance of laws (above and beyond what can be indicated by the previous tabulations) is emphasized by considering what we would *like* to have as reliable indicators. To what extent do laws, once enacted, follow a mortmain principle, never being repealed? Or is it the case that they are subject either to more or less well-timed revision and consolidation or to wholesale repeal or cancellation when regimes change, a question of particular concern in Central Europe? If repeal is an indicator of major political change, then consolidation or revision is an indicator of adaptation, and non-repeal indicates continuity—or, conceivably, dysfunctional persistence because of a failure to adapt.

The growth of regulations, statutory instruments, and other secondary legislation (i.e., measures enunciated by administrators under authority delegated by statute) raises questions about the scope of legislation affecting society. Regulations may simply be filling in details of established laws and therefore concentrating government more intensively in areas long covered by legislation (e.g., regulation of trade and commerce or of industrial safety). Alternatively, regulation may reflect an expanding scope, leading government to areas that it has previously not sought to regulate (e.g., the ramifications of equal opportunity regulations as interpreted by American federal compliance officers).

To attempt to assess what proportion of society's total activities today are regulated by legislation is an impossible ideal, for its presupposes a comprehensive account of all of society's activities. We could think in terms of weighing laws in terms of the following attributes (Rose, 1970: 196ff), which would give a rough guide to their importance: (1) scope (what proportion of society is meant to be affected?); (2) the probability of a law affecting people (laws about elementary education will affect more people than laws about university education); (3) the intensity of the impact (e.g., university education may have a higher impact upon a smaller number of individuals); and (4) the frequency of impact (laws affecting transportation in use every day will have more regular effect than emergency codes affecting government in wartime).

(2) Public revenues. The ways in which government raises its revenues are multiple and separate. A tax on income is not the same as a tax on sales; taxes set in fixed-money terms will have a different rate of growth to that of a tax expressed as a percentage of money volume. Revenue received by nationalized industries is not conventionally considered a tax, but rather a fee for service, yet it is money that government controls just as much (or as little) as earmarked taxes paid in the expectation of pensions or health care. Last and not least, income in the form of loans—from within a nation or from foreign sources—constitutes present revenue in exchange for claims against future revenue. In a period of fiscal stress the political difference between loan income and tax income makes this source particularly subject to relatively rapid growth, as long as a government's credibility holds.

Although public revenue and public expenditure are both measured in money terms, the two are not interchangeable. In policy terms they are complementary (see Rose and Page, 1981: Table 7). At the aggregate level revenues are considered part of the costs of government and expenditure as benefits. When the categories of revenue and expenditure are examined, the difference is very evident. The great bulk of public revenue is not raised as earmarked taxes. Taxes that allocate revenue to specific expenditure purposes are disliked in principle by public finance experts and are decreasingly used. Alterations in public revenue are neutral in terms of expenditure programs, and alterations in expenditure are neutral about how revenue should be raised to finance them. Expenditure and revenue may even vary inversely; for example, in a recession, spending on income maintenance programs will increase and tax yields will fall.

Inflation creates peculiar problems in time-series analysis within a country, for revenues will grow in money terms, but the purchasing power of that revenue will not increase in proportion to its current money growth in value.

There have been three main sources of growth in public revenues in the past decade: increases produced by raising tax rates; increases produced by higher tax yields from a real growth in the national economy; and increases produced by inflation. The last is by far the greatest cause of growth in public revenues in the past decade. For example, in the 1960s inflation accounted for about half the increase in current value public revenue in both the United Kingdom and the United States. By the 1970s inflation accounted for eighty-six percent of the increase in American federal revenue and for ninety-three percent in the United Kingdom (Rose, 1980b: Figure 1).

In public expenditure accounting there is some justification for evaluation expenditure in terms of constant value (misleadingly labeled real money) insofar as the purpose of such accounts is to obtain measures of the volume of goods and services. Even here there are very considerable questions about how constant are constant value sums, given the cumulative bias of the relative price effect, and year-on-year instabilities in this deflator. Public revenue must first of all be examined in current money terms, for it is levied and collected in actual money. This term was invented by a British treasury official (Clarke, 1973: 159), who was in despair about the consequences for revenue raising of analyzing public expenditure only in real or constant money terms. Taxes, fees, user charges, and loans are all denominated in current money terms. Moreover, there are important and unanswered behavioral questions about the extent to which taxes feel the same when they increase 300 percent in real terms, though remaining level in constant terms—as can be the case, say, in the United Kingdom in the past decade.

In international comparisons the meaning of money is not constant across space or time; floating national currencies in the 1970s led to a quantum jump in the volatility of exchange rates. To reduce money figures to the U.S. dollar is simply to invite the question: How much was the U.S. dollar worth in X, Y, and Z currencies on the day your measure was employed?

(3) Public employees. To count the number of people who work for government we must first of all define the bounds of public employment. Official statistics on the civil service are very misleading, for the officially denominated civil service accounts for less than one-sixth of total public employment in Britain or the United States, and for less than half in most Western nations. The majority of public employees work in local government, nationalized industries, health services, and other fringe or parasitical institutions. Moreover, the proportion of public employees denominated as civil servants is variable cross-nationally. The result is that the OECD has found it extremely difficult to compile measures of public employment that are fully valid cross-nationally because it relies upon national government as sources of its data (see Martin, 1980: 3; Economic Commission for Europe, 1979)

As the Centre for the Study of Public Policy we have defined public employment organizationally; public employees are those persons working for organizations that are either headed by elected officials or by appointees of an elected government (e.g., nationalized industries), or are government owned, or are principally at the margin, but it has a high degree of validity, and, given that large public organizations are invariably good record keepers, its application is reasonably reliable and capable of use cross-nationally (Rose, 1980c). Defining employees in terms of attributes of the employer, rather than of the employee, avoids many problems in cross-national comparability.

One point immediately apparent in any analysis of public employment is the heterogeneity of public employees. Heterogeneity is expressed in many different ways. Employees differ in their functional characteristics: higher level administrators, refuse collectors, teachers, postmen, soldiers, coal miners, and other substantial groups of public employees are not interchangeable. They also differ according to whether they produce collective goods, marketable goods that are given away (e.g., free health care), or marketed goods that are sold (even if at a loss, e.g., postal or railway services). Aggregating public employees into a single category may be necessary for purposes of macro-level analysis, but it tells one little about the composition or purpose of public employment.

A systematic five-nation comparison of trends in public employment since the early 1950s has found no similarity in size or cross-national changes in aggregate public employment. The nations fall into four categories: (1) initially high and high growth (Sweden, twenty-one to thirty-one percent of labor force); (2) initially high and low growth (Britain, twenty-six to thirty percent); (3) initially low and high growth (Italy, ten to twenty-two percent, and Ireland, fourteen to twenty-six percent); and (4) initially low and remaining low (United States, sixteen to eighteen percent; Rose, 1980c: Table 1). The study found a similar pattern of expansion in the numbers of public employees in education and in health, and also, a similar pattern of nonexpansion or contraction in military defense. If public employment is disaggregated into functional components, the same government can be changing in different directions at the same time.

(4) Organizations. In institutional terms government is not a single organization, but a complex or a maze of institutions. The difficulties of enumerating the organizations that constitute government face public officials as well as social scientists. For example, President Carter's Reorganization Project (1977: 2) required forty-five pages to produce a one-line-per agency description of the executive branch of the American federal government. This having been done, the compilers cautioned;

> It is important to emphasize that this categorization of organizational elements does not constitute an exhaustive accounting of the whole federal gov-

ernment. Rather, its purpose is to establish a definition of the executive branch for the reorganization process. We anticipate changes as the reorganization study groups learn more about the executive branch.

Before the unit could complete its explorations into the jungle of Washington, it was itself disbanded. The negative moral is clear: Whatever else government is, it is *not* a single organization.

Interorganizational analysis makes evident the importance of disaggregating government into a complex of institutions (see, e.g., Hanf & Scharpf, 1978). In this body of literature, relations between organizations nominally working for the same government can take on properties of bargaining between separate national governments. Valuable as this approach is, it has two deficiencies. The first is that it does not pay any attention to the borderline between government organizations and private sector institutions. The borderline is debatable, and modern organization theory can even discuss the client as part of the organization. The fact that the borderline is unclear does not deny that it exists. Second, the interorganization approach tends to conflate all organizations into a single category as if each were as independent as a member of the United Nations, ignoring differences in size and dependency between them.

Once a boundary is stipulated, the question then remains: What is the primary unit of analysis and tabulation? It cannot be government organizations, for on that basis the U.S. federal government would count only as one among 78,268 state, local, and special-purpose institutions (Wright, 1978: 10). Multipurpose jurisdictions—especially national governments—must be subdivided functionally. In a previous work disaggregation to the level of the ministry (or analogous units in local government, say, education, health, police and fire, housing and land use planning) was deemed sufficient for a very broad brush portrait of comparative analysis of functions of government across a century (Rose, 1976). However, for systematic analysis of government today, ministries themselves must be disaggregated; the nation, that is, "the largest community which when the chips are down effectively commands men's loyalty" (Emerson, 1960: 95) is likely to be smaller than a ministry. In operational terms ministries are themselves holding companies of more or less related but still discrete functions; it is the bureau or the agency or the division within the ministry that comes closest to having its hands on the action. Moreover, such bureaus or agencies can command strong loyalties both to institutional values and to external client groups. Disaggregation at this level emphasizes the heterogeneous character of individual ministries; for example, in the United Kingdom most ministries do not even have uniform territorial responsibilities; for some purposes a ministry will be concerned with England or England and Wales only, for others

Great Britain, and for yet others with the United Kingdom as a whole (Rose, 1982: ch. 5).

Establishing units of account is particularly important insofar as reorganization has been a common panacea (or placebo) of Western governments in the past twenty years (Leemans, 1976). Change in the U.K. government appears to have led to the reduction of the total number of ministries by creation of superdepartments or by hiving off of functional agencies. Concurrently, in the United States it has led to the proliferation of cabinet-level agencies, as well as birth, death, and/or merger of many more agencies (cf. Kaufman, 1976; Starbuck & Nystrom, forthcoming; Hood, 1979).

(5) Programs: Organizations combine the resources of government together in a wide variety of mixes in order to produce programs. It is the programs—specific activities of indentifiable organizations authorized by law to spend public funds and to employ public personnel for statutory purposes—that constitute the principal outputs of government. The mix of resources varies greatly from program to program. For example, pensions are money-intensive; education is labor-intensive; and marriage and divorce programs are law-intensive. However each program requires all three resources—laws, personnel, and money—and organizations to assume program responsibilities. In aggregate, there is wide scope for interprogram conflicts or inconsistencies. However, program is free-floating, that is, without an anchor in statutes and institutions, and without personnel and appropriations. Any policy that is not embodied in a program is best described as a goodwill intention rather than a concrete activity of government.

The concept of program is important in several senses. First, it concentrates attention upon the multiplicity of resources and organizations required for any significant action of government. Second, it calls attention to the fact that government activities are not, at least in the day-to-day observational sense, reducible to a single homogeneous flow of outputs. Theoretical economists in the land of *Weissnichtwo* may write about government producing welfare, but anyone working elsewhere will observe very big differences between programs however these differences are typologized. Military defense, managing the economy, and providing welfare services may be not unrelated; but they are also not identical. Not least in importance, programs reflect the purposes that politicians and citizens see in actions of government. Any large-scale study of the size and growth of government cannot concentrate upon the evanescent or latent purposes attributed to government. Nonetheless, it is important to realize that the specific activities of government are not simply self-serving and reflexive, but are justified by purposeful intent.

Logically, programs could grow in throughput without any increase in number. Without enacting any new legislation on pensions, a government could find that it was paying more and more for pensions as people lived longer. Without making any statutory changes, a government could find that it was spending more and more on health programs if demographic changes resulted in a change in the number of people entitled to claim particular benefits or in the claiming of these entitlements.

An important question about the growth of government is whether growth comes through the adoption of new programs, or whether it is primarily a consequence of the expanded volume of throughput in established programs. At any given point the greatest political attention is likely to focus upon new programs. These will be the cause of political controversy prior to adoption and of administrative difficulties in their implementation for the first time. Subsequently, they may also cause dispute insofar as anything done for the first time will be evaluated as less successful than hoped, or produce unintended and unexpected consequences (Rose, 1981).

The expansion of government programs in many Western nations in the 1960s and early 1970s was a desire to produce achievements that outran well tested means-ends technologies. The easy-to-do things have already been done. For instance, building bridges, sewers, or roads were techniques known to the Romans as well as to present-day governments. However, the Romans did not know how to end poverty any more than do contemporary governors—but contemporary governors are more anxious to achieve this ideal.

Much of the growth of government as measured by the volume of claims upon resources simply reflects inertia tendencies of established programs. In size, the marginal claims of established programs upon resources can be much greater than those of new programs that, because of their novelty, are likely to be small initially. The bigger the existing program commitments and the scarcer marginal resources, the less significant new programs are going to be. One qualification must be added to this hypothesis: There are grey areas between new and established programs. For example, raising the number of years that children are required to remain in school does not create something entirely new, especially if half the pupils are already voluntarily remaining at school. Yet it does alter the compulsory entitlement to a merit good, and is a notable claim on marginal resources. Expansion of education, health, and other major welfare state programs typically shows an expansion in the numbers and criteria for entitlement, as well as demographically determined increases in effective demand (OECD, 1976 et seq.).

The differentiation of government programs could be continued almost endlessly. Functional budgets of government, which consist of listings of programs, can enumerate literally hundreds of different programs, which themselves consist of aggregations of many more specific laws, personnel groups, and elements. For example, the seventeen functional categories of expenditure in Britain are in turn each disaggregated into as many as a dozen programs under each heading (Cmnd. 8175, 1981). The functional categories of the U.S. federal budget take a dozen pages to list and in turn are disaggregated into 180 pages of more detailed budget accounts (Office of Management and Budget, 1981: 269-548; 566-277d). It is not necessary to pursue disaggregation further. A brief review of important properties of basic elements of government is sufficient to emphasize the differences between these elements and, therefore, the need to disaggregate the concept of government. The alternative is to risk either of two equally attractive errors: letting one party of government stand for many disparate properties, or trying to add up incommensurables in a way that can only misrepresent variety within government.

Analyzing a Complex Construct

Because government is a complex construct, we cannot reduce it to a single measure that can be monitored for change or growth. Government is not a single variable; it is a family of variables whose constituent terms can change in different directions at different rates simultaneously.

Logically, different terms of government can change in opposite directions or in the same direction but at different rates. For example, there has been an inverse relationship between the growth of public expenditure and growth in government organization, where expenditure for local government has increased while the total number of local government units has decreased. In the United States a reduction of 33 percent in local government units since 1952 has been accompanied by an increase of 139 percent in the number of their employees (Wright, 1978: 10-12). Where different terms of government have grown in the same direction, they have not grown at the same rate. For example, in every major Western country public revenues have grown at a much faster rate than public employment if only because of the importance of money-intensive (but not labor-intensive) income maintenance programs. It is also possible for some terms of government not to grow at all; for example, public employment in the United States has remained relatively steady as a proportion of the total labor force, but the composition of public employment has shown major changes in opposite directions in its defense and civilian components (Peters, 1980).

Empirically, attempts to reduce government to a single composite construct by such clustering techniques as factor analysis will be infirm. The different elements of government do not share a common metric. Public revenue and public employment can each be measured as a continuous variable, but there is no equivalence between one unit of revenue and one public employee. The chief thing that laws and programs have in common is that each consists of a family of objects that are more important than their quantitative features, and the same is true of programs. Organizations can in principle be counted, but the difference is vast between one organization, one employee, and one unit of revenue. Nor is there a ready-made definition of what constitutes a single organization. Is a ministry of defense or a catchall interior ministry equivalent in scale to a ministry for sport or a single local government unit? A complex statistical analysis of Whitehall ministries by Hood and Dunsire (1981) has even shown how large the differences are between ministries in the relatively simple (sic) organizational environment of Whitehall. The lack of a common metric means that simple correlations or statistical causal models cannot provide appropriate models of the dynamics of government change.

A general theory of the growth of government can only be validated by disaggregating government to test under what circumstances and to what extent it may be effective. For example, a theory of institutionalized inertia can purport to explain slow but continuing change in government as a consequence of political, economic, bureaucratic, and legal inertia forces within government. However, it still remains necessary to stipulate the nature of the inertia force applicable to particular elements of government. In one context it may refer to continuing growth in welfare expenditure and in another to a tendency of organizations to resist change. It is also necessary to stipulate the rate of inertia or incremental change. Dempster and Wildavsky (1979) have argued that incremental change is best defined as persisting regularity rather than as change of a given size. However, applying this concept to disaggregated elements of government can lead to destablization of the system. The reason is simple; the steady compounding of different growth rates—and differences here are likely to be very substantial (e.g., of the magnitude of five or ten to one) as between revenues, public employees, and laws—will cause systemic change by altering the relationship between different resources, and mixes of resources, organizations, and programs (Rose and Page, 1981).

At the other extreme it is possible to analyze the growth of government in terms of changes in particular policy arenas. This denies that there need be any generic tendency for government to change at rates that can be deduced from first principles or inferred by statistical analyses of an aggregate or disparate program. Comparing the same programs in different countries (e.g., education) may be more likely to reveal common patterns than comparing different programs in the same country (e.g., health care and defense). Behind the argument for analyzing government programmatically rather than holistically is an extremely important implicit premise, namely, that growth in government is *purposeful*. The causes of inertia growth are not just ghosts within a machine; change can occur because representative governments have made particular choices to provide programs benefits collectively.

Interdependencies between programs make it important to go beyond the analysis of single policy arenas; a distinctive characteristic of government is the multiplicity of its program outputs, resource inputs, and organizational forms. When big government is the object of study (and the government of nearly every Western nation today is big by historic and absolute standards), then important consequences of size and growth are likely to reflect changes in the relationship between different programs (Rose, 1981). When government has many program commitments, any increase in programs is likely to affect an area of life already intensively affected by preexisting public policies. Unless one believes in a hidden hand mechanism perfectly coordinating the multiple activities of government (which is more like a swamp of alligators than a single octopus), then the chances of contradiction increase disproportionately. As Wildavsky (1979: 65) argues, "Interdependence among policies increases faster than knowledge grows." In an effort to deal with the pathologies of interdependence, "policy becomes its own cause" and its own justification for further growth.

In a very practical sense all government programs have some things in common, for they compete with each other at the margin of growth for limited resources of revenue and public employment, and also for the limited capital that politicians are willing to invest in new legislation or organizational change. This is specially important today when public expenditure tends to grow faster than the gross national product (Rose and Peters, 1978; Taylor, 1981). It is true whether pressures upon the *total* resources of government arise as an unintended byproduct of particular program changes or because of macro-economic calculations or miscalculations.

The different programs and parts of government can and must be linked together by a model that can see government as a *system with particular subsystems* having distinctive rates of change in resources, organizations, and programs. A systems-dynamic philosophy of modeling provides a better orientation toward this complex structure than does a rational deductive model. The former is flexible, incorporating whatever influences are empirically important; the latter is inflexible, excluding everything of importance that cannot be recognized. Equally important, a systems-dynamic approach is more appropriate than analysis by regression statistics, in circumstances in which the phenomena being modeled cannot be reduced to a common metric. Systems dynamic models can accommodate all kinds of variables and model stochastic processes. Moreover, a systems-dynamic model provides an accounting framework in which those subsystem terms that are generic (e.g., revenue claims) can be linked to the system as a whole and system terms (e.g., revenue constraints) can be input to subsystem models.

Whatever analytic strategy is adopted to cope with the complex character of government, a further choice must still be made about the time-and-space universe for testing propositions. An analysis of one subsystem by one country by one year would be far less generalizable than a systems analysis of one hundred countries by one hundred years. However, the latter could become so impossibly vast a task as to be self-defeating. Or, to make the task manageable, the amount of information collected might be reduced to data that were conveniently handy rather than that which was theoretically necessary to test theories of growth and change in government properly. No general rules can be prescribed for choosing a particular mixture of concepts, countries, and years. The choice should be instrumentally determined by the problem at hand. Just as with most choices, it involves trade-offs between competing claims, and it is important to recognize the implications of different strategies.

   The World Handbook of Political and Social Indicators is the best-known and geographically most inclusive compendium of data about growth and change in government in the post-1945 world. As its title emphasizes, it is truly global in its coverage. Moreover, it is also very inclusive in its definition of what social scientists may want to know about world systems; it includes social and economic as well as political data. However, analyzing the tables for the forthcoming third edition of the *World Handbook* by concepts outlined here calls attention to the inevitable imbalance of subjects covered in this worldwide compendium. There is nil information about legislation, about government organizations, or about public policy programs, and there is very scanty information about public personnel (see Table 9.1). There are many tables about public expenditure and revenue. The explanation is simple: The only possible way in which a political indicator can be produced on a global basis (154 different countries) is to concentrate on financial data. Two inferences can be drawn, and both are valid. The first is that a global record should be maintained and the time series of that record extended. The second points in the opposite direction: There is a complementary need to concentrate upon a limited range of countries in order to obtain a better understanding of the growth of government, for the disparate and few indi-

TABLE 9.1   An Imbalance of Social Science Indicators of Government

Indicators in World Handbook III	N	Percentage of total variables (N = 326)
Revenue	12	4
Public Expenditure	25	8
Personnel	6	2
Laws	0	0
Organizations	0	0
Programs	0	0
	43	13

Source: Charles Lewis Taylor and David A. Jodice (1979).

cators available at a global level are inadequate partial proxies for government as a system.

Within a Western political perspective, the most obvious subset of the global system for analysis is the Western world (here operationally taken to mean the OECD). This differs from a European universe, excluding Eastern Europe and including non-European nations with high levels of economic development. Taking OECD countries as a universe for analysis has theoretical justification in terms of relating growth of government to socioeconomic mobilization and modernization. It also has a practical justification; the OECD regularly collects and publishes masses of data. However, OECD data have a clear and, within their own terms, proper economic bias. The OECD provides excellent and comparable data on national income accounts, public expenditure, and public revenues. Upon occasion it publishes studies that both report and analyze data about major programs, albeit these publications are typically one-off studies. It does not produce data about laws or organizations, nor has it yet begun to monitor public employees consistently. In short, OECD data greatly increase the information available about the political economy; but doing this only unbalances understanding of the growth of systems of government.

The HIWED (Historical Indicators of West European Democracies) project directed by Peter Flora has shown it is possible to abstract noneconomic statistical series from European government publications and to do so for some measures going back to 1815. Forthcoming is the large compendium of HIWED data that will extend the *World Handbook* coverage in order to present data about public employment (but on a much restricted and less consistent definition from that cited above) as well as public revenue and public expenditure data. However, the problem of measuring laws, organizations, and programs of government will remain.

There are two alternatives that should be high priority areas for understanding the growth of government. Both are now being pursued at the Centre for the Study of Public Policy at the University of Strathclyde. The first is a strategy of concentrating upon elements of government that can be made amendable to cross-national analysis with reasonably reliable, valid, and comparable indicators. These terms include public revenues and public employment, as well as public expenditure in aggregate and under program headings. Pilot work already undertaken on changes in public employment since the early 1950s in five Western countries has been encouraging and thought-provoking. It shows that it *is* possible to obtain comparable data about public employment from a multiplicity of national sources. By starting from a model of public employment with seven basic concepts, each of which relates to others, we have limited the amount of digging required, yet have also committed ourselves to do a substantial amount of research in national sources. Preliminary results are at hand (see Rose, 1980c; Parry, 1980; Peters, 1980; Pignatelli, 1980). With the aid of a two-year Anglo-German Foundation grant, the study is now being extended to incorporate the two missing major European nations, Germany and France. This will help establish whether there is a central tendency in public employment patterns or if there are culture-specific patterns. The study is also being enlarged to cover the interaction of public employment, nation employment, and nonemployed persons, in particular pensioners and the unemployed who receive their primary income from government, so that we can analyze cross-nationally the interaction between the social system and this attribute of government.

While cross-national analysis of a single term in government proves encouraging, expanding such work is inhibiting if countries can only be added at the rate of a few per year, given the difficulties and intensity of data collection. Yet a study need not be limited intellectually simply because it refers to a limited number of countries. We did not have to wait for studies of voting in all OECD nations to have general propositions about voting behavior (see, e.g., Lipset, 1960). Most comparative studies in politics are more nearly single nation than global studies (Dogan and Pelassy, 1981). The important point is that the countries chosen should be selected with a specific research strategy in mind, so that it is possible to test some generalizations of wide interest.

The second approach, the configurative analysis of the growth of government in one country since 1945, is even more low level by comparison with the *World Handbook* analysis; yet by the same token it can maximize advantages that the other must minimize. The country chosen is the United Kingdom, which is sufficiently rich in historical records to emphasize that conceptualization, not information for its own sake, is the fundamental task of understanding. The British Social Science Research Council has given the Strathclyde Centre for the Study of Public Policy a £250,000, five-year program grant to examine the growth of government in the United Kingdom since 1945, in accord with the framework outlined in this chapter. A series of five monographic volumes is planned, one for each major term examined here, plus an introductory volume and final synthesizing study.

Concentrating attention upon the growth of government in one country over a period of more than three decades should have the following distinctive advantages:

(1) Greater intensity of data coverage for conventionally analyzed concepts (e.g., the full variety of revenue sources and program headings of public expenditure).
(2) Greater variety in the approaches to analysis of conventionally quantified data (e.g., analyzing the territorial distribution of public employment or distributional properties of public expenditure or revenue raising).
(3) The collection and analysis of quantified data for concepts conventionally not subjected to systematic analysis (e.g., public employment).
(4) Developing measures to analyze changes in concepts that are not conventionally quantified (e.g., laws, and organizations).

(5) Last, and not least, analyzing the dynamics of the system of government by relating change (and nonchange) in resources, organizations, and programs to each other.

This program of studies of the growth of government is about Britain, but it is not solely a study of British government for its own sake. The object is to develop and apply a generic model of the growth of government. The choice of a country that was the home of the Industrial Revolution and has fortuitously been spared the disruptions of Central Europe simplifies the work and widens its potential generality. Just as the *World Handbook* examines properties of all nations as a means of understanding specific nations so the intensive examination of one country may, by virtue of its value as a leading case, generate a more refined understanding of the way in which readily quantifiable, not so easily quantifiable, and nominal variables interact in the process that is commonly labeled the growth of government.

REFERENCES

ALLISON, G. (1971) Essence of Decision. Boston: Little, Brown.

CLARKE, R. (1973) "The long-term planning of taxation," in B. B. Crick and W. A. Robson (eds.) Taxation Policy. Harmondsworth: Penguin.

Cmnd. 8175. (1981) The Government's Expenditure Plans, 1981-82 to 1983-84. London: Her Majesty's Stationery Office.

DEMPSTER, M. A. H. and A. WILDAVSKY (1979) "On change: or, there is no magic size for an increment." Political Studies 27: 3.

DEUTSCH, K. W. (1963) The Nerves of Government. New York: Free Press.

DI PALMA, G. (1977) Surviving Without Governing. Berkeley: University of California Press.

DOGAN, M. and D. PELLASSY (1981) "The choice of countries in comparative research." Werner-Reimers Stiftung, Bad Homburg: Committee on Political Sociology Conference.

Economic Commission for Europe (1979) "Employment in general government in industrial market economies." Economic Bulletin for Europe 30: 2.

EMERSON, R. (1960) From Empire to Nation. Boston: Beacon Press.

FLORA, P. (forthcoming) Handbook HIWED. Frankfurt: Campus Verlag.

HANF, K. W. and F. W. S. SCHARPF (eds.) (1978) Interorganizational Policy Making. London: Sage.

HOOD, C. (1979) The Machinery of Government Problem. Studies in Public Policy 28. Glasgow: University of Strathclyde.

———— and A. DUNSIRE (1981) Bureaumetrics. Farnborough: Gover Press.

KAUFMAN, H. (1976) Are Government Organizations Immortal? Washington, DC: Brookings Institution.

LARKEY, P. C. S. and M. WINER (1981) "Theorizing about the growth of government." Journal of Public Policy 1: 2.

LEEMANS, A. F. (ed.) (1976) The Management of Change in Government. The Hague: Martinus Nijhoff.

LIPSET, S. M. (1960) Political Man. New York: Doubleday.

MARTIN, J. P. (1980) "Public sector employment trends in Western industrialized economies." Paris: OECD (unpublished)

Organization for Economic Cooperation and Development (1976, 1977, 1978) Public Expenditure on Education (Studies in Resource Allocation, 2; Public Expenditure on Income Maintenance Programmes (3); Public Expenditure on Health (5). Paris: OECD.

Office of Management and Budget (1981) The Budget of the United States Government: Fiscal Year 1982. Washington, DC: Government Printing Office.

PARRY, R. (1980) United Kingdom Public Employment: Patterns of Change, 1951-1976. Studies in Public Policy 62. Glasgow: University of Strathclyde.

PETERS, B. G. (1980) Public Employment in the United States: Growth and Change. Studies in Public Policy 63. Glasgow: University of Strathclyde.

PIGNATELLI, A. C. (1980) The State as Paymaster: the Italian Experience, 1951-1976. Studies in Public Policy 64. Glasgow: University of Strathclyde.

President Carter's Reorganization Project (1977) Current Inventory of Organization Units within the Executive. Washington, DC: Executive Office of the President. (photocopy)

ROSE, R. (1982) Understanding the United Kingdom: The Territorial Dimension in Government. London: Longmans.

_____ (1981) "What, if anything, is wrong with big government?" Journal of Public Policy 1: 1.

_____ (1980a) Do Parties Make a Difference? London: Macmillan.

_____ (1980b) "Misperceiving public expenditure: feelings about 'cuts'," in Charles H. Levine and Irene Rubin (eds.). Fiscal Stress and Public Policy. Beverly Hills, CA: Sage.

_____ (1980c) Changes in Public Employment: A Multi-Dimensional Comparative Analysis. Studies in Public Policy 61. Glasgow: University of Strathclyde.

_____ (1978) What Is Governing? Englewood Cliffs, NJ: Prentice-Hall.

_____ (1976) "On the priorities of government: a developmental analysis of public policies." European Journal of Political Research 4: 3.

_____ (1970) People in Politics. London: Faber & Faber.

_____ and EDWARD C. PAGE (1981) "Incrementalism or instability?" Glasgow: University of Strathclyde. (unpublished)

_____ and GUY PETERS (1978) Can Government Go Bankrupt? New York: Basic Books.

SARTORI, G. (1970) "Concept misformation in comparative politics." American Political Science Review 64: 4.

STARBUCK, W. H. and P. C. NYSTROM (forthcoming) "Designing and understanding organizations," in P. C. Nystrom and W. H. Starbuck (eds.) Handbook of Organizational Design. London: Oxford University Press.

TAYLOR, C. L. (1981) "Limits to governmental growth" in R. Merritt and B. Russett (eds.) From National Development to Global Community. London: Allen & Unwin.

_____ and M. C. HUDSON (1972) World Handbook of Political and Social Indicators: Second Edition. New Haven, CT: Yale University Press.

_____ and D. A. JODICE (1979) Updating and Expanding the World Handbook Data Collection. Berlin: International Institute for Comparative Social Research, IIVG/pre 79-6.

WILDAVSKY, A. (1979) Speaking Truth to Power: The Art and Craft of Policy Analysis. Boston: Little, Brown.

WRIGHT, D. S. (1978) Understanding Intergovernmental Relations. Belmont, CA: Duxbury.

CHAPTER 10

THINKING ABOUT
PUBLIC SECTOR GROWTH
Conceptual, Operational,
Theoretical, and
Policy Considerations

B . G U Y P E T E R S
M A R T I N O . H E I S L E R

The growth of government and of its involvement in the lives of citizens has
become more than merely the concern of political economists. It is now the
concern of ordinary citizens as well as the focus of an increasing number of
political movements. Even persons in government are worried about its
growth, but they appear to have very little ability to control the expansion. It
is imperative that scholars, policy makers, and the public be disabused of the
assumption that we can easily know what is being measured, or what is
growing, how, and why. Nevertheless, measurement and analysis of the
growth of government across long periods of time and across countries are
important. They should provide the basis for theories of development and
change, for assessments of performance, for the determination of the recip-
rocal influences of government, politics and policy, and for analyzing the
impacts of government on changing conditions and preferences in society.

AUTHORS' NOTE: The order of the coauthors' names was determined by the flip of a coin
rather than by their respective contributions to the manuscript.

"Normal Science" and
the Study of the Growth of Government

Work to date in this genre has been "normal science," in Kuhn's terminology. Until now it has been relatively standard procedure to test associations of political variables, such as progressive democratization, the ideological balance in governments, and the size of bureaucracies with the relative magnitude of government expenditures, and, on occasion, indicators of outcomes or performance.[1] These same dependent variables also have been related to demographic factors, resources available to governments, and the objective needs of societies. However, there has been virtually no questioning of this approach.[2]

Normal science studies of the growth of public expenditure and other interval-level indicators of changes in magnitude are in themselves important and interesting, but their usefulness is severely limited in the analysis of the growth of government. This general inductive approach—measuring what is most readily available and quantifiable—misses entirely some of the most important questions that need to be considered; and it may actually obscure more than it reveals. While such studies were adequate as means of initiating cross-national diachronic examinations of policy and government, they no longer suffice and even have serious drawbacks as guides for policy makers.

First, in the modern period—especially in the last thirty to fifty years, depending upon the country or policy area—many important activities of Western governments have taken forms that are not measurable by such standard indicators as expenditures or the size of the bureaucracy. There has been increasing use of formally mandated self-regulation in several policy areas (as distinguished from simply not having a policy), the use of guidelines both for policies and for such components as price and wage increases, jaw-boning, informal negotiations, and loan guarantees. Further, government regulation imposes public and private economic costs that do not show up as public expenditures;[3] and negative expenditures—such as tax expenditures—influence the use of societal resources and have important substantive policy implications in, for example, housing. However, such costs are not usually counted as a part of public spending.[4]

Second, both direct government action (e.g., public expenditure) and less direct policy influences carry opportunity costs and have displacement effects. The measurement of these costs and effects is difficult, if not impossible at times, but nonetheless they have important consequences for society and its utilization of scarce resources. Also, the involvement of government, directly or indirectly, in an area of policy may crowd out or preempt private activity, again with potential costs (or benefits) to the society; and the measurement of such effects is also often problematic or intractable.

To a substantial extent this analysis parallels criticisms of standard work in economics—criticisms made by some leading members of that discipline. Many of our points in this section reflect concerns that are the counterparts to Robert L. Heilbroner's paper, "On the Limited 'Relevance' of Economics" (1970). Heilbroner notes the failure of economists to address "real," "relevant" and "important" problems in large part because of what he considers to be conservative orientations that militate against such work; but Robert Solow, in his response, "Science and Ideology in Economics" (1970), defends economics against such charges. However, here we are raising questions about the *usefulness* of the current line of research on the growth of government, without imputing its shortcomings to the value biases of researchers.

The essential point we seek to make here is that, as Olson and Clague recognize (1976), the impact of the operating norms of standard, hard-nosed social science on the valuation of scholarly work is such that work involving quantification and formalization seems to militate against the investigation of questions that do not now lend themselves to such rigor. We would argue that posing the difficult questions, or contextualizing in a broader framework the presently approachable ones, need not—and should not—wait until the questions become more tractable.

This position is not contrary to good science. Indeed, many major theoretical leaps in physics and astronomy (for those who favor using the natural sciences as exemplars) during the past century have followed such a pattern: dissatisfaction with existing theory grows from the perception of gaps in explanatory scope due to gross specification errors, insufficient contextualization, and consequent lack of robustness; a new approach is posited *before* current techniques of measurement can test it; and the subsequent refinements or major innovations in measurement—often stimulated by the suggestiveness of the nonrigorous, partially empirical framework—which permit testing. (In the case of the general theory of relativity, the wait was one of decades.)

Measurement and Analysis of
the Growth of Government

To date much of the analysis of the growth of government has been like the search of the proverbial drunkard, who looked for a lost house key under the lamppost, because the light was better there. We have been looking for governmental growth in forms for which data are more readily available, in quantifiable form, ubiquitous units, and preferably in interval form. There are, for example, reasonably reliable statistics on the levels of public expenditures in virtually all industrialized societies. These statistics often extend backward for a century or more. However, as exponents of the social indicators movement have pointed out, the usefulness of the measuring rod of money is quite limited when considering governmental activity and its impact.[5] Further, many of what we shall argue are the crucial and most interesting questions about the growth of government do not involve direct financial transactions.

In addition to heavy reliance on fiscal indicators, government employment has also been an important, interval data-level measure of the growth of government. It has the advantage that employees are real and are less susceptible to changes in value over time than money.[6] However, the measurement of growth through the counting of people presents many of the same problems encountered with money: We must be able to establish what is a public purpose, and who are public employees (Peters, 1980). As we shall see forthwith, these are far from easy questions to answer with confidence.

Not only have we seen changes in absolute size but also in the instruments used by government to exercise control over society. Some government activities, especially regulative and self-regulative policies, were less important and perhaps of a different nature in earlier periods. As noted, these types of policies and their impacts are not readily quantifiable even today; and their impact is even more elusive for the nineteenth and early twentieth centuries. Thus if we select indicators principally on the basis of their ability to travel well over time—that is, to provide continuity and consistency of measurement—we may obscure vital change in both the quantitative and qualitative dimensions of growth.

The form and potential magnitude of such a risk can be gauged by contemplating some of the implications of the illustration given above: the costs incurred by the private sector in conforming with government regulations. A researcher following an inductive design, and naive in the sense that he or she is unaware of the relative increase in regulative and self-regulative outputs over the more expenditure-intensive outputs of government, might well conclude that the rate of government growth has been more or less arithmetic since World War II in most highly industrialized societies (Rose and Peters, 1978: 54-56). Further, he or she might conclude that government has grown at roughly similar rates in most industrialized societies.

Yet, if prevailing impressions of the real record are correct, and both regulative and self-regulative policies have grown at a more rapid and uneven pace in recent decades—and with substantial variation from country to country—such conclusions would be far off the mark. If, as we suspect, self-regulative outputs have become especially significant aspects of government in "corporate pluralist" regimes (such as those of the smaller European democracies and, to a lesser extent, the United Kingdom) but have remained relatively less important in the United States, neither longitudinal or cross-country comparisons could be accurate (Salisbury, 1977; Heisler, 1974: ch. 8).

Regulative and self-regulative policies influence the private sector and utilize social, political, and economic resources not generally thought to be public. The use of private resources, often in a manner that is contrary to or at least not evidently consistent with economic rationality and self-interest, may be required to compensate for negative externalities occasioned by government regulations.

These impacts constitute an extension of governmental influence without *commensurate* extension of governmental apparatus or expenditure. The resources required flow from the private or quasi-public sectors of the economy and not merely from the governmental apparatus and the public sector. Such elusive concepts as quiescence, obligation, and the ability and willingness to work with a shifting social contract become important, and the nature and form of the effective domain of the state's defining concept—authority—become important considerations. In addition, the boundaries and transactions between the public, private, and quasi-public sectors must be more carefully scrutinized.[7]

The allusion above to the state as a concept and an entity that may have to be distinguished from government in the consideration of growth points to another occasionally confounding, often hidden, conceptual problem. It would be foolhardy for us to attempt a thorough or formal statement of the nature of the state here; however, it is necessary and useful to point to some of the problems that arise when the distinction is not made and to some of the potential benefits that may follow from more directly addressing the distinction.

In the classic sense the state represents a compact among citizens regarding their mutual obligations, and in it reside the more transcendent values employed in the governance of society. The mechanisms used for implementing the compact are sets of authority relationships; and a particular government in a given time and setting merely exercises the state's authority.[8] The nature of those authority relationships changes over time and with context, and the mutual relationships and expectations among citizens—the compact—may also change. It may even be possible to conceive of authority within a polity growing or shrinking over time, as well as changing in form and meaning (Nisbet, 1975). In addition, it is possible to see that the actions of governments of the day may affect the long-run authority of the state and the nature of the compact among citizens either positively or negatively. Thus our conception of authority and the state at any point in time is necessarily only one frame of a rather slow-moving motion picture of the relationships among citizens and the structures of authority designed to govern them.

The response to a conditioning of many of the expectations of citizens by the governments of modern welfare state have legitimized interventions by those governments into the market economy for several generations now. These interventions often began as temporary measures, or as the ad hoc responses to crisis, or politically instigated redistribution of income. The beneficiaries of such interventions, however, associate them not with a particular situation or a government of a particular political complexion, but rather with the state. In this sense the fundamental compact has been altered, such that a government that sought to roll back benefits or programs of long standing would probably not be tolerated as legitimate by citizens.[9]

As Bell (1974: 39) has noted, the politics of the contemporary welfare state are the politics of "rising entitlements" rather than rising expectations. Citizens believe themselves to be entitled to certain goods and services, and that they have real, and perhaps justiciable, claims against the state. The growth in entitlements occurs in the range of *claims against the state* rather than in the domain of the activities of government. The two may be highly correlated; but many entitlements may remain dormant for long periods of time (e.g., pensions, education for childless couples anticipating a family), and many will, citizens' hope, never be taken up (e.g., unemployment insurance or disability benefits). They remain, however, as (arguably) legal and moral commitments on the part of the state the citizens believe they can expect to receive, if the conditional statements involved are fulfilled. For many programs citizens do in fact have a virtual contractual arrangement, since payments have been made into the programs for many months or years. As Franklin Roosevelt said at the time the social security system of these United States was created:

> We put those payroll contributions there so as to give the contributors a legal, moral and political right to collect their pensions and employment benefits. With those taxes in there, no damn politician can ever scrap my social security program [Leuchtenberg, 1963: 133].

This obtains as well for what have become the largest items in the budgets of most local and many national governments, and items that are certain to increase in magnitude: public payrolls and retirement programs (Peters, 1980). Altering contracted payrolls and retirement benefits is much more than a political or moral undertaking. On the basis of straightforward projections based on the number and age of current government employees, a sharply and continuously growing public financial burden can be predicted for advanced industrial societies well into the next century. Thus governments striving to hold down the rate of growth trends are confronted with politically, morally, and legally conditioned expectations. In brief, in many and important ways, some aspects of the *social* contract are also *legally* binding.[10]

The purposes of government also have changed. When government was occupied with the traditional "defining functions," such as defense and justice, the instruments and organizations required for performing such tasks were captured quite well by traditional measures (Rose, 1976). However, as the economic and social functions of government have become more important, so too have the instruments and organizations become more complex— and the transactions between the public and private sectors even more complex. Even in defense, the maintenance of a high-technology and capital-intensive defense force require much greater interaction with the private sector than was true previously, and a blending of public and private activity follows.

In short, the time has arrived to move beyond uniscalar analyses in the study of the growth of government. It is now appropriate and necessary to develop a more subtle and much more complex contextualization of the growth of government. The hoped-for outcome will be a more accurate and sophisticated understanding of governmental activity and growth, of the tools for effective policy management and of likely impacts—and perhaps a better grasp of changes in the nature of the contemporary state. The costs associated with this strategy will also be high: initial losses in theoretical parsimony and in diachronic and synchronic comparability. However, the eventual and attainable benefits seem to warrant these temporary losses.

We propose as a beginning the restatement of some of the fundamental questions of political science and public policy. The increased complexity of governmental activity, the increased blurring to the always fuzzy distinctions between the public, quasi-public, and private domains in society and economy, the frequent confounding of government and the state, and the inchoate exhaustion of the theoretical utilities of the standard approach militate in favor of this departure from the modern tradition.

Problems in Conceptualizing
the Growth of Government

To this point we have been discussing the difficulties of understanding and conceptualizing the growth of government at a very general level. In this section these problems are examined more thoroughly through two salient terms in the literature on growth: government and public sector. We shall attempt to differentiate between these overlapping concepts and also to show some difficulties encountered in using each of them.

The concept of government. The most frequently used term in describing the growth of the collective choice sector is the growth of *government*. As noted at several places above, one can regard the growth of government rather simply as increases in taxing, spending, and employment in institutions that are formally designated as governmental. However, clearly, this conceptualization needs to be examined and extended to include a much wider range of concerns.

Government is, most fundamentally, the institution that imparts direction to its society by various means of collective decision making and exercises the state's authority on a daily basis. The root words of government have to do with piloting or steering; and the most basic task of government is to steer what might otherwise be a drifting or floundering ship of state (Rose, 1973).

If we concentrate on this conceptualization of government as steering or directing, we might be tempted to say that government has actually shrunk—rather than grown—over the past decade in many societies. Evidence from a variety of sources points up the extent to which citizens no longer believe that governments are capable of supplying direction to society; or they may believe that government *should not* provide such direction.[11] In addition to this subjective perspective, the capability of governments appears to have diminished in an objective sense as well. Whereas once many observers considered the economy and society to be amendable to governmental control, and indeed even to fine tuning, the bulk of the population and many analysts have seemingly lost faith in this ability to control forces and to cope with challenges from the environment.

Paradoxically, despite the apparent loss of effectiveness in exercising control over society, governments are more deeply involved in a wider range of policy areas than ever before. Whether the genesis of that growth lies within or without government is perhaps not as important here as the large-scale shift in the *number* of activities influenced by governmental action and the *extent* to which they are influenced.[12] Unfortunately, as we have already pointed out, the extent of the influence of government is not readily measured through direct, simple, comparable indicators such as expenditures and employees.

First, the costs imposed on society, economy, and polity by regulations— and the benefits produced by those regulations—are extremely difficult to isolate and quantify, even for the current time period (Viscusi, 1979). These regulatory impacts are, of course, substantial. One estimate for the costs associated with federal regulations in the United States for 1979 is in excess of $121 billion (Weidenbaum, 1978, 1979). To attempt to estimate those costs for any significant span of time would be an exercise in futility; and yet, without data over time, the measurement of growth in this aspect of governmental growth is not possible. The point remains, nevertheless, that the regulatory and self-regulatory activities of government have come to represent a substantial part of its overall impact on society and economy.

A second form in which governments direct resources without actually spending them is through not collecting certain types of expenditures through the tax system. Virtually all tax systems have some preferences built into them and these preferences direct the resource of the economy and society, usually according to the interests or values of identifiable constituencies. For example, in the United States tax expenditures for property taxes, interest, and deferral of capital gains taxation amounted to a housing subsidy of over $30 billion in 1981 (U.S. Bureau of the Census: Table 419). This subsidy accrues mostly to the middle classes and also diverts attention from multiple family rental dwellings. Even the United Kingdom, with its large-scale council housing program, provided £2.33 billion in tax expenditures for the owners of private homes in 1976 (Willis and Hardwick, 1978: 93-94). In Denmark and elsewhere, such subsidies or tax expenditures have become important political issues, not only because of their distributive impacts but also because they are seen by many as excessively indirect policy instruments.

We could proceed to calculate different types of subsidies and discuss their effects in various settings, but our point is a theoretical rather than an empirical one. Taxation as well as expenditure define the interests and extent of the state, but the structure of revenue collection is not often counted or conceptualized in discussions of the size of government. It *does* matter how the government collects—or chooses not to collect—its revenues (Peters, 1979). It is, in fact, the state-defining aspect of the subsidization of middle-class mortgage holders in Denmark that underlies much of the debate, alluded to above, regarding this particular form of tax expenditure.

A third manner in which the government may influence society with only minimal expenditures for regulation or control is through its contracting powers (Singer, 1979). Clearly, the writing of equal employment or affirmative action requirements into federal contracts in the United States, even given spotty enforcement, has been a more cost-effective means of producing greater employment opportunities for women and minorities than an attempt at direct controls would have been. This is not to say that it has not been costly, but, rather that much of the cost has been displaced upon private employers and hence onto consumers. We are dealing here with a form of taxation intended to achieve a collective objective. We do not want to raise the question of whether such taxation at several removes through the private sector is proper or costly. Rather, we wish to emphasize the incomplete and insensitive nature of existing conceptions of growth in the case of our illustration, perhaps more of the state than of government. Finally, the contracting powers of government as a major purchaser of goods and services may allow it to influence, even control, such factors as prices without resort to direct, formal controls.

One good example of the influence of the contracting powers for purposes of influencing the economy and society in the United States is the Davis-Bacon Act, requiring federal contractors to pay prevailing union wages whether they use union labor or not.[13] Although this legislation does not require the use of unions, it does make it easier to use union labor, as there are no direct economic advantages to using nonunion labor.

A fourth means by which government can influence its society without direct expenditure is through insurance (Aharoni, 1980). The use of insurance may obligate governments to spend money under certain conditions, but in all except the most exceptional circumstances the actual outlays will be much less than the potential obligations. Also, those outlays will be much less than probable impact on the society or economy. These types of public insurance, especially on bank deposits and on crops, are common in many countries. The socialization of risk in Western societies has allowed the public sector substantial influence over the economy and the utilization of resources with the expenditure of only relatively small amounts of money and manpower.

With the use of regulatory and self-regulatory policies, tax expenditures, contracting powers, and insurance obligations we see that government can attempt to control societal activities without directly intervening through large and costly expenditures or bureaucracies. Governments can structure individual or organizational choices without directly compelling action, as with tax expenditures (Schultze, 1977). The use of incentives for private action provides an alternative—or, perhaps more accurately, a complementary—means of governing, which may or may not be more efficient than conventional expenditure—intensive programs. In any case these controls might never be counted in a normal science conceptualization of the growth of government. This is especially important as taxpayer resistance forces governments to seek lower costs options for action at the same time that most citizens have come to expect the mitigation of most social and economic ills through government action.

The public sector. The second term commonly applied to the metaphenomenon we are investigating is the public sector. It is usually defined in rather narrow economic terms, rather than as the scope of activity or authority of governments. There are, however, fundamental problems in the prevailing conception and usage of the term "public sector." There is a commonplace assumption that what is public can be differentiated from what is private. In fact, that distinction is generally very elusive; and in some circumstances it cannot be made meaningfully at all. Perhaps the most outstanding feature of the mixed economy welfare state is the blending and confounding of public and private. Some of these problems are detailed below in our discussion of economic classifications of public and private activities; but at this juncture it may be useful to point out the increasing tendency to mix public and private roles through political and institutional practices (Nadel, 1975).

The inceasing blending of public and private roles appears to follow from pressures by both public and private actors. On the one hand, public institutions in many advanced industrial societies have sought increasingly to employ private agencies to implement public policies. This takes the form, first, of the use of nominally private actors—most frequently interest organizations—to perform many public functions, including the legitimate (indeed, often mandated) inputting of information and advice for decisions. More significant, they are often used in the actual administration of public programs in the name of the state. The literature on corporate pluralism or interest intermediation abounds with examples of the use of interest organizations in these capacities; and for some systems there is now evidence of the comprehensive, institutionalized, legitimate operation of such practices throughout the policy universe (Olsen, 1981). Governments have also sought to use privatized means to accomplish their goals, perhaps due to a desire to reduce or obscure accountability. The creation of a corporation to administer the foreign relations of the United States with Taiwan, though not without historical parallel (e.g., the British East India Company), represents a "hiving-off" of one of the fundamental, traditional functions of the state.

The process of admixture of public and private roles operates from the other direction as well. As Johan P. Polsen has pointed out, "governmental agencies frequently operate as representatives of organized interests" (Olsen, 1981: 502). The literature on corporate pluralist regimes abounds with illustrations of this tendency (Heisler, 1974; Kvavik, 1976), and it can be found in a wide array of modern societies that are not generally characterized as corporate pluralist. Thus, for instance, in the United Kingdom "quangos" (quasi-nongovernmental organizations) are prime examples of the development of organizations outside normal lines of authority and control. They perform public functions, spend public money, and their members often have Crown appointments, but yet are not made easily accountable to elected political officials for their actions (Hogwood, 1979; Hood, 1981). The literatures on contemporary Danish, Belgian, Dutch, Israeli, Australian, and American policy structures also abound in illustrations of this trend.

Private actors have also placed pressures on governments for the *deinstitutionalization* of many of the activities nominally reserved for government acting as agent for the state. Both the state and interest organizations may stand to benefit from the corporate pluralist and other arrangements noted above. Likewise, private firms have sought special arrangements and financial assistance from governments in order to assure their continued existence or even their profit levels, as negotiations between Chrysler and the American government in 1979, the French government's assistance to the steel industry, and numerous British examples of bail outs would indicate.[14] Viewed in this light, the impression that in many cases government is becoming little more than a collection of numerous private interests does not seem entirely unfounded; and the attempt to differentiate those activities that are truly public from those that are truly private may have become a virtually futile exercise.[15]

When we move to the economic components of the public sector, we encounter a number of important problems in definition and conceptualization. The public sector is frequently narrowly defined in terms of levels of taxation, expenditure, and debt creation. The treatment of the activities of state enterprises often differs, although the most common approach is to count only the trading balance of these enterprises in public accounts[16] Thus if a public enterprise loses money, the amount of subsidy needed to meet operating costs (leaving aside the many complex questions involving subsidies coming from capital grants and tax exemptions) is counted as a component of public expenditure. If, as with the British Post Office and British Gas in 1978, a public corporation should make a profit, then in many accounting schemes this would be a net *reduction* of the size of public expenditure and, thus, of the public sector. When government is a monopoly provider of a service this is a real problem; but in cases in which there is competition between governmentally owned and private-sector firms (assuming for the moment that such delineation can be made sharply and with confidence), this form of accounting may actually obscure the growth of the public sector. The growth of the trading revenues of a public enterprise may be an indication that this enterprise is crowding out the private firm, while the accounts would show a negative contribution to public expenditures and hence a smaller public sector. Since there are numerous nontrivial cases in which public and private firms compete, for example, in broadcasting and air traffic in several countries, this is a significant problem in conceptualization and measurement; and as the admixture of public and private business together with the tendency in a number of countries to reprivatize is growing, we think it a problem of increasing importance.[17]

What is left out of the public sector? At least three elements must be added to the narrow definition of the public sector in order to make it a useful concept for political—and even perhaps for economic—analysis. The first, following directly from the discussion above, is a more complete measurement of the operations and impacts of government-owned, operated, and controlled firms. While this may entail the opening of an immense Pandora's box, it does address the complexity of the problem. The most fundamental question here is under what circumstances is a firm or enterprise owned by the government or the state? Some industries, for example, the railroads of most European countries, British Steel, or Gaz de France, are clearly and directly nationalized. However, when we begin to look at a more varied range of examples, the dividing line between public and private firms becomes very blurred indeed. Some firms may be only partially owned by the state, with the government being only one of numerous stockholders, as in the case of the Scandinavian

Airlines System. In Belgium, *intercommunales*, as the name implies, are consortia established to provide services that cannot be provided by individual municipalities or where the economies of scale clearly militate in favor of joint enterprises. However, *intercommunales* are legally private entities; they often operate like private firms or associations despite producing public services and their status as product of agreements among local governments. Those providing basic public goods and services—such as gas, water, electricity, and public transportation—might lend themselves to classification with public sector activities more readily than those charged with generating capital for regional development and planning and implementing such development. However, even the activities of the former class of *intercommunales* do not permit straightforward accounting treatment, since their capital generation, investment, and other financial operations fit readily into neither governmental nor private sector molds.[18]

In other countries the dividing line between public and private enterprises may be even more obscure. In Italy, for example, despite the fact that the two large holding companies, IRI and ENI, are public holding companies, many of their subsidiaries operate very much as if they were accountable only to market forces (Holmans, 1978: 7). In similar fashion the National Enterprise Board in the United Kingdom has used public funds to buy up shares in private firms, frequently as a means of supporting declining or infant industries. Especially when those firms are only partially owned by government, they tend to continue to function very much as private entities, for example, the *statligt aktiebolaget* in Sweden. In the United States anyone riding an Amtrak or a Conrail train may wonder whether he or she is using a public or a private conveyance. In Israel the close connection between the government, the major labor union federation, and several important firms makes the sorting out of public from private still more difficult (Sharkansky, 1979). Similar or even more confounding arrangements can be found in many other countries as well.

A development in France in September 1978, noted in passing above, provides perhaps the sharpest illustration of this conundrum and of the general problem of distinguishing the public and private sectors. The five largest steel-producing firms in France have been in severe financial difficulty for some years (due mainly to intense competition from Japanese exports and to structured inefficiencies). They had received numerous, sizable government loans; and the prospects for repayment were ebbing. Consequently, accompanying its response to the industry's recent and most severe financial crisis, the government created three holding companies taking control of two-thirds of the stock in the five companies and leaving the remainder in the hands of the private owners of the firms. In return for its controlling interest, the government is forgiving the firms' debts. Yet, notwithstanding its two-thirds interest and massive financial participation, the government does not consider that it owns the firms. It expressly denied during public discussions of its 1978 actions that the new arrangements were tantamount to nationalization; and it stressed that it expected the firms to operate—presumably in the future, since they clearly had not in the past—in terms of profit-making principles.[19]

This action was far from unique. It is part of a growing pattern in Europe and is not unlike American actions with regard to railroads. Further, the mercantile policies of the Japanese government, pursued during the past two decades and seemingly expanding, represent a variant of government intervention in the interest of profitability in internationally competitive sectors and often in order to preserve jobs in threatened industries (or to sustain an industry deemed politically or symbolically essential). If Japanese industries encounter unfavorable conditions in the future, it seems reasonable to predict that bail out measures would be taken by the government.

Such actions and the resultant structures defy classification in terms of the common rubrics public and private; and they confound notions of governmental control. The point here is that governmental control need not be total or clear-cut. Increasingly, it is partial and takes the form of debt management, regulation, management policy influence, and the like; but the firm affected remains at least partially in the market sector. However, such a nominal distinction between the public and private sectors obscures the magnitude of changes in the size of the public sector (and of government) and perhaps even the direction of such changes. Political expediency, economic necessity, and varied patterns of historical development (not to mention ad hoc responses to specific events or needs) may well muddy the dividing line between public sector and private sector organizations (Myrdal, 1960: 64-66). Equally or perhaps even more difficult problems are presented by the broad sector of *parastatal* operations, which can be classified as one will. However, such entities and their classification are crucial in gauging accurately the magnitude of public sector growth.

A second category of firms that have obvious public sector implications are those whose primary client or purchaser is government. The defense industry in any country is an obvious example, as are firms producing goods as diverse as school buses, police equipment and, in some societies, commercial aircraft and hospital equipment. Even when government is not in a monopsonistic position, it may well be the principal purchaser of some goods and therefore in a position to influence substantially the activities of a firm. And governments, beginning from low baselines, seem increasingly inclined to use their purchasing power to regulate the quality, nature, and price of the goods produced in the private sector, with regard to safety features, for example, often preceding formal regulation in that policy area. (Governments in most countries also can use their purchasing leverage for gaining compliance with policies or even guidelines regarding price and wage levels, employment and management practices, investment policies and virtually all other policy or political desiderata.)

In the monopsonistic case, and to some degree in cases of less complete purchasing control, firms in the role of purveyor to government cannot be said to be entirely private in the last quarter of the twentieth century. Their existence is largely dependent on the procurement decisions of government agencies, especially in defense, and their policies and behavior must be related to that special association with government. This need by no means be a disadvantage for such firms, however; and many profit, some perhaps excessively, from their connections with the public sector. They may also become less effective competitors on the market (particularly internationally), and thus progressively more dependent on government. At that juncture the practices discussed in conjunction with the first point in this section may become operative.

Third, some consideration must be given to organizations and firms that exist with special licenses and virtual mandates from government. Public utilities, communications media in countries where these are not governmentally owned or directly controlled, and to a lesser and varying extent some professions owe their standing to actions taken by some agency of government. These organizations are licensed to work in the public interest, although the nature of the public interest is defined largely by public regulatory activity, and by the often highly political interactions of the regulated and the regulators.

One might extend this already very broad conception and argue that almost everything in a modern society is actually in the public sector, since all activities in such societies are regulated to some degree, more or less directly. However, there is a substantial difference between the corner grocer, whose products are regulated for a variety of reasons and whose occupational safety practices are regulated to accord with public standards, and a large public utility or privately owned broadcast facility, which could not exist without the monopoly market granted it by government and whose prices and profits as well as business practices are determined by government. Again, the conceptual reasons for including these types of firms in a comprehensive delineation of the public sector are compelling. There are real definitional and operational problems; but attempts to ignore or avoid those problems can only lead to confusion and perhaps serious self-deception: the illusion that we have indeed measured the thing we purport to have measured.

Implications

We have discussed the conceptual problems involved in assessing the growth of government, the public sector, or whatever name one wishes to attach to the mechanisms for collective choice in modern society. The numerous points made concerning the deficiencies of each concept as commonly operationalized were not intended to deny the validity of many useful studies but rather to point up the need to conceptualize more clearly and to delineate what is meant when each term is used and, at the same time, to understand better the nature of the elephant we as blind men confront. Conceptualization and operationalization do influence findings, and our belief is that in this case operationalizations have tended to understate significantly the magnitude and nature of the increase in government over the past several decades. There have been a number of recent discussions of the growth of government or the public sector of late. Some have been academic, some popular, and some polemical (Rose and Peters, 1978; Gallaway, 1976; Larkey, 1981). If our belief concerning the even greater growth of government is indeed correct, then these studies have even greater importance than is commonly understood.

Our most fundamental concern with the growth of government is that of a certain paradox of power. At the same time that government has been growing in terms of the number, range, and extent of its regulations of society, it appears to have lost effective power and authority over the society and indeed its broader environment. It is perhaps the very extent of its activities, their frequently unintended consequences, the presence of contradictory goals of agencies, and the extension of activities to include policy areas not obviously amendable to collective control or the quick technological fix that have led to this unhappy situation (Beer, forthcoming). On the other hand, it may be in the manner in which power has been exercized, rather than the internal nature of the public sector, which has led to the apparent waning of control over the society. Nisbet argues that the Leviathanlike nature of the modern state and its imperial nature have led to a sense of impotence and disaffection by ordinary citizens (Nisbet, 1975: 13-20). Likewise, the system of institutionalized lying that characterized government (in the United States at least) during the late 1960s and early 1970s (if not before or since) is argued to be crucial in the decline of authority. Government may be perceived by the average citizen as a remote and uninfluenceable creature out of control.

As correct as Nisbet may have been for the United States for a very limited time period, a more general case rather contradictory to his can be made. One cause for the weakening of government may be its tendency to subdivide and deinstitutionalize its control over society, using a wide variety of instrumentalities to accomplish this end (Sharkansky, 1979). This change in the exercise of authority results in part from democratic and participatory pressures resulting in direct grants of power to extragovernmental actors, allowing them to control their own affairs. It also results from technocratic initiatives, based upon the expertise of a group as a means of avoiding policy conflicts. Finally, it may result from the inability or unwillingness of governments and partisan politicians to make decisions about the hard issues on which they are sure to offend most if not all voters.[20]

From whatever sources these developments sprang, however, self-regulatory or virtually neofeudal administration of programs may ultimately damage the ability of the state or an individual government to govern (Natchez and Bupp, 1973: 96). The problems of incoherent details, escalating costs, and a general loss of control may frustrate even the hardiest politician. Those elected to office may find it impossible to hold unelected, or unofficial, policy makers responsible for actions having obvious impacts on the society and that are blamed on or credited to the elective officials. Finally, those in government must face the almost inherent illegitimacy of actions taken by individuals or groups lacking discernible legal or constitutional connections of public authority.

The exercise of state authority by parastatal actors may bring into question the whole authority of the state. This frequently results in the inability of the *parastataux* to act either as proper private organizations, that is, they do not make a profit, or to act as public organizations with direct lines of accountability to public, elective officials. Their positions as neither fish nor fowl may make citizens question the efficacy of these forms of organization for accomplishing public purposes, the effectiveness of current governments, and the overall effectiveness of the state. The exercise of authority by corporate-pluralist actors, for example, interest groups acting in public roles, may be equally problematic.[22] Despite the popular dislike for such quasi-governmental arrangements, they may be expected to increase in use as those in government attempt to hide some of the costs of government from citizens and to eliminate controversial issues from their direct control. Paradoxically again, actions that may be optimal for the individual politicians may be decidedly suboptimal for the governing system as a whole.

As government grows through its fiscal operations and through regulation, and as citizens increasingly have contact with government, it appears that many citizens will seek to avoid additional contacts. That is not to say that government is a public bad, or that there are magical limits twenty-five or sixty percent to the percentage of tax in GNP.[23] Rather, it is to point to the frustration, fear, and hostility apparently generated by big government among many citizens. This alienation from government is at times manifested through rather blunt instruments such as Proposition 13 and its sequels, but also may be manifested through more sophisticated and covert actions such as tax evasion and the demonetization of the economy. It may also be manifested through more sophisticated political activity, such as movements for deregulation.

Perhaps ironically, but certainly with significant implications for those unwilling to exercise discipline in thinking, writing, or talking about the phenomenon of the growth of government, the developments alluded to in the preceding paragraph imply an erosion of authority relationships upon which the state is built. Thus the growth of government conceptualized in our broader terms may imply a shrinkage of the state, that is, its domain of effective authority. Thus if the standard measures of the growth of government do not effectively capture developments either in government or in the more elusive public sector, they fail in an even more important manner and degree to reflect changes in the state.

The major questions raised in this chapter concern the form and nature of the contemporary welfare state, as well as its size. It appears that these two issues are inextricably interrelated. As important and interesting as studies in the normal science approach of measuring expeditures and employment have been, they are not sufficient to document the growth of government. We must seek to understand the emerging form of the state and government and the impacts of those forms on citizens. These and related questions are not readily operationalizable. However, they are not inherently philosophical in the sense that they will be intractable to ultimate quantification in some form. Consequently, the choice before us is whether to wait to raise the basic questions until we are able to raise them in a form sanctioned by contemporary social science, or to pose them now without being able to treat them rigorously. By choosing the latter course, we hope to stimulate others to join us in the pursuit of rigorous operationalizations and data better to understand the contemporary state.

NOTES

1. We have performed several studies of this kind in the past, but the complexity of the questions involved in the growth of government have now led us to reexamine seriously the fundamental nature of the enterprise in which we had, until recently, engaged rather uncritically. See Peters (1972); Peters and Klingman (1977); and Heisler and Peters (1978: 149-175).

2. See, for example, Moss (1973).

3. For example, Kneese and Schultze estimate that the cost of environmental regulations passed in 1970 and 1972 would amount to between 280 and 500 billion. See Kneese and Schultze (1975: 73ff); and Schultze (1977: 46-57). See also Weidenbaum (1978); Viscusi (1979).

4. See Bleckman et al. on tax expenditures. (1978: Appendix).

5. Bertram Gross deems the emphasis on the GNP "economic philistinism" (Gross, 1966: ch. 3). See also Hirsh (1977). He argues that growth rates should be discounted because of the inability to increase positional goods in the same way as with manufactured goods.

6. For a comparison of the growth of public employment see Rose (1981) and Eichenberg (this volume).

7. For the most part this chapter is an argument that such boundaries as do exist are very permeable and very fuzzy. We ignore private governments that would make this argument even more complex. See Bachrach (1967: 101-103); Lakoff and Rich (1973); and especially Nadel (1975).

8. This is a dynamic relationship, and the short-run behavior of individual governments will affect the long-run authority of the state.

9. For example, after being reelected in October 1976, Chancellor Schmidt attempted not to index pensions the following January. The political opposition was sufficient to force him to reverse the decision. A similar initiative under the Clark government in Canada produced a very similar reaction, as have current attempts by the Reagan Administration. Arguments that circumstances had changed, or the new government's electoral mandate called for termination rather than continuation of benefits, would tend not to be accepted by many or even most citizens. This would be true not simply because these terminations would be regarded as inimical to the interests of the beneficiaries of specific programs, but also because changes in programs would be regarded as *ultra vires* for any single transient government, as they would be altering the nature of the more permanent bargain that had evolved between citizens and the state.

10. It is important to note that these entitlements are conceptualized as emanating from the state rather than from any particular government of the day. This means effectively than any set of governors may be expected to provide those benefits to citizens: The citizens are, after all, entitled *as citizens*. Some entitlements may continue after the end of a state (e.g., West Germany continues to pay benefits to the widows and veterans from two former regimes, as well as to compensate the victims of one). The summary point for this brief discussion of changes in the nature and scope of the modern state is that changes in its fundamental dimensions do not necessarily covary with or reflect changes in the scope of government, and governments can not always affect ebbs and flows in the scope of the state. Just as a simple (and, as we have sought to show, simplistic) measurement of the size of government does not capture effectively, in either a theoretical or policy-related sense, actual changes in the scope and domain of government activity and influence, so too even the more complex and broadly contextualized assessment of change at the level of government fails to reflect accurately alterations in the nature and magnitude of the state. Thus to assume, as a multitude of writers have in recent years, that increasing governmental activity and involvement in social and economic relationships per force denotes an increment in the power of the state is unwarranted and possibly wrong.

11. For example, Inglehart (1977). For a more polemical view see Harris and Selden (1979).

12. While most studies express these concerns conceptually, the measurements used stress only expenditures and/or unemployment.

13. Of course, a good deal of the cost of this mandate is reflected in public expenditure.

14. The Chrysler bail out is by no means unique either cross-nationally or within the United States. In the United States the examples of Lockheed and the railroads are most instructive.

15. One of the strongest statements of this position is in Lowi (1979).

16. For example, the SNA system excludes the operation of state enterprises except when subsidies must be paid. For a discussion of the ensuing problems see Holmans (1978).

17. Public and private airlines operate on approximately the same routes and timetables but apparently with quite different costs, at least in the Australian case.

18. For a general treatment of intercommunales in Belgium, see Hautphenne (1966).

19. See "Giscard Steels Himself for Nationalization" (Economist, 1978).

20. For an analysis of the United States Congress in these terms, see Fiorina (1977).

21. This is evidenced by the current round of "quango bashing" in the United Kingdom.

22. This is evidenced by the Danish electoral campaign in the fall of 1979 in which perhaps the major issue was the role of interest groups in policy making. See "Ungovernable Denmark Turns a Shade Less So" (Economist, 1979: 51).

23. Long ago Colin Clark argued that twenty-five percent was the upper limit of government spending that would not produce significant inflation. More recently, Milton Friedman has argued that government spending over sixty percent would threaten political freedom.

REFERENCES

AHARONI, Y. (1980) The No-Risk Society. Chatham, NJ: Chatham House.

BACHRACH, P. (1967) The Theory of Democratic Elitism. Boston: Little, Brown.

BEER, S. H. (forthcoming) "Political overload and federalism," in Victoria Shuck and Josephile Milburn (eds.) New England Politics. Cambridge, MA: Schenkman.

BELL, D. (1974) "The public household—on fiscal sociology and the liberal society." Public Interest 37 (Fall): 76-81.

BLECKMAN, J. et al. (1978) Setting National Priorities: the 1979 Budget. Washington, DC: Brookings Institution.

Economist (1979) "Ungovernable Denmark turns a shade less so." 27 October.

_____ (1978) "Giscard steels himself for nationalization." September 23: 95-96.

FIORINA, M. (1977) Congress: Keystone of the Washington Establishment.New Haven, CT: Yale University Press.

GALLAWAY, D. (1976) The Public Prodigals. London: Temple Smith.

GROSS, B. (1966) "The state of the nation," in Raymond Bauer (ed.) Social Indicators. Cambridge: MIT Press.

HARRIS. R. and A. SELDEN (1979) Over-Ruled on Welfare. London: IEA.

HAUTPHENNE, P. (1966) Les associations de communes en Belgigue.Bruxelles: Union de Villes et Communes Beleges.

HEILBRONER, R. L. (1970) "On the limited relevance of economics." Public Interest 21 (Fall): 80-93.

HEISLER, M. O. with R. KVAVIK (1974) "Patterns of European politics: the European polity model," in Martin O. Heisler (ed.) Politics in Europe. New York: David McKay.

_____ and B. G. PETERS (1978) "Comparing social policies across levels of government, countries and time," pp. 149-175 in Douglas E. Ashford (ed.) Comparing Public Policies. Beverly Hills, CA: Sage.

HIRSCH, F. (1977) The Social Limits of Growth. London: Routledge & Kegan Paul.

HOGWOOD, B. W. (1979) The Tartan Fringe: Quangos and Other Assorted Animals in Scotland. Studies in Public Policy No. 34. Glasgow: University of Strathclyde.

HOLMANS, S. K. (1978) The Italian Public Expenditure System. Government Service Working Paper 3 (May) London: Her Majesty's Treasury.

HOOD, C. (1981) "Axeman, spare the quango," in Christopher Hood and Maurice Wright, (eds.) Big Government in Hard Times. Oxford: Martin Robertson.

INGLEHART, R. (1977) "Political disaffection and mass support for social change in advanced industrial societies." Comparative Political Studies 10: 455-472.

KNEESE, A. V. and C. L. SCHULTZE (1975) Pollution, Prices and Public Policy. Washington, DC: Brookings Institution.

KVAVIK, R. B. (1974) "Interest groups in a 'cooptive' political system: the case of Norway," in Martin Heisler, (ed.) Politics in Europe. New York: David McKay.

LAKOFF, S. and D. RICH (1973) Private Government. New York: Scott, Foresman.

LARKEY, P. D., C. STALP, and M. WINER (1981) "Theorizing about the growth of government." Journal of Public Policy 1: 157-220.

LEUCHTENBERG, W. E. (1963) Franklin D. Roosevelt and the New Deal, 1932-1940. New York: Harper & Row.

LOWI, T. J. (1979) The End of Liberalism. New York: Norton.

MOSS, M. (ed.) (1973) The Measure of Economic and Social Performances. New York: Columbia University Press.

MYRDAL, G. (1960) Beyond the Welfare State. New Haven, CT: Yale University Press.

NADEL, M. V. (1975) "The hidden dimension of public policy: private governments and the policy-making process." Journal of Politics 36 (February): 2-34.

NATCHEZ, P. B. and I. C. BUPP (1973) "Policy and priorities in the budgetary process." American Political Science Review 67: 313-328.

NISBET, R. (1975) The Twilight of Authority. New York: Oxford University Press.

OLSEN, J. P. (1981) "Integrated organizational participation in government," pp. 492-516 in P. C. Nystrom and W. H. Starbuck (eds.) Handbook of Organizational Design. New York: Oxford University Press.

OLSON, M. and C. K. CLAGUE (1976) "Dissent in economics: the convergence of extremes," pp. 79-99 in Ryan C. Amacher Robert D. Tollison, and Thomas D. Willett (eds.) The Economic Approach to Public Policy: Selected Readings. Ithaca, NY: Cornell University Press.

PETERS, B. G. (1980) "Public employment comes home: the growth of public employment in the United States." Studies in Public Policy 63. Glasgow: University of Strathclyde.

————— (1979) "The determinants of tax policy." Policy Studies Journal 7: 787-794.

————— (1972) "Economic and political effects in the development of social expenditures in France, Sweden and the United Kingdom." Midwest Journal of Political Science 16: 225-238.

————— and David Klingman (1977) "Patterns of expenditure development in Sweden, Norway and Denmark." British Journal of Political Studies 7: 387-412.

ROSE, R. (1981) Changes in Public Employment. Studies in Public Policy 6. Glasgow: University of Strathclyde.

————— (1976) "On the priorities of government: a developmental analysis of public policy." European Journal of Political Research 4, 3: 247-289.

————— (1973) "Models of governing." Comparative Politics 5: 465-496.

————— and B. Guy Peters (1978) Can Government Go Bankrupt? New York: Basic Books.

SALISBURY, R. (1977) "Corporatism in America." Presented at 1977 meeting of American Political Science Association, Washington, D.C.

SCHULTZE, C. L. (1977) The Public Use of Private Interest. Washington; DC: Brookings Institution.

SHARKANSKY, I. (1979) Whither the State? Chatham, NY: Chatham House.

SINGER, J. W. (1979) "The determinants of tax policy." Policy Studies Journal 7: 787-794.

SOLOW, R. M. (1970) "Science and ideology in economics." Public Interest 21 (Fall): 94-107.

U.S. Bureau of the Census (1981) Statistical Abstract of the United States, 1981. Washington: Government Printing Office.

VISCUSI, W. K. (1979) "The impact of occupational safety and health regulation." Bell Journal of Economics 10, (Spring): 117-140.

WEIDENBAUN, M. (1979) "The high cost of government regulation." Challenge 22: 32-39.

————— (1978) The Costs of Government Regulation. St. Louis, MO: Centers for the Study of American Business.

WILLIS, J. R. M. and P. J. W. HARDWICK (1978) Tax Expenditures in the United Kingdom. London: Heinemann.

PART V

Explaining
Public Sector Growth

CHAPTER 11

THE FUNCTIONAL STRUCTURE OF PUBLIC EXPENDITURES
Long-Term Changes

J Ü R G E N   K O H L

The notion of the use of public expenditure data for indicators of state activities is an old one. Adolph Wagner argued that "the law of growing state demand for expenditures is but the *financial* formulation of the general law of expanding state activities" (Wagner, 1893: 892, translation by author). Some objections can be raised, however. These stem primarily from the argument that different spending or costs intensities apply to different activities (Zimmermann, 1973). Governments may use other resources than fiscal intervention; regulation by law and effective sanctions may be important to a government's range of control, but they will not show up in the budget figures.[1] Structural shifts may occur in the mix between activities that lead to over-or underestimations of the scope of state interventionism. For example, new political tasks such as the provision of welfare may be more cost-intensive than older tasks such as preserving law and order. A related argument is that as productivity increases more slowly in the public sector than in the private, expenditure data are likely to give an inflated measure of the growth of the real volume of public goods. On the other hand, the real growth of government may be obscured by budget figures because governments may

AUTHOR'S NOTE: The research reported here was carried out under the aegis of the Historical Indicators of West European Democracies (HIWED) project, directed by Professor Peter Flora at the Universities of Mannheim and Cologne. It was funded by grants from the Volkswagen Foundation. I am especially grateful for Franz Kraus, who generously made available to me his dataset on national income and product and to Richard Eichenberg for his competent advice and support in preparing the machine-readable data files.

shift their activities towards less cost-intensive forms of intervention and shift costs from the public to the private sector.[2]

There is considerable question as to whether or not the shifts have indeed taken place. This is all the more reason why they should be examined empirically, but the actual structure of public expenditure must be taken as a starting point. Expenditure commitments do not necessarily bring a realization of goals or a better quality of services, but because appropriations have opportunity costs, they do reveal hidden preferences of governments. Hence, information on the historical development of the size and structure of public expenditures seems to be interesting in its own right but should also form the facts to be explained by a positive theory.

Cross-national analyses of public expenditures have confined themselves primarily to comparisons of aggregate expenditure levels and to explanations in terms of economic growth and levels of socioeconomic development. An overview of these analyses is found in Musgrave (1973). Longitudinal studies of single countries have taken changes in the composition of expenditures into account (Peacock and Wiseman, 1967; Andic and Veverka, 1964; Weitzel, 1968; Edmond-Grange, 1963). These analyses have tended to interpret changes in terms of the peculiarities of national histories. The approach in this chapter is to combine the advantages of both perspectives by extending the time perspective, by disaggregating expenditure levels, and by analyzing multiple countries simultaneously.

Particular factors may explain only certain portions of public expenditure or they may affect different expenditure items in different ways. Disaggregation is required to study the different effects of selected demographic, technological, or socioeconomic factors and to detect the prime movers behind general expenditure growth. Classification schemes for public expenditure items, developed along policy areas, lend themselves more easily to political and sociological interpretations than do economic distinctions such as public consumption, public investment, and transfer expenditures that were developed for other purposes.

Some Problems of
Public Expenditure Classification

Conceptualizations of state functions underlying the classification scheme presented here were developed by Deutsch (1980), Rostow (1971), and Rose (1976) (see Table 11.1). In spite of variations in labeling, the three of them have some consensus on the relevant functions. The following is an attempt to reconcile their theoretical conceptions with the statistical categories needed for empirical research. A classification scheme for expenditure by policy area or purpose should meet these requirements:

TABLE 11.1 Matching Public Expenditure Categories to Theoretical Concepts of State Functions

Expenditure Categories	Functional Complexes	State Functions According to: Rostow (1971)	Rose (1976)	Deutsch (1980)
Defense	Defense	(External) Security	Defense of territorial integrity	Maintenance of order against external threats: pursuit of power
General Administration Judiciary and Police	Administration and justice	Constitutional order	Mobilizing finance Maintaining internal order	Maintenance of order against domestic threats
Industry and Commerce, Agriculture Transport and Communications	Economic and environmental services	Growth	Mobilizing physical resources	Pursuit of wealth (by economic development)
Social Security	Social services (in a narrow sense)	Welfare	Providing social benefits	Provision of welfare through social, medical, or educational services
Health				
Housing	(in a broader sense)			
Education and science				
Debt Interests				

- the functional categories should be sufficiently general in application and stable over time as to allow comparability;
- they should be concrete and familiar enough to be matched with the classifications used in national reports without undue discrepancy;
- total expenditures should be allotted as completely as possible to specific functions without large residual categories;
- the categories should not be too large in number and should represent important shares of total expenditures.

Ten separate categories were identified.[3] The aggregation to more comprehensive groupings, however, improves cross-national comparability. By summarizing expenditures in adjacent policy areas, some blurred distinctions are likely to disappear. On the other hand, the detailed categories may be sufficiently comparable over time to be suitable for interpretation within the national context. Moreover, the disaggregated figures allow alternative means of summing.

Whenever available, existing appropriate functional classifications of expenditures were used. Usually with the nineteenth-century data one must resort to administrative classifications and list expenditures according to the responsibilities of departments. Unfortunately, the same or similar functions may be performed by different departments and agencies, and the same department or agency may perform functionally different kinds of activities. Relying exclusively on department or agency breakdowns would thus lead to serious distortions in both historical and cross-national comparisons. It is helpful, therefore, to disaggregate the institutions; administrative subdivisions within a department frequently correspond more closely to functions as defined in Table 11.1. This is particularly true of the nineteenth-century ministries of the interior, which later gave birth to ministries of justice, industry and commerce, agriculture, labor, social affairs, and so on.

Since national official statistics are the predominant data sources, temporal comparisons are generally more reliable than cross-sectional ones. This suggests that the most appropriate strategy for comparison is first to examine historical trends and structural changes within countries and then to compare developmental trends cross-nationally. Direct comparisons of levels of expenditure and shares of functional categories cross-nationally are risky.[4]

Changing Priorities in the Structure of Public Expenditures

It was suggested above that the functional structure of public expenditures can be perceived as reflecting the preferences of governments in the allocation of resources. The changing priorities of government are more sensitively revealed that way than by any analysis of departmental differentiation. Shifts in priorities can be indicated even when there is no change in organization. That the bulk of expenditures are fixed by legal obligations is no contradiction to this view. It only means that in contemporary states, actual priorities change slowly, perhaps sometimes in dramatic contrast to the program statements of politicians. However, in the medium or long run, systematic changes can be unmistakably observed.

Examination of the changing structure of public expenditures in four major West European and four Scandinavian countries demonstrates the basic developmental pattern suggested by Rose (1976). From as far back as data sources go until about one hundred years ago, the defining activities of the state (defense of its territory, maintenance of internal order, mobilization of finance) absorbed the largest share of total expenditures (see Figure 11.1).[5] If interest on the public debt, then incurred mostly because of war, is added to these activities, they account for three-fourths of all expenditures. The military was especially important in the nineteenth century. Its share was seldom less than twenty percent of the total and often reached forty percent. Governments were preoccupied with striving for international power and status or with preserving their territorial integrity. Economic and social concerns were mostly ignored or left to local government. Most of the social expenditures that were allocated were devoted to education rather than welfare.

Even prior to World War I, however, a slow but continuous trend toward an increasing share of public expenditure for social purposes began. This trend was reinforced between the wars and in the period since World War II. Moreover, in the interwar period claims for social welfare and health expenditures surpassed education expenditures. Expenditures for economic and environmental services, however, have not gained predominance in the budgets of any of the countries.

In 1970 no Western European central government spent less than forty percent of its resources on social services (including education). The long-term shift toward this category is certainly the most significant structural change in the composition of public expenditures during the last century. Although social policy relies more heavily than other policies on "intervention by money," its predominance in contemporary budgets gives a hard data meaning to the notion of the welfare state. Expenditures for the military have declined to about ten percent more or less, and expenditure shares for general financial and judicial administration are even smaller.

These secular changes are brought out more clearly in Table 11.2, which categorizes countries by the predominant functions in their budgets (Deutsch, 1980). The first predominance type is defined as one in which outlays for defense and administration are larger than all economic and social service expenditure together. The second is defined as a type in which the reverse is true. The third is characterized by the prevalence of social

…

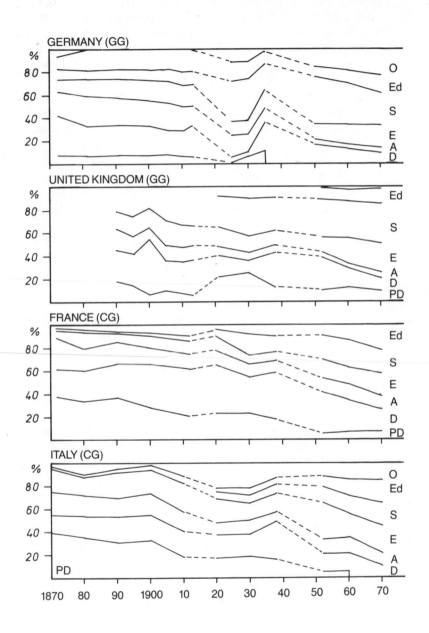

FIGURE 11.1:   The Changing Structure of Public Expenditures

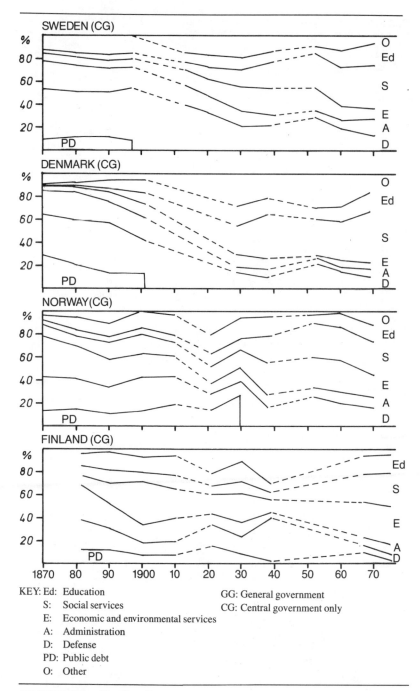

KEY: Ed: Education
   S: Social services
   E: Economic and environmental services
   A: Administration
   D: Defense
   PD: Public debt
   O: Other

GG: General government
CG: Central government only

FIGURE 11.1 (Continued)

TABLE 11.2 A Typology of States by Structure of Public Expenditures

Country	Level	Type 1	Type 2	Type 3
Belgium	Central 1835-1900		1931-1938, 1953-1975	1934-1936, 1959-1975
Denmark	Central 1869-1901		1929/1938, 1952-1975	1929/1938, 1952-1975
	General		1929/1938, 1952-1975	1929/1938, 1952-1975
Finland	Central 1882-1884, 1918-1920, 1939-1945		1885-1917, 1921-1938, 1946-1951, 1967-1975	1967-1975
France	Central 1822-1931, 1933/1937/1938, 1952/1953		1932/1934-1936, 1947-1951 1954-1975	1962-1975
Germany	Central 1913		1925-1932, 1950-1975	1925-1932, 1950-1975
	General 1872-1900		1906-1913, 1925-1935, 1948-1975	1925-1934, 1948-1975
Italy	Central 1862-1904, 1906/1907, 1909-1920, 1922 1925-1930 1934-1944		1905/1908, 1921/1923/1924, 1931-1933, 1945-1973	1958-1973
Netherlands	Central 1850-1922, 1933, 1937-1939, 1948-1954		1923-1932, 1934-1936, 1955-1975	1958-1975
Norway	Central 1865-1918		1919-1939, 1946-1975	1920-1938, 1946-1975
	General		1915/1920, 1925-1971	1920, 1925-1971
Sweden	Central 1865-1897, 1913-1920, 1924 1940-1944		1922, 1926-1938 1946-1975	1948-1975
	General 1940-1944		1913-1938 1946-1958	1913/1914, 1920-1938, 1946-1958
United Kingdom	Central 1890-1920, 1938		1921-1937, 1950-1975	1923-1936, 1950/1951, 1956-1975
	General 1890-1900, 1915-1918		1905-1913, 1920-1975	1921-1975

NOTE Type 1: Outlays for defense and administration are larger than all economic and social service expenditures.

Type 2: Outlays for economic activities and social services are larger than defense and administration expenditures

Type 3: Social service expenditures alone are larger than defense and administration outlays expenditures over defense and administrative expenditures; thus it is a subset of the second type. This typology allows a rather precise determination of the qualitative changes in the structure of the budgets. Since the countries fall into different types in successive periods, these may also be interpreted as developmental stages.

The turning point at which economic and social services began to predominate in general government budgets was just after World War I. This point, when resources spent for welfare exceeded outlays for defense and financial and judicial administration, might be called the beginning of the modern welfare state. This decisive structural break occurred almost simultaneously in all Western European countries. Because defense and foreign relations are almost exclusively tasks of the central government and social responsibilities are shared among the levels, the turning point at the central level came later than for general government. In the United Kingdom, Germany, and the Scandinavian countries, this point was reached early in the interwar period. For the Netherlands, Belgium, Italy, and France it did not come before the end of the 1950s. This difference cannot be attributed simply to different degrees of centralization. It has to be examined, however, whether it is shaped by different degrees of integration of social security institutions into the central government budget.

In assessing the priorities of government, expenditure shares in the budget seem to be adequate indicators. However, when the degree of state interventionism is to be assessed, the share of government expenditures in the national product has additionally to be taken into consideration.

The assertion that "a change in policy concerns of a state must mean growth" (Rose, 1976: 263) is based on the assumption that the abandonment of activities by governments proceeds at a slower pace than the instigation of activities. In expenditures it is possible that growth can occur in the absence of structural changes, so that all activities grow. It is also possible that priorities may change within a given limit of resources. Figure 11.2 indicates that both types of changes have occurred historically. Primarily, however, changes in priorities have occurred in the context of long-run increases in expenditure levels. Prior to World War I public expenditure levels in the major Western European countries (Germany, the United Kingdom, France, Italy) did not exceed fifteen percent of the GNP. During the interwar period, these countries' public expenditure levels reached twenty to thirty percent and have not been raised substantially since. Scandinavian public expenditures, on the other hand, were initially much lower (about five percent of GNP) and they remained below ten percent during the interwar period. Their major growth came after World War II, when public expenditure levels doubled within two decades.[6]

This growth in the share of gross domestic product devoted to public expenditure means that new budget priorities have not required the reduc-

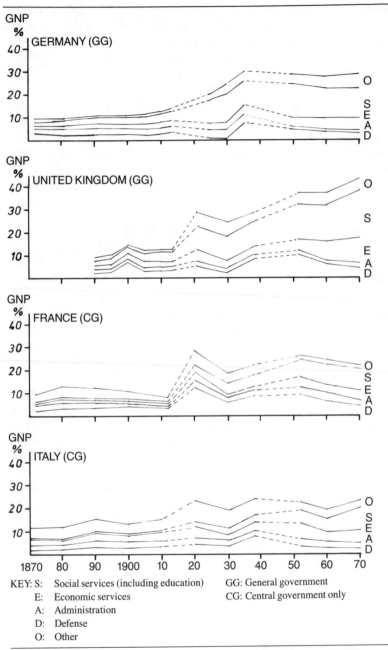

FIGURE 11.2   The Changing Size and Structure of Public Expenditures

tion in older activities. Welfare and educational expenditures have not only gained predominance in the states' budgets but have increased their share in GNP more than tenfold. However, resources spent for military purposes although they rank lower in the priorities of the budgets today absorb larger shares in GNP than a century ago.

Two Models of Developmental Change

We can finally only sketch two models that may help to integrate long-term public sector development into broader theories of economic and political development, respectively.[7] According to Walt Rostow's theory on politics and the stages of growth (1971), creation of the preconditions for take-off to development was primarily a matter of building social overhead capital. The take-off period itself is characterized by the rapid formation of a suitable political, social, and institutional framework for economic growth. This includes the formation or modernization of a rational bureaucratic administration in the Weberian sense, particularly in financial and judicial administration. Expenditures for the institutional infrastructure and public investments in the material infrastructure must be paid for from a national product that is still relatively small. Hence, there is a sharp rise in the state's claims on total economic resources. Later, during self-sustaining growth and the drive toward technological maturity, labor movements and political parties that accompany the process of industrialization demand new social policies including social insurance systems and educational systems with compulsory schooling. At the same time, economic growth supplies the public sector with increasing revenues so that the share of GNP in the public sector need not rise rapidly. This continues into the stage of mass consumption. Later, in what Rostow has called the "search for quality," fundamental value changes bring increasing strains to the political system. Negative external effects of extensive industrial growth are realized. A growing awareness of the deficient provision of public goods and services and an emphasis on redistribution issues lead to growing demands for welfare and education services. Since all of this happens in the context of declining economic growth rates, a rapid rise in the ratio of public expenditure to GNP must be expected. This model is graphically represented in Figure 11.3.

An alternative model of public expenditure development, presented in Figure 11.4, is based upon Stein Rokkan's theory of state and nation building (Rokkan, 1970, 1975). According to Rokkan, nation states in Western Europe were formed through a succession of major developmental crises, the most recent of which were the participation and the distribution crises (see also Almond and Powell, 1966: 73ff; LaPalombara, 1971). In the participation crises the modes and channels of interest articulation and aggrega-

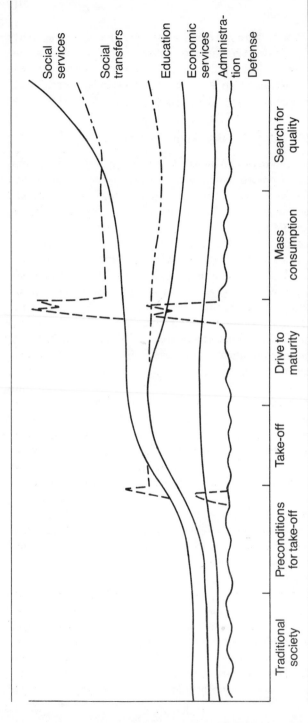

FIGURE 11.3   Public Expenditure Development and the Stages of Economic Growth

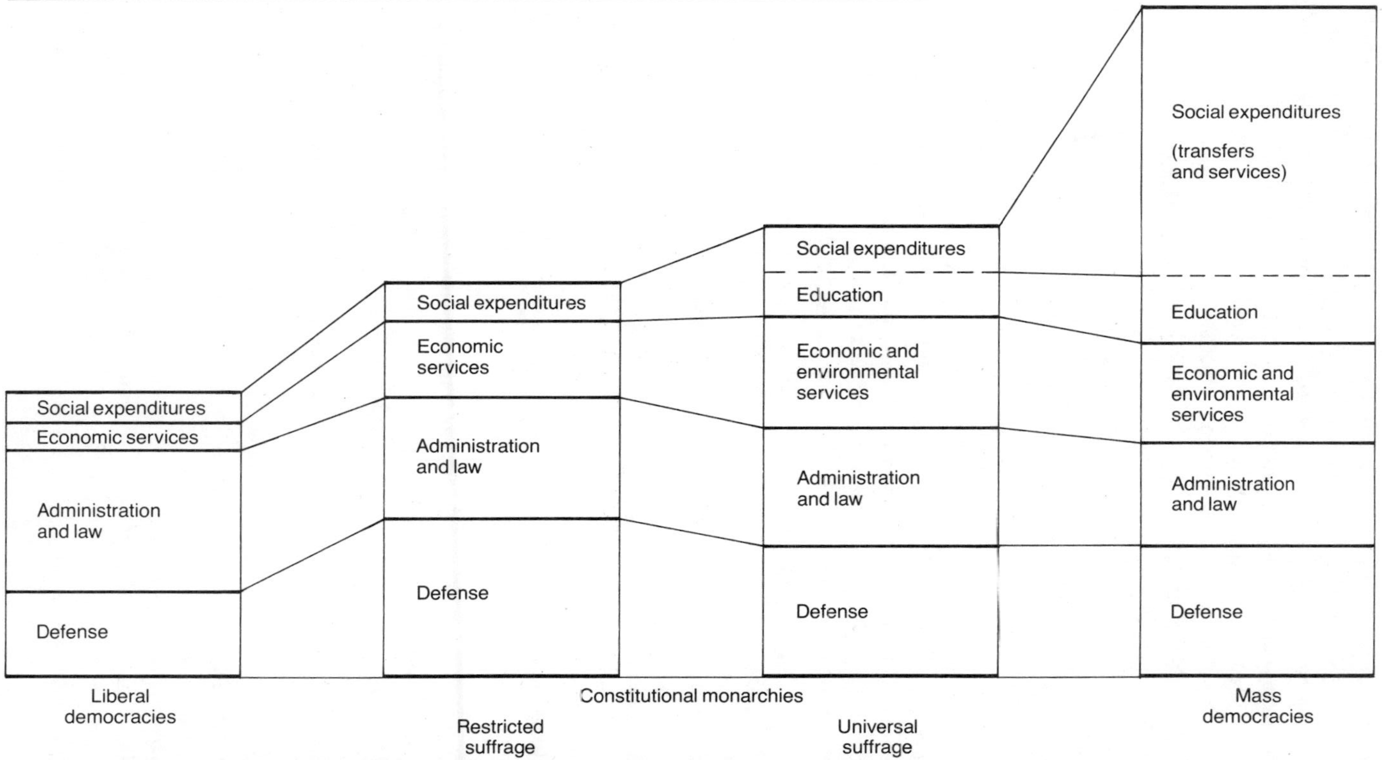

FIGURE 11.4   The Size and Structure of Public Expenditures in Different Political Systems

tion are fundamentally restructured. This is likely to have an impact on political decisions concerning mobilization and allocation of resources and concerning the distribution of benefits and burdens among individuals and groups in society. Hence, the modes and timing of the institutionalization of political participation are particularly relevant in accounting for the specific problems and options in the distribution crisis.

Early bourgeois democracies are characterized by governmental responsibility to parliament, but also by restricted suffrage for their citizens. They are hypothesized to have kept the scope of state activities and therefore the level of state expenditures as low as possible. Restricted suffrage by economic qualifications favors the wealthy, and backed up by the doctrines of economic liberalism, they are strongly opposed to economic and social policy interventions which will disturb the market mechanism. The proper realm of the state's responsibility is seen as the maintenance of general conditions for peacefully living together and for the pursuit of individual self-interest. One would expect expenditures for public order and safety, for the administration of justice, and for other tasks of administration to constitute the largest part of the budget. Governments not fully responsible to parliament are expected to have comparatively higher levels and somewhat different structures of expenditure. Military expenditure especially played a greater role. With less powerful middle classes, they were less subject to the doctrines of economic liberalism. They also had fewer obstacles against economic activities in the mercantilist tradition, and they sometimes even engaged in modernization from above. The scope of social and educational policy depends upon the degree of institutionalized political participation. When the suffrage is restricted, expenditures by parliament on welfare and education are also restricted. As the suffrage is extended, governments become more inclined toward social interventions, partly to divert people from political demands by offering material compensation, and partly to buy the loyalty of the lower strata and to integrate them into the national community. Contemporary mass democracies are characterized by enormous expansions of the politically relevant publics and by a higher responsiveness of the political institutions. Opportunities for participation offered by universal suffrage are made effective by an organizational infrastructure of associations and parties that is reinforced by the mechanisms of competitive party systems. Politically articulated demands tend to produce increasing expenditure levels, with disproportionate increases in social expenditures.

These two models are largely compatible in their conclusions with regard to development trends and typical structural changes of public expenditures. The economic model appears to account for the uniformities of secular tendencies of expenditure development. The political model emphasizes structural differences among political systems independent of the level of socioeconomic development. The economic model leads to more conclusive propositions concerning the level of total expenditure since it takes into account the resources of financing expenditures. The political model allows for more specific hypotheses regarding the functional structure of expenditures by relating them to structural characteristics of the political system.

Carefully constructed time series for a larger number of economic and political variables are needed for a stricter testing of these models. However, matched historical comparisons within broader analytical frameworks such as those developed by Walt Rostow (1971) and Stein Rokkan (1970, 1975) will certainly give us a much better understanding of the changing priorities among governments and of the corresponding changes in the structure of public expenditure over the last one hundred years.

NOTES

1. These functions, of course, require resources also, but the resources expended are not proportionate to the importance of the tasks performed.

2. See Peters and Heisler in this volume.

3. These may be aggregated into more functional complexes. Education, for example, may be considered part of social services or may be kept separate. Debt interest is not strictly a functional category and does not appear with the theoretical concepts; it nevertheless constitutes a part of total expenditure that is of high political significance.

4. Cross-national comparability is diminished by the fact that for most countries data on functional structure of expenditure are available only for the central government. In longitudinal perspective, however, the risks of misinterpretation are minimized. These can be further reduced if the centralized ratio, that is, central government to total government, is known.

5. For graphic presentation, time points in decade intervals (approximately) have been selected from a data collection of annual time series, which is documented in Kohl (1979).

6. The results for the Scandinavian countries are not given here in graphic presentation, but they can be found in the respective chapters, prepared by the author, in Flora (1982).

7. These models have been elaborated in greater detail in Kohl (1979).

REFERENCES

ALMOND, G. and B. POWELL (1966) Comparative Politics: A Developmental Approach. Boston: Little, Brown.
ANDIC, S. and J. VEVERKA (1964) "The growth of government expenditure in Germany since the unification." Finanzarchiv 23: 169-278.
DEUTSCH, K. W. (1980) "Functions and transformations of the state: notes toward a general theory." Wissenschaftszentrum-Berlin. Berlin: International Institute for Comparative Social Research.
EDMOND-GRANGE, J. (1963) Le Budget Fonctionnel en France. Paris: Editions Universitaries.
FLORA, P. (1982) State, Economy, and Society in Western Europe. Frankfurt: Campus.
KOHL, J. (1979) "Staatsausgaben in Westeuropa. Ansätze zur empirischen Analyse der langfristigen Entwicklung der öffentlichen Finanzen in Westeuropa." Ph.D. dissertation, University of Mannheim.

LaPALOMBARA, J. (1971) "Distribution: a crisis of resource management," pp. 233-282 in Leonard Binder et al. Crisis and Sequences in Political Development. Princeton, NJ: Princeton University Press.

MUSGRAVE, R. A. (1973) Fiscal Systems. New Haven, CT, and London: Yale University Press.

PEACOCK, A. T. and J. WISEMAN (1967) The Growth of Public Expenditure in the United Kingdom, London: Allen & Unwin.

ROKKAN, S. (1975) "Dimensions of state formation and nation-building: a possible paradigm for research on variations within Europe," pp. 562-600 in Charles Tilly (ed.) The Formation of National States in Western Europe. Princeton, NJ: Princeton University Press.

————— (1970) "Methods and models in the comparative study of nation-building" and "Nation-building, cleavage formation, and the structuring of mass politics," pp. 46-71 and 72-144 in Stein Rokkan, Citizens. Elections. Parties—Approaches to the Comparative Study of the Processes of Development. Oslo.

ROSE, R. (1976) "On the priorities of government: a developmental analysis of public policies." European Journal for Political Research 4: 247-289.

ROSTOW, W. (1971) Politics and the Stages of Growth. Cambridge: Cambridge University Press.

WAGNER, A. (1893) Grundegung der politischen Ökonomie. Leipzig.

WEITZEL, O. (1968) "Die Entwicklung der Staatsausgaben in Deutschland." Ph.D. dissertation, University of Erlangen-Nürnberg.

ZIMMERMANN, H. (1973) "Die Ausgabenintensität der öffentlichen Aufgabenerfüllung." Finanzarchiv 32: 1-20.

CHAPTER 12

THE GROWTH OF PUBLIC EXPENDITURES
Theory and Evidence from
Six Advanced Democracies

FRANK GOULD

Considerable research has been carried out on the growth of public expenditures relative to gross domestic product (GDP) in the industrialized democracies; yet the question still remains whether or not there are general factors or phenomena, economic, political, social, that explain the observed variation among these countries. The purpose of this chapter is to explore the form of any associations in the data in terms of the major explanatory hypotheses that have been proposed. This analysis will be made at both the aggregated and disaggregated levels, using time-series data for the period 1950 to 1978.

The public expenditure data used in this study have been compiled from national sources because, although there are some internationally compiled public expenditure time series, they are not available for the appropriate length of time at the level of coverage and the degree of functional breakdown required by this study. The data used here cover current and capital expenditures on goods and services and on transfers of both central and local government and provide the most comprehensive measure of the degree of *involvement* of government in the economy. Including transfers is appropriate in attempting to assess government's overall impact on the economy. It is after all

AUTHOR'S NOTE: I am grateful to Roderick Goodyer for valuable research assistance in the assembling of the public expenditure data and for other contributions.

total government expenditure that has to be funded, and it is the level of this aggregate that influences the levels of taxation, borrowing, and interest rates and possibly through them, investment, economic growth, and inflation.

Since our interest is in the growth of public expenditures relative to the economy as a whole, the data are analyzed in terms of annual growth rates of various categories of public expenditure relative to the corresponding growth rates of GDP. All are based upon current market prices and are expressed as a ratio of the former to the latter. Such a measure raises a number of problems; one is that the numerator of the ratio of public expenditure to GDP contains transfers which are not contained in the denominator. Nevertheless, it provides a valid basis of comparison between countries of the degree of total government involvement and is widely used for this purpose. Even though there is no universal functional breakdown of public expenditures, the major categories are still comparable. We are not concerned with attempting to measure how much each country spends on each function but rather with growth rates of particular subcategories and functions within countries. Such differences in definition and coverage as exist do not present a problem.

Countries included in the study will be extended in number at a later time. Apart from some cultural bias (i.e., the preponderance of Anglo-Saxon countries), the current six represent a fiscal cross-section. There are countries with fast-growing public sectors relative to GDP (Sweden, Ireland, the United States), countries with slow-growing public sectors relative to GDP (Germany, New Zealand, the United Kingdom), countries with relatively small (the United States), medium (Germany, New Zealand, the United Kingdom), and large (Ireland, Sweden) public sectors; countries with a high degree of fiscal decentralization (Germany, the United States, Sweden) and a high degree of fiscal centralization (the United Kingdom, New Zealand, Ireland).[1]

Public Expenditures at
the Aggregate Level

In Figure 12.1 total public expenditure (including current and capital expenditures on goods and services and on transfers) of general government is shown as a percentage of GDP for the six countries annually over the period approximately 1950 to 1978. The same raw data are expressed as a ratio of the growth rates of total public expenditure relative to the corresponding growth rates of GDP decade by decade and for the whole period of study in Table 12.1.

Figure 12.1 shows that the ratio of total public expenditure to GDP rose for all six countries over the period of study. However, there is considerable variability between the six countries, with a rapid expansion of the public

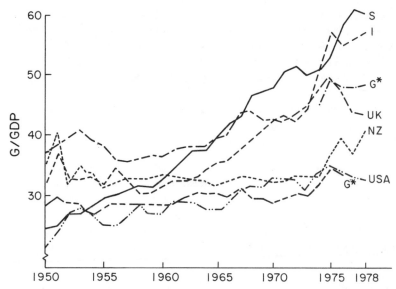

*The broken series for Germany 1950-1976 and 1974-1978 represents a change in both the coverage of the financial statistics and the method of presentation in 1974. Following this change the coverage of social security expenditures was greatly expanded. The old time series therefore understates total government expenditure by several percentage points, as the chart shows. For sources of data of this and subsequent figures, see Appendix.

FIGURE 12.1   General Government Total Expenditures (G) as a Percentage of GDP: Six Advanced Democracies

TABLE 12.1   Ratios of Annual Growth Rates of General Government Total Expenditures to Annual Growth Rates of GDP, 1950-1978

Country	1950-1959	1959-1969	1969-1978	1950-1978*
Germany	1.00	1.03	1.19[1] (1.30)[2]	1.04[3]
Ireland	0.92	1.37	1.26	1.21
New Zealand	0.93	1.03	1.22	1.10
Sweden	1.39	1.51	1.28	1.42
United Kingdom	0.97	1.26	1.03	1.08
United States	1.47	1.23	1.01	1.18

NOTE: For sources of data for this and subsequent tables see the Appendix.
*Growth rates calculated using three-year averages at beginning and end of period:
1. 1969-1974—old series
2. 1974-1978—new series
3. 1950-1974—old series

sector in Sweden, Ireland, and the United States and a more modest expansion in Germany, the United Kingdom, and New Zealand. Table 12.1 shows actual growth rates of total public expenditures relative to GDP. There was an acceleration of the rate of growth of public expenditures to GDP over the whole period in Germany and New Zealand, but the growth rates declined throughout for the United States. In three countries, Ireland, Sweden, and the United Kingdom, the growth ratios peaked during the 1960s. However, all the ratios for the whole period exceed unity, indicating a long-term expansion of total public expenditures relative to GDP.

Wagner's Law. This law, formulated in the late nineteenth century, is generally interpreted to imply that as industrial societies develop and become more prosperous, the state will be called upon to supply an increasing number of services, in particular defense, education, communications, and infrastructure, and these will require an increasing *share* of the nation's resources (Rechtenwald, 1978). Figure 12.1 and Table 12.1 appear to confirm Wag-

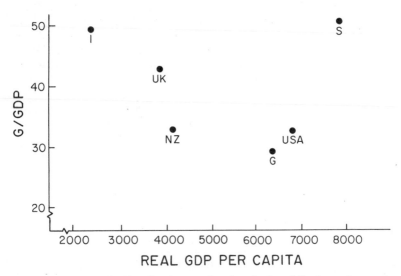

NOTE: The years 1970-1972, directly preceding the adoption of floating exchange rates throughout the world, were selected so as to minimize the distorting effect of subsequent exchange rate fluctuations of GDP conversions to U.S. dollars. However, it should be noted that this does not eliminate distortion since it has been found in a sample of thirty-eight developed and developing countries that conversion at official exchange rates resulted in estimates of per capita GNP that were wrong by an average of twenty-five percent (Barlow, 1977). There are unfortunately no readily available adjusted exchange rate calculations for all six countries of this study.

FIGURE 12.2   General Government Expenditures (G) as a Percentage of GDP and Real Per Capita GDP

ner's law, as indeed do studies using a much longer time period (Peacock and Wiseman, 1967; Andic and Veverka, 1964; Musgrave, 1969; Bird, 1970). However, it has been observed that while there is such a long-term tendency within countries, cross-sectional data among the most developed countries do not confirm Wagner's law in that the levels of development, measured by per capita GDP, are not positively correlated with the relative size of the public sector (Musgrave and Musgrave, 1980: 151; Gupta, 1969).

In fact, from the evidence in Figure 12.2 and from evidence in studies already referred to, there appears to be, if anything, a negative relationship among developed countries between degree of development and relative size of the public sector. The exception in Figure 12.2 is Sweden, which is the only one of the six countries to have had a left of center government for almost the whole of the period of study.[2] Further discussion of this point will be taken up later.

Wagner's law might have been a reasonable prediction of the future course of industrialized societies when formulated, but it contains a number of obvious inherent weaknesses. First, it assumes no revenue constraints on governments as the ratio of public expenditure to GDP rises. In fact, governments have experienced increasing resistance to tax burdens as the growing budget deficits relative to GDP, particularly in the last decade, indicate. Moreover, Wagner did not foresee that at more advanced states of prosperity consumers might wish to substitute private for public consumption in order to gain more freedom of choice. The hypothesis also ignores the effect of ideology—that is, the partisan composition of government—on the growth of the relative size of the public sector.

The observed tendency towards a negative, rather than positive, relationship between the relative size of the public sector and the degree of economic advance might suggest that the ratios are statistical artifacts and that the crucial factor producing differences in the relative size of the public sector is the rate of economic growth (real GDP). It might thus be hypothesized that among interdependent countries there is a tendency for public demands on public provision to be roughly similar, with the result that real public expenditure grows at roughly similar rates in these countries; that is, there may be a strong international demonstration effect in operation, the product of the growth of world trade, tourism, worldwide communications, and international trade unionism. The considerable variability between countries in economic growth rates leads to variability in the capacity to pay for the rising volume of state provided services and the ability to absorb such increases with the public sector's share of GDP rising. Thus the statistical relationship between the growth of public expenditures and GDP among countries will vary negatively with economic growth rates. Figure 12.3 shows this relationship. It does appear to be negative but there is only a poor fit in the data.

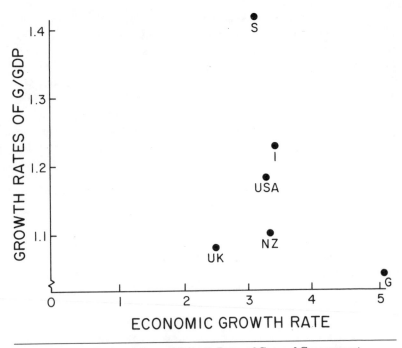

**FIGURE 12.3   Ratios of Annual Growth Rates of General Government
Expenditures to GDP and Rates of Economic Growth
(1950-1978)**

Another way of examining the hypothesis of the international demonstration effect is to consider whether there is any evidence of catching up by countries that commenced the period of study with relatively smaller public sectors. There is some evidence that countries commencing the period with the smallest public sectors experienced the fastest subsequent ratios of growth of public expenditure to GDP (r rank = .49). This relationship is examined in Figure 12.4. Although negative, as would be expected by the catching-up hypothesis, there is clearly a poor fit in the data. While in Ireland there could be an element of catching-up (Lyons, 1973; Kennedy and Dowling, 1974), the case of Sweden suggests subsequent rapid growth of the public sector might be more related to the uninterrupted rule of a left-of-center government. In summary, then, there is no confirmation from the data of Wagner's law among the six countries but some suggestion that its reverse may be true.

The Displacement Effect. This hypothesis, developed by Peacock and Wisemen in 1961 for data over a much longer period of study than this, states that major social upheavals such as wars will lead to a reduction in taxpayer's

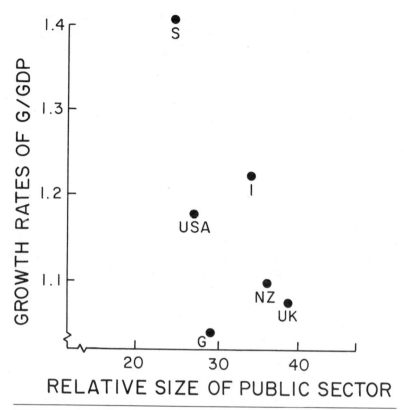

FIGURE 12.4 Ratios of Annual Growth Rates of General Government Expenditures to GDP (G/GDP) and Relative Size of Public Sectors at Outset of Study (average of first three years)

resistance to higher levels of taxation and thus make it possible for governments to fund the higher (required) level of public expenditure. However, because of a ratchet effect, neither public expenditure nor taxation levels subsequently fall back on the precrisis levels and so the public sector is permanently enlarged, displacing private expenditure (Peacock and Wiseman, 1967).

Figure 12.1, however, shows that in the six countries of this study, as for other industrialized democracies (OECD, 1978: 14-15), there has been a long-term upward trend in the ratio of public expenditure to GDP in the absence of a major social upheaval during the postwar period 1950 to 1974. This observation clearly disconfirms the Peacock and Wiseman hypothesis. The United States, which was heavily involved in two wars during this period, shows only a moderate increase in the public expenditure/GDP ratio. However, Figure 12.1 shows clear evidence of a displacement effect in the aftermath of the oil price rise of 1973-1974, which could be described as a major social upheaval. This was followed in all countries by a sharp rise in the public expenditure/GDP ratio ranging from approximately four percentage points (Germany and the United States) through five (the United Kingdom), seven (New Zealand), eight (Sweden), and thirteen (Ireland). Thus from this and other studies examining data covering both world wars of this century, there appears to be unambiguous evidence of the displacement effect (Peacock and Wiseman, 1967; Andic and Veverka, 1964; Musgrave, 1969; Bird, 1970; Rechtenwald, 1978). However, this still leaves the long-term upward trend of 1950 to 1974 unexplained. The Peacock and Wiseman hypothesis clearly explains short-term variations in the ratio of public expenditure to GDP but not the long-term upward trend.

Population increases and demographic changes. An increase in population may lead to demographic change. Depending on the source of the increase, for example, immigration or an increase in births, the subsequent demographic change will make increased demands on particular areas of publicly provided services. One type of demographic change common to most advanced countries has been an aging population. This of course will put increased demands on the various forms of income maintenance and public health expenditure. Examination of these hypotheses will therefore be deferred until later, when the data are disaggregated to the functional level.

The partisan composition of government. There has been a considerable controversy in the social science literature on the extent to which public policy outturns have generally been shaped in the post-World War II period by economic, technological, and social forces rather than by ideological ones. This argument has been formulated in terms of "convergence theory," "decline of ideology," or "consensus politics" (Bell, 1960; Lipset, 1960; Downs, 1957). A number of studies have examined the specific hypothesis that total public expenditure grows faster under governments of the left than right (Burstein, 1979; Gould and Roweth, 1978; Wilensky, 1975). The rationale of this hypothesis, which is not particularly controversial, is that, notwithstanding actual outturns, parties of the left generally claim to favor more strongly increased state intervention, greater public expenditure, and general policies intended to produce a greater redistribution of income than parties of the right. The latter, on the other hand, generally emphasize more strongly individualism, less government intervention, lower taxes, and therefore lower public expenditure.

The findings of these studies are inconclusive. In a recent study Gould and Goodyer examined this hypothesis, using time series data, at both aggregate and functional levels for a number of countries best exemplifying alternating single party or near single party government (Gould and Goodyer,

TABLE 12.2 **Ratios of Annual Growth Rates of General Government Total Expenditures Relative to Corresponding Growth Rates of GDP During All Years in Office, 1950-1978, by Country and by Party[1]**

Country	Party	Party
Germany[2]	SPD/FDP 1.24	CDU/CSU[3] 1.03
Ireland	Fine Gael/Labour 1.61	Fianna Fail 1.14
New Zealand	Labour 1.38	National 1.01
United Kingdom	Labour 1.17	Conservative 1.12
United States[4]	Democrat 1.15	Republican 1.68

1. The coverage for the particular countries as follows:
   Germany, 1950-1976; Ireland, 1948-1977; New Zealand, 1951-1977; United Kingdom, 1951-1977; United States 1952-1978.
2. Grand Coalition of 1966-1968 omitted.
3. CDU/CSU were joined intermittently by other splinter parties.
4. Civilian expenditure only because of distorting effect of defense expenditure.

forthcoming). The five countries were West Germany, Ireland, New Zealand, the United Kingdom, and the United States. The strength of partisan commitment was measured by the ratio of annual growth of public expenditures relative to GDP during all periods of office of the particular parties over the period 1950 to 1978. The details are summarized in Table 12.2. This table shows that in four out of five countries total public expenditures relative to GDP increased more rapidly under governments of the left than right, thus confirming the predicted left-wing outturn. The exception is the United States. Because of the nature of the American party system and the separation of executive and legislative powers in matters of public expenditure, the United States had in any case been assigned a lower probability of fulfilling the prediction of the hypothesis. The overall outturn in Ireland for the Fine Gael/Labor coalitions is heavily influenced by the very rapid expenditure increases which took place under the first interparty government of 1947 to 1951. Irish historians recognize this government as having a strongly influential and ideological element in the cabinet (Lyons, 1973: 560-561, 572-573; O'Leary, 1979: 38). The expenditure performances of the two subsequent Fine Gael/Labor coalitions were very similar to those of the party forming the alternative government—Fianna Fail. This is consistent with the hypothesis because these subsequent Fine Gael/Labor coalitions lacked the partisan element of the first coalition, thus making them ideologically very similar to the Fianna Fail governments (Gould, 1981).

Thus it can be concluded that where partisan differences have existed between governments, there have been differences in public expenditure outturns in a predicted left/right direction. Looking at the industrialized democracies as a whole although there has been a tendency for faster growth in those countries where government has been dominated by left-of-center parties, for example, Sweden, Norway, Denmark (OECD, 1978), there are also examples of very rapidly growing public sectors, for example, the Netherlands, Ireland, and Canada, where right-of-center governments have predominated. Therefore, a left-of-center government predominance does not seem to be a necessary condition for a rapid expansion of the public expenditure relative to GDP. However, in the group of countries of the OECD study, there are no examples of a relatively *slow*-growing public sector where left-of-center governments have predominated.

Although it is clear from single-country studies that a number of independent variables have made a contribution to the growth in the ratio of public expenditure to GDP, the fit of the cross-section public expenditure data at the aggregate level to the major explanatory hypotheses is generally poor. In the next section public expenditure will be examined at a disaggregated level to explore further possible associations in the data. In addition, two hypotheses that are more appropriate to the disaggregated level will be introduced.

Public Expenditures at
the Disaggregated Level

The ratios of growth rates of public expenditures on current and capital goods and services and on transfers relative to GDP by central and local government are shown in Table 12.3, both for subperiods and the whole

TABLE 12.3   Ratios of Annual Growth Rates of Total Public Expenditures, Relative to GDP, by Central and Local Government, 1950-1978*

Country	Central Government	Local Government
Germany	1.02[1] (1.42)[2]	1.11[1] (0.84)[2]
Ireland[3]	1.31	1.14
New Zealand	1.09	1.03
Sweden[4]	1.30	1.42
United Kingdom	1.03	1.12
United States	1.24	1.31

*Growth rates calculated using three-year averages at beginning and end of period.
1. 1950-1974—old series
2. 1974-1979—new series
3. A breakdown of the Irish data is available only from 1953 onward.
4. A breakdown of the Swedish data is available only from 1963 onward.

period of study. It can be seen that in four of the countries, Germany (1950-1974 but not 1974-1978), Sweden, the United Kingdom, and the United States, there was a faster overall growth of local government expenditures relative to GDP than central government expenditures. In Ireland and New Zealand, local government expenditures grew more slowly than central government expenditures. However, comparing central and local government expenditures, including both goods and services and transfers, is not entirely satisfactory since central government expenditures include a much larger element of transfers (ranging from thirty-seven percent to seventy-seven percent of central government total expenditure) than local government. It is therefore more appropriate to compare central and local government expenditures on goods and services.

Expenditures on goods and services–Central and local government. The ratios of central government and local government expenditures on goods and services to GDP are shown in Table 12.4. It is to be noted that in almost every case (except New Zealand where the local government sector is exceptionally small) local government expenditures expanded faster than central government.[3] This finding has considerable economic importance because, as noted earlier, it is public expenditures on goods and services which are the resource consuming element of total public expenditure. It is also contrary to the prediction of increasing centralization made by Peacock and Wiseman (1967). In fact, if we relate the growth of local government expenditure on goods and services relative to GDP to the size of the local government sector at the outset of the study, there appears to be a positive correlation between the two. This suggests that the larger the local government sector was relative to the public sector as a whole, the faster it grew. This relationship is shown in Figure 12.5. Although not a very close fit, the correlation coefficient ($r = .68$) indicates a moderately significant positive linear correlation between the two variables.

TABLE 12.4   Ratios of Annual Growth Rates of Central and Local Government Expenditures on Goods and Services, Relative to GDP, 1950-1978

Country	Central Government	Local Government
Germany	1.08 (0.90)	1.12 (0.80)
Ireland	1.15	1.16
New Zealand	1.11	1.02
Sweden	1.03	1.41
United Kingdom	1.01	1.11
United States	1.06	1.35

NOTE: See note for Table 12.3.

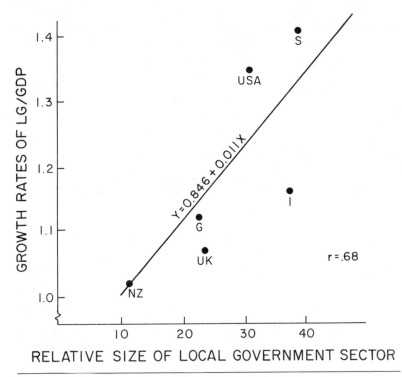

FIGURE 12.5   Ratios of Annual Growth Rates of Local Government Expenditures on Goods and Services Relative to GDP (LG/GDP) and the Relative Size of the Local Government Sector at Outset of Study (average of first three years)

A number of possible explanations might be hypothesized for explaining this finding among the six countries:

(1) It may be a consequence of central governments transferring more and more statutory functions to local governments.

(2) Some of the functions for which local governments are responsible, for example, health or education, may have grown faster than the functions for which central governments are usually responsible, for example, defense (Gould and Roweth, 1980).

(3) Budgetary control systems in local government may be both less sophisticated and less effective than in central government.

(4) The bureaucratic process described by Niskanen, summarized in the phrase "budget-maximizing bureaucrats," may operate more strongly at the local than at the central level.

Expenditures on goods and services and on transfers. In Table 12.5 growth rates of general government expenditures on goods and services and

TABLE 12.5   Ratios of Annual Growth Rates of General Government Expenditures on Goods and Services and on Transfers, Relative to GDP, 1950-1978

Country	Expenditures on Goods and Services			
	1950-1959	1959-1969	1969-1978	1950-1978
Germany	0.98	1.06	1.27 (0.86)	1.07*
Ireland	0.36	1.22	1.22	1.14
New Zealand	1.07	1.06	1.14	1.10
Sweden		1.34	1.22	1.26
United Kingdom	1.03	1.16	0.92	1.00
United States	2.24	1.19	0.88	1.26
	Expenditures on Transfers			
	1950-1959	1959-1969	1969-1978	1950-1978
Germany	1.04	0.97	1.05 (1.31)	1.02*
Ireland	0.84	1.55	1.18	1.28
New Zealand	1.69	0.88	1.38	1.08
Sweden		2.20	1.26	1.59
United Kingdom	0.65	1.43	1.18	1.11
United States	1.72	1.34	1.47	1.39

NOTE: Notes as for Table 12.3.
*1950-1974—old series

on transfers (defined to include transfer payments, subsidies, and interest) relative to GDP are shown both for the subperiods and the whole period of study. The data show that in Ireland, Sweden, the United Kingdom, the United States, and Germany (1974-1978 only) expenditures on transfers grew faster than expenditures on goods and services.[4] In New Zealand and Germany (1950-1974) transfers grew moderately more slowly than expenditures on goods and services. (The transfers data for Germany, however, are incomplete over this period.) It can be observed from the subperiods that there has generally been no steady acceleration in the rates of growth of either goods and services or of transfers over the whole period (Bell, 1976: 232-243), nor did the 1960s show an acceleration in growth rates for three cases out of five (Germany, Ireland, and the United Kingdom). In only two cases out of six were growth rates in the 1970s faster than the 1960s (Germany and New Zealand). Only one country (Germany) experienced a steady acceleration of expenditures on goods and services over most of the period of study. This slowed in the second part of the 1970s. Turning to transfers, the 1960s show an acceleration of growth rates over the 1950s for three countries out of five (Ireland, New Zealand, and the United States). (The acceleration in Germany in the second part of the 1970s was particularly rapid.) Thus in only one country (New Zealand) was there a steady acceleration of the growth of transfers over the whole period.

230 _Explaining Growth_

TABLE 12.6   Ratios of Annual Growth Rates of General Government Social Security Expenditures Relative to GDP, 1950-1978

Country	Expenditure on Social Security
Germany	1.01 (1.58)
Ireland	1.34
New Zealand	1.13
Sweden	1.67
United Kingdom	1.23
United States	1.68

NOTE: Notes as for Table 12.3.

TABLE 12.7   Budget Deficits as a Proportion of GDP, Selected Years

Country	1960	1970	1975	1978
Germany	0.29	1.17	6.47	3.22
Ireland	3.83	6.82	14.78	16.78
New Zealand		1.53	2.94	9.37
Sweden	−2.40	1.51	4.02	10.04
United Kingdom	2.56	−0.29	9.66	5.50
United States*	−0.05	0.25	3.10	2.48

NOTE: Signs reversed: negative sign = surplus.
*Federal Government

The largest single component of transfers is social security payments. The rates of growth of social security payments relative to growth rates of GDP are shown in Table 12.6. It can be seen that in every case except Germany for 1950 to 1974 (the period of incomplete coverage of social security in Germany), the ratio of social security payments growth to GDP growth was greater than the ratio of transfer payments to GDP. Further discussion of social security will be postponed until the functional analysis below. The other interesting component of transfers is interest payments. The combination of the increasing average size of budget deficits as a proportion of GDP (Table 12.7) and rising average level of interest rates have added a sharp impetus to the relative growth rates of interest payments on public debt, especially during the 1970s. This is now becoming a major factor in central governments' difficulties in controlling the growth of public expenditures.

Incrementalism.[5] According to the hypothesis of incrementalism in public budgeting, there is a tendency to base this year's budget very much on what it was last year, rather than to make a radical reconsideration of expenditure programs. These adjustments tend to be made incrementally (Wildavsky, 1974). This hypothesis has obvious implications for the growth

TABLE 12.8   Observations of Percentage Point Changes in Individual Functions Shares of Total Public Expenditure in Selected Ranges*

Country	Decade on Decade Changes			
	less than 1	*greater than 1 and less than 2*	*greater than 2 and less than 4*	*greater than 4*
Germany	17	4	7	2
Ireland	14	6	7	2
New Zealand	22	15	6	2
Sweden	12	5	5	0
United Kingdom	23	9	10	3
United States	16	10	11	6
Changes from Beginning to End of Period				
Germany	2	1	4	3
Ireland	0	2	2	2
New Zealand	6	3	4	2
Sweden	6	0	3	2
United Kingdom	5	6	0	5
United States	5	2	3	5

*For decade changes and for changes from beginning to end of period of study, six countries, three-year averages.

of public expenditure relative to GDP. In principle, as long as incremental adjustments upwards were offset by incremental adjustments downwards, there would, ceteris paribus, be no rise in the average level of public expenditures. However, as the earlier analysis has attempted to show, while there have been many upward pressures on public expenditure over the past thirty years, it is difficult to identify any downward pressures. The outcome is a rise in the average level of public expenditure. Table 12.8 shows the overwhelming tendency to incrementalism among the six countries. Taking the change in functional percentage shares of total public expenditures for the beginning and end periods for each country for which data were available (N = 73), one-third of the changes were at the level of less than one percentage point (N = 24); over half, at less than two percentage points (N = 38); and nearly three-quarters, at less than four percentage points (N = 54).

Taking the decade-by-decade changes (N = 214), nearly half were at a level less than one percentage point (N = 104); three-quarters, less than two percentage points (N = 153); ninety-three percent, less than four percentage points (N = 199). Given the extremely small degree of change that has generally taken place in public budgeting, it is perhaps not surprising that more radical techniques such as zero-base and sunset-law budgeting have been proposed.

A high income elasticity of demand for social welfare goods. At the functional level it is appropriate to consider the major subcategory of total public expenditure that has long been thought to be the engine of public expenditure growth, namely social welfare expenditures. This broad category has been so defined here as to include public expenditures on social security, education, health, housing, and personal or community social services.[6]

Publicly provided social welfare goods and services and transfers can be broadly described as "merit" goods in the sense that both individuals and the community consider them desirable. While rivals in consumption they nevertheless contain elements of public goods in the sense that their consumption contains quite large externalities. Together they form the core of the welfare state idea, namely, that it is in both society's and its individual members' best interests if (1) all members of society have access to a guaranteed minimum standard of social welfare facilities and (2) these minimum standards are pitched at a reasonably generous level. In addition, the demand side has been affected over this period by (1) rising expectations of social welfare standards,[7] (2) the growing awareness of the contribution of social welfare provision to general standards of living, (3) the recognition of new needs for social provision, and (4) the rapid translation of these needs into demands. Thus as a result the demand for social welfare provision is highly income elastic.[8] Such a combination of pressures would indeed have considerable implications for the growth of total public expenditures because the social welfare area, as defined, constitutes approximately fifty percent of total public expenditures in the six countries.

From Table 12.9 it can be seen that social welfare expenditures as a whole have increased more rapidly than GDP for all countries of this study, ranging from a ratio of 1.06 in Germany to 1.49 for the United States. This confirms an elasticity greater than unity, as suggested for such merit goods. Looking at the time trend of social welfare expenditure with respect to GDP, it can be seen that the ratio accelerated in the 1960s compared to the 1950s in Ireland, New Zealand and the United Kingdom and decelerated in Germany and the

TABLE 12.9   Ratios of Annual Growth Rates of Social Welfare Expenditures Relative to GDP

Country	1950-1959	1959-1969	1969-1978	1950-1978
Germany	0.94	0.88	1.49	1.06
Ireland	0.94	1.42	1.26	1.25
New Zealand	0.93	1.05	1.37	1.16
Sweden		1.83	1.37	1.53
United Kingdom	0.96	1.45	1.14	1.17
United States	2.23*	1.42	1.24	1.49

NOTE: Notes as for Table 12.3.
*1952-1959

TABLE 12.10   Ratios of Annual Growth Rates of Social Welfare Expenditures Relative to Total Public Expenditure

Country	1950-1959	1959-1969	1969-1978	1950-1978
Germany	0.95	0.86	1.21	1.00
Ireland	1.03	1.03	0.99	1.01
New Zealand	1.09	1.04	1.68	1.07
Sweden		1.21	1.07	1.12
United Kingdom	1.09	1.15	1.10	1.11
United States	2.23*	1.05	1.18	1.35

NOTE: Notes as for Table 12.3.
*1952-1959

United States. It accelerated in the 1970s compared to the 1960s in Germany and New Zealand, while decelerating in Ireland, Sweden, the United Kingdom, and the United States. Only New Zealand experienced continuous acceleration over the whole period of study.

In order to examine the hypothesis that social welfare expenditure has been the engine of public expenditure growth, its growth must be related to the growth of total public expenditures. This is done in Table 12.10. Here it can be seen that in no country did social welfare expenditures increase more slowly than public expenditure, although in Germany and Ireland the difference between the two rates is very small. In New Zealand, Sweden, and the United Kingdom, social welfare expenditure increased moderately more rapidly. Only in the United States is there very big difference. Again the time trends show that the growth rates of social welfare expenditures relative to total public expenditures have not accelerated continuously over the period of study. In four out of five countries (Germany, Ireland, New Zealand, and the United States) there was a deceleration in the growth rates in the 1960s compared to 1950s. The growth rate accelerated in the 1970s compared with the 1960s in only three countries (Germany, New Zealand, and the United States).

Thus, although we can conclude from the evidence that social welfare expenditures have an income elasticity of demand greater than unity, we cannot conclude that it has been the engine of total public expenditure growth. Once again there is no general pattern. In Ireland, a country with one of the fastest growing public sectors, the growth of social welfare expenditures only equalled the average growth rate of total public expenditures.

Population increase and demographic change. Figure 12.6 shows the relationship between rates of growth of social welfare expenditures relative to GDP and population growth. Figure 12.6b shows rates of growth of social welfare expenditure relative to GDP and the degree of change in the size of the dependent population as a proportion of total population. In neither scattergram is there any clear evidence of a strong relationship in the direction

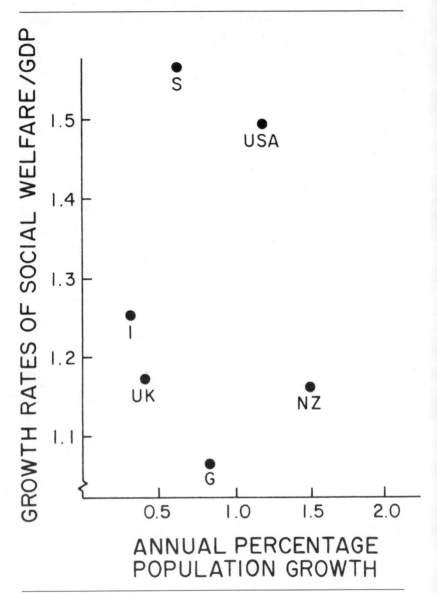

FIGURE 12.6a   Ratios of Annual Growth of Social Welfare Expenditures
Relative to GDP and Annual Population Growth, 1950-1978

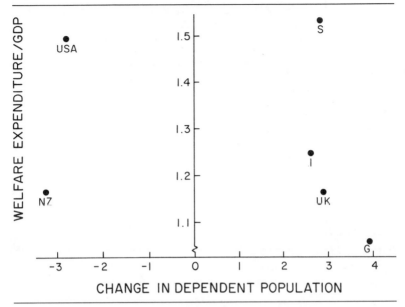

FIGURE 12.6b **Ratios of Annual Growth Rates of Social Welfare Expenditures Relative to GDP and Change in Dependent Population on Percentage of Total Population, 1950-1978**

expected. This seems to confirm that while population increase and demographic change may have contributed to the growth of public expenditures relative to GDP in general and social welfare expenditures in particular, they do not help to explain variations between countries. It is therefore of interest to examine other possible influences on the growth of social welfare expenditures.

The partisan composition of government. Evidence was adduced above to show that the rate of growth in total public expenditure relative to GDP was related to the type of political party that had held office. Total public expenditure relative to GDP had tended to grow faster under governments of the left than of the right. At the functional level the evidence of the effect of the partisan composition of government on expenditure outturns is even more persuasive. Gould and Goodyer (forthcoming) found that certain functions tend to be politically sensitive. For the Left these included functions reflecting general government administration/intervention and those embodying policies that attempt to reduce inequality by redistributing cash (social security) or by the provision of subsidized services such as public education, health and housing. For the Right, they included functions emphasizing law and order and in certain circumstances defense.

TABLE 12.11   Number of Functions Confirming or Disconfirming Left/Right
Prediction of the Effect of Partisan Composition on
Goverment, Five Countries, 1950-1978.

Country	Number of Functions Confirming	Number of Functions Disconfirming
Germany	5	1
Ireland	4	1
New Zealand	8	1
United Kingdom	4	4
United States	4	5

NOTE: Notes as for Table 12.2.

Of thirty-seven politically sensitive functions among the five countries, it was found that sixty-eight percent emerged with higher spending ratios over the whole period of office in the left/right direction predicted. In the welfare state area the effect of the partisan composition of government emerged even more strongly. Of twenty-four functions falling directly within the social welfare category some seventy-five percent had higher spending ratios in the predicted left/right direction. These results are summarized in Table 12.11. In the United States there was no evidence of difference in the effect of the partisan composition of government in the predicted left/wing direction. Differences between the major parties in the United Kingdom were weaker than expected. Otherwise, the relationship was rather strong. Perhaps then, it is not surprising that the association with population increase and demographic change appears so weak. The growth of social welfare expenditure is clearly influenced by the ideological stance of governments.

Conclusion

At the aggregate level this research has found a poor fit between the public expenditure cross-section data and a number of explanatory hypotheses. Although public expenditure increased as a proportion of GDP in all six countries, Wagner's law is not confirmed using per capita GDP as a measure of development. In fact, there is some evidence that the level of economic development is negatively related to the size of the public sector. There is also some evidence of a negative relationship between economic growth and the relative expansion of the public sector, and some evidence of a catching-up process in terms of the relative growth rates between the six countries, but the variables are poorly correlated.

There is universal evidence of a Peacock and Wiseman displacement effect in the aftermath of the 1973-1974 oil price shock, but this hypothesis does not explain the long-term upward trend in the ratio of public expenditure to GDP over the period of 1950 to 1974. Differences in population growth and demographic change in the six countries are not related to differences in the relative expansion of public expenditures to GDP. However, where partisan differences between governments have existed, there is some confirmation of its influence on public expenditure outturns in a predictable left/right way. In addition it is possible, at the extremes, to adduce further support for this hypothesis from public expenditure data of countries experiencing single party dominance of either left-of-center or right-of-center governments, although there are some notable exceptions here.

At the disaggregate level two main growth areas of public expenditure were generally identified: transfers, predominantly the responsibility of the part of the central government, and local government expenditures on goods and services. While the growth of transfer payments is heavily influenced by the growth of its largest component, social security, which in turn appears to have been strongly influenced by the partisan composition of government where it existed and the high income elasticity of demand for social welfare goods in general, there seems to be no simple explanation for the variability in transfer payments growth between countries. The almost universally faster growth of local government over central government expenditures is a finding of considerable interest and significance. A number of possible explanations were adumbrated and this area is being further investigated. At the functional level the strong influences of incrementalism and the partisan composition of government were noted, the latter particularly in the area of social welfare expenditures. However, there seemed to be, surprisingly, no relationship between the growth of social welfare expenditures and the indicators of demographic change. It was also noted that while social welfare expenditures had expended faster than public expenditure in some countries, this was not always the case.

This research overall demonstrates the considerable diversity among this group of countries, and, it may be presumed, among advanced democracies in general. Very few patterns in expenditure outturns common to all countries exist; this is even less so at the aggregate level than at the disaggregated level. This, and the findings at the disaggregated level, confirm the difficulties (and failures) to find a good fit in the aggregated public expenditure data with one or two independent variables. For example, the study by Cameron (1978) claimed that the openness of the economy coupled with high industrial concentration and powerful trade unions provided the best predictor of the expansion of the public economy. While it can be easily seen how such a combination might influence the behavior of central governments, particularly in the area of some transfer payments, it is difficult to conceive of such a highly centralized mechanism influencing the behavior of tens, sometimes over one hundred different and fragmented local governments in a similar way.

Appendix:
Data Sources

Germany (FRG): All expenditure data from the Central Statistical Information System of the Statistisches Bundesamt, Wiesbaden.

Ireland: Expenditure data from *National Income and Expenditure Green Books*, various numbers, except for functional breakdown before 1963; the latter from a highly authoritative private academic source.

New Zealand: All expenditure data from *Public Expenditure and its Financing: 1950-1979*, Wellington: New Zealand Planning Council, 1979.

Sweden: All expenditure data from *Statistiska meddelanden*, National Central Bureau of Statistics. (No functional breakdown of capital transfers available.)

United Kingdom: All expenditure data from *National Income and Expenditure Blue Books*, various numbers. There was a change in presentation in 1976 excluding capital investment of the public corporation; figures from earlier Blue Books have been reconciled with this later presentation.

United States: All expenditure data from *Survey of Current Business*, various numbers.

Election data: from Keesing's *Contemporary Archives* (various years from 1950); *The Stateman's Yearbook*, London: Macmillan, annual; T. Mackie and R. Rose, *The International Almanac of Electoral Behavior*, London: Macmillan, 1974.

Economic growth data: 1960-1978 from OECD *National Accounts* 1950-1960 as follows: Germany, IMF *International Financial Statistics* Ireland, Kennedy and Dowling (1974); New Zealand, OECD *Economic Survey of New Zealand, 1979* Sweden, *Statistiska meddelanden* United Kingdom, *National Income and Expenditure Blue Books* United States, Office of Management of the Budget.

Demographic data: from OECD *Labour Force Statistics* (various numbers).

Real per capita GDP data from OECD, *National Accounts*, vol. 1, 1950-1978.

NOTES

1. For the relative positions of these six countries among all industrialized democracies in terms of public expenditure, see OECD (1978).

2. The social Democratic Party was the governing party continuously from 1932 to 1976.

3. Preliminary analysis of the Canadian data reveals the same finding.

4. Preliminary analysis of the Canadian data further confirms this finding.

5. The functional analysis for this section was carried out by calculating the percentage share of the individual functions in total expenditure, using three-year averages for beginning and end of period and for intervening ends of decade. See Table 12.8.

6. Coverage of each of these functions is not identical in all six countries but since we are

comparing growth rates rather than shares of public expenditure or of GDP, this is of minor importance.

7. Bell (1976) for example, argues that over time expectations have become translated into entitlements.

8. It should be noted that in practice it is not possible to separate income and price elasticities because consumers do not have to meet directly the increasing relative price of most public services.

REFERENCES

ANDIC, S. and J. VEVERKA (1964) "The growth of government expenditure in Germany since the unification." Finanzarchiv 23, 3: 169-278.

BARLOW, R. (1977) "A test of alternative methods of making GNP comparisons." Economic Journal 87 (September): 450-459.

BELL, D. (1976) The Cultural Contradictions of Capitalism. London: Heinemann.

―――― (1960) The End of Ideology. New York: Free Press.

BIRD, R. M. (1970) The Growth of Government Spending in Canada. Toronto: Canadian Tax Foundation.

BURSTEIN, P. (1979) "Party balance, replacement of legislators and federal government expenditures, 1941-1976." Western Political Quarterly 32 (June): 203-208.

CAMERON, D. R. (1978) "The expansion of the public economy: a comparative analysis." American Political Science Review 72: 1243-1261.

DOWNS, A. (1957) An Economic Theory of Democracy. New York: Harper & Row.

GOULD, F. (1981) "The growth of public expenditure in Ireland, 1947-1977." Administration (December): 115-135.

―――― and B. ROWETH (1980) "Public spending and social policy: the United Kingdom, 1950-1977." Journal of Social Policy 9, 3: 348-349.

―――― (1978) "Politics and public spending." Political Quarterly 49, 2: 222-227.

―――― and R. GOODYER (forthcoming) "Does politics matter? The evidence from five industrialized democracies."

GUPTA, S. (1969) "Public expenditure and economic development—a cross-section analysis." Finanzarchiv 28, 1: 26-41.

KENNEDY, K. A. and B. R. DOWLING (1974) Economic Growth in Ireland: The Experience Since 1947. Dublin: Gill & Macmillan.

LIPSET, S. M. (1960) Political Man. Garden City, N.J: Doubleday.

LYONS, F. S. (1973) Ireland Since the Famine. London: Collins-Fontana.

MUSGRAVE, R. A. (1969) Fiscal Systems. New Haven, CT, and London: Yale University Press.

―――― and P. B. MUSGRAVE (1980) Public Finance in Theory and Practice. New York: McGraw-Hill.

Organization for Economic Development (1978) Public Expenditure Trends. OECD Studies in Resource Allocation. Paris: OECD.

O'LEARY C. (1979) Irish Elections, 1918-1977. Dublin: Gill & Macmillan.

PEACOCK, A. T. and J. WISEMAN (1967) The Growth of Public Expenditure in the United Kingdom. London: Allen & Unwin.

RECHTENWALD, H. C. (1978) "The public sector in transition," in H. C. Rechtenwald (ed.) Tendances a long terme du secteur public. Paris: Editions Cujas.

WILENSKY, H. (1975) The Welfare State and Equality. Berkeley: University of California Press.

WILDAVSKY, A. (1974) The Politics of the Budgetary Process. Boston: Little Brown.

CHAPTER 13

MARKET FAILURE AND GROWTH OF GOVERNMENT
A Sociological Explanation

F R A N Z   L E H N E R
U L R I C H   W I D M A I E R

The advanced capitalist societies have experienced continuous and rapid growth in the public sector and in government intervention into the economy throughout this century. Today government spending in these countries amounts to thirty or fifty percent of the GNP, and government intervention by means of financial incentives or regulation covers an overwhelming part of economic transactions. This development has provoked an ongoing debate on the role of government in advanced capitalism and various attempts to understand the causes and reasons for government growth. In this chapter a sociological explanation and a dynamic model of the development of the public sector in capitalist societies is presented. Market failure, growth of government, and government failure are explained in terms of socioeconomic structure and organization, societal differentiation, and the scope and density of the organization of interests. The explanation and the model consider both the fiscal and the regulatory activities of government.

Our analysis is concerned with the sociological rather than the economic aspects of growth. These are of crucial importance but are neglected in the literature. Neoclassical economists often explain and justify government intervention in terms of market failure. Government intervention is justified if the provision of goods and services by the market is inefficient and if government can provide these goods and services more efficiently. Not all government activity is determined by market failure; in fact, market failure often results from government intervention.[1] Given these facts, an explanation of government intervention and growth in terms of market failure seems not to be very fruitful. This may be true if we define market failure in the rather narrow sense of economic efficiency. We can, however, reach a more fruitful and realistic explanation if we consider that even when markets work in an economically efficient way they may produce results—that is, prices, income distributions, or conditions of competition—that are not accepted by a smaller or larger proportion of the population. Such *lack of social accept-ance* is much more likely to create demand for government intervention than cases of economic inefficiency. In this view the motor of government growth is social market failure (nonacceptance of market allocation) much more than economic failure (inefficiency). Economic inefficiency may frequently be a reason for nonacceptance of market allocation, but more often market conditions will or will not be accepted irrespective of their efficiency or inefficiency.

Following this approach it is necessary to find the conditions that make markets fail socially in order to understand the continuous and large growth of government over the last decades. Moreover, we have to understand the conditions that determine the transformation of perceived market failure into government action.

Socioeconomic Development and Market Failure

The development of capitalist societies is paralleled by conditions that are likely to increase social (and economic) market failure and that also facilitate the transformation of perceived market failure into government action. Two conditions are of crucial importance:

(1) the increasing *density of economic organization,* that is, increasing size of firms, scale of production, and concentration; and

(2) increasing *societal differentiation,* that is, increasing status differentiation, enhanced by an increasing division of labor, and accentuated regional and sectoral differences or even disparities.

Both these conditions have primarily *technological roots.* The development and application of increasingly complex technologies, the rationalization of production and distribution, and increasing world market integration imply an increasing scale of production, size of firm, and complexity of organization. Beyond technological grounds, political and economic factors often enhance the formation of large and complex economic organizations. The complexity of economic organization and of technology also inevitably creates a complex division of labor that in turn results in societal differentiation.[2]

The formation of large enterprises and of oligopolistic market structures is a major cause of economic market failure in a highly organized economy where the price mechanism is only partially effective. A considerable amount of economic transactions are determined by corporate planning and economic power. This often results in features of economic inefficiency that may justify government intervention. This partially explains government growth. However, in our view most government growth is not caused by economic but by social market failure.

Markets possess an inherent tendency to fail socially. The reason for this is that the qualities and quantities of goods and services produced and distributed by the market are not directly connected to the needs and preferences of the members of a society, but rather determined by available prices and profits. On an aggregate level, available prices for goods and services depend not only on the aggregate preference structure, but also on the aggregate distribution of income (and wealth). Consequently, the production and distribution of goods and services resulting from spontaneous market coordination fits the societal distribution of preferences only to the degree in which the distribution of buying power (wealth and income) corresponds to the distribution of preferences. This correspondence is not guaranteed by the market mechanism.[3]

The basic social problem of the market working within a given distribution of income and wealth is that it often provides goods and services in quantities and at prices that are not consistent with the needs and preferences of certain parts of the population. This is likely to produce considerable dissatisfaction with market allocation. Dissatisfaction will, in turn, under certain conditions that will be described later, result in pressure for government intervention (Widmaier, 1978).

While this problem may occur in simple as well as in differentiated societies, it is more strongly accentuated and increased by societal differentiation. As a general hypothesis we assume that *the likelihood of social market failure and of its transformation into pressure for government intervention increases with increasing societal differentiation.* Societal differentiation has three features which are of relevance in this context:

(1) Societal differentiation resulting from division of labor consists primarily of a *differentiation of status, income, and power.* This is combined with the differentiation of socioeconomic conditions, values, needs, and interests. Economically, this is expressed in the differentiation of preferences and demands for goods and services.
(2) Societal differentiation in terms of values and interests always amounts to some *decomposition of a society* and its class structure into a larger number of different interest layers and social groups with particular value structures. As a result, social control and the legitimization of societal institutions by means

of ideologies, norms, and values declines. This is combined with a rather low amount of societal consensus.

(3) The decomposition of society into particular interest layers and social groups creates an *increasing organization of societal interests*. Hence, societal differentiation is combined with an increase in the scope and density of societal organization because it facilitates the rise of new interest organizations. These new organizations, however, are often rather fragile and structurally weak. This weakness produces an organizational dynamics characterized by a low degree of flexibility and considerable radicalism. Parallel to this we often find a strong tendency for unconventional behavior (see Janowitz, 1976; Buchanan, 1974; Budge et al., 1972; Ingelhart, 1977; Ionescou, 1974; Lehner, 1979).

In a world in which valuable resources are scarce, a differentiated structure of preferences and demands for goods and services inevitably creates considerable problems for any system of coordination of production and distribution. However, this does not, in principle, pose difficulties to economic efficiency; in terms of economic efficiency, the market is better capable of coping with a high differentiation of preferences and demand than government.[4]

The increasing differentiation of preferences and demands increases the likelihood that partial dissatisfaction with the ultimate outcome of market coordination will occur. Furthermore, under such conditions we may expect this dissatisfaction to vary greatly, becoming rather widespread and extending over a number of different issues and societal groups. Finally and most important, the differentiated structure of needs and preferences is paralleled by the *acceleration, expansion,* and diffusion of expectations and demands, which in turn creates dynamic dissatisfaction with the actual outcome of the market (and of government too). This process is dialectically accelerated if the market efficiently copes with differentiation: *The more provision of goods and services is differentiated, the higher is the number of goods and services for which new demand may occur.* Moreover, the better the provision of material goods and services, the greater the demand for nonmaterial goods and services (e.g., demands for ecological qualities) will be. Altogether, in a differentiated society the market is likely to produce a large, widespread, and increasing potential for dissatisfaction and social market failure.[5]

Societal institutions often have a general legitimacy that is more or less independent from their actual performance. This legitimacy protects institutions to some extent in cases of bad performance and secures their survival even if their perceived performance is bad over a long time. The market is provided with such a general legitimacy by the liberal ideology dominating capitalist societies. Liberal philosophy is, however, a rather weak source of ideological legitimacy, as its underlying utilitarian ethics enhances the evaluation of institutions in terms of their material performance. Utilitarian ethics and the spirit of capitalism contain a rather simple ideological perspective: that of the maximization of individual utility and the evaluation of interactions and institutions in terms of resulting profit. This perspective creates the type of rational behavior that is the necessary condition for the operation of the market and the success of a capitalist economy, but at the same time, provides little protection for the market in case of dissatisfaction with its outcomes (Habermas, 1973; Offe, 1975).

In this context we should note that governmental institutions generally have much stronger legitimacy than the market because they are based not only on utilitarianism but also on an ideology that contains some strong non-utilitarian and altruistic elements, such as beliefs in democratic fairness, political justice, and national identity. These elements provide a dignified legitimization for political institutions that is minimally affected by material performance. This fact facilitates the transfer of functions from the market to government in case of perceived market failure but inhibits the opposite transfer in case the government fails. Note, however, that this effect is likely to decrease since increasing government intervention increases the material impact of government on individuals. Consequently, the legitimacy of government may be increasingly questioned on material grounds.

Societal differentiation is paralleled by the *corresponding differentiation of the distribution of income and wealth.* Instead of the polarized distribution in the class structure of early capitalism, the income distribution of advanced capitalism is more continuous, although not necessarily more egalitarian. This, in turn, changes the structure of individual and collective expectations regarding income and other valuable properties. These expectations are shaped by social comparison processes. That means that any individual evaluates his or her income and other properties in terms of those individuals who are in similar positions and share similar social attributes. In a society with a clear-cut class structure, social comparison is thus always limited by class borders, while in a more differentiated society the scope of social comparison is much broader. The ultimate result of this is rising expectations with respect to income (and to a lesser degree property). The legitimacy of income distribution and of the underlying distribution of property rights declines to the extent in which these expectations cannot be satisfied within the market coordinated economy and demands for governmental redistribution increase (Atkinson, 1974; Widmaier, 1978).

Altogether, capitalist societies have a strong inherent tendency to create a multifarious social market failure; while they rely on the market as a central steering mechanism, they cannot safeguard its legitimacy. Similarly, but to a lesser degree, increasing organization and concentration of production and distribution creates the increasing likelihood of economic market failure.

Political Organization, Interest Intermediation, and Government Activity

Perceived market failure, especially nonacceptance of market outcomes, is likely to provoke demands for government intervention. This is not surprising because government has always been a major institution for steering production and distribution. A government that is confined to safeguarding the operational conditions to the market but keeping out of the control of production and distribution plays an important role in some economists' books, but it has never existed in reality. The ancient Roman or Greek state and the early liberal state were welfare states to a considerable degree. The difference between them and the modern welfare state is not one of quality but rather of quantity. This difference is crucial because the growing scope of government has had and still has a large impact on its functions (Deutsch, 1974: 74ff).

It is therefore of interest to investigate not why perceived market failure creates demands for governmental intervention, but rather under which conditions such demands can be effectively carried through, and what changes have occurred allowing for the remarkable growth of government over the last decades. Finally, we have to analyze the feedback effects of governmental growth on the conditions that have initiated it.

In democratic systems demands for governmental action can be intermediated primarily through three channels that constitute different conditions for the effectiveness of interest intermediation:

(1) The traditional and politically most legitimate way to intermediate interest is the one that works via elections or votes, parties, and parliamentary decisions (conventional political participation). In order to use this channel effectively, interests have to be sufficiently organized to mobilize mass support.

(2) A less legitimate but often more effective way of intermediating interest is constituted by the interactions and the interlocking of organized interests (including large firms), bureaucracies, and politicians (pressure politics). Effective pressure politics generally require a high capacity of interest to get organized, to control scarce resources or special functions, and to engage in political conflicts.

(3) Finally, there are often strategies to serve intermediate interests such as protests, strikes, and similar activities (unconventional political participation). While the effectiveness of such political participation is generally rather low and difficult to predict, it is quite clear that it requires at least some capacity to

get organized, to mobilize support, and to prevent the production and distribution of valuable goods and services. Unconventional participation thus
combines elements of both conventional participation and pressure politics.

For the purpose of this chapter, it is not necessary to analyze these three
channels and the corresponding conditions for effective interest intermediation in detail. Rather, it suffices to state that in any case the effectiveness of
interest intermediation is determined by an interest's capacity (1) to get organized; and (2) to mobilize mass support, and/or to control scarce resources
or special functions (Offe, 1972).

The capacity of interests to meet the above conditions varies a great deal.
In all capitalist societies there are particular interests, which, although they
include only a small proportion of the population, are nevertheless very
powerful. At the same time the interests of large numbers of people often
cannot be sufficiently carried into effect. The organization of interest is, as
Mancur Olson shows, generally a difficult task since it is concerned with
collective goods. Individuals are not necessarily motivated enough to contribute sufficiently to the costs of a common interest organization and tend
instead to behave as "free riders." This tendency is proportional to the size of
an interest group. In order to be effective, large interests have to be capable
of providing selective social and material incentives to a caucus of activists
or functionaries, while small interests can often rely on purposive or nonse-
lective social incentives. This implies that the larger the potential group is,
the more difficult and ineffective the organization of an interest will be.[6]

Conditions under which even large interests can be effectively organized
are

(1) If the interests of a large social stratum are severely hurt in a society, a larger
    number of the members of this stratum may be sufficiently motivated by pur-
    posive incentives to join and to work for a common interest organization. The
    financial contributions of a large membership may thus enable the organiza-
    tion to provide sufficient selective incentives.
(2) The degree of organization an interest group needs to be effective also de-
    pends on the channel it uses to intermediate demands. Interests working via
    conventional political participation, for example, often do not need to have a
    strong organizational apparatus. Rather, a small caucus that mobilizes mass
    support during elections may be sufficiently effective. Similarly, a small cau-
    cus mobilizing punctual support of generally rather passive members and sup-
    porters can be effective for interest groups with unconventional participation.
(3) Another important set of contextual conditions for the organization of large
    interests is provided by the institutional structure of government. We can rea-
    sonably assume that a highly centralized government requires much more
    powerful organization than a highly decentralized one. Centralized govern-
    ment thus reduces the chances of large interests to become effectively orga-
    nized, while decentralized government is more favorable. Similarly, a highly

fractionalized party system has better chances of influencing politics via conventional participation than a highly integrated one.

These conditions may partially reduce the bias of organized interest intermediation resulting from the above described general logic of interests organization.

Historically, large but weak organizations (social movements) have been of crucial importance for the development of the welfare state. In many countries social security systems have been created by government in order to cope with increasing socioeconomic unrest, protest, and strikes, and to avoid mass mobilization by unions and socialist parties. Governments often did not react to organized political power in terms of pressure or electoral power, but rather acted to prevent effective organization of working-class dissatisfaction by unions and socialist parties. Social security interests thus often have been carried into effect without strong organization; a small caucus of activists was capable of mobilizing strong support of a large number of strongly dissatisfied people. We can observe similar patterns of interest intermediation with respect to the ecologists or the peace movement (Barnes et al., 1979; Janowitz, 1970, 1976; Oberschall, 1973; Widmaier, 1978).

These examples demonstrate that interests need not have a strong capacity of organization if they receive large-scale mass support on the basis of purposive motivation. Purposive incentives, however, have a rather limited applicability and motivational strength. They are bound to specific goals and their motivational strength is directly related to the importance of that goal for the concerned individuals. They are also somewhat dialectically related to the success of an organization: The closer the goal, the less its motivational impact. Generally we cannot expect that a large organization can be maintained over a long time on the basis of purposive motivation of its members and supporters. However, purposive motivation of a large number of individuals may be a good starting point for the formation of a powerful interest organization. The history of trade unions in Western Europe illustrates this case.

There remains a systematic bias of organized interest intermediation in favor of small and specialized interests, which we will show in the next section of this chapter as a major determinant of the dynamics of interest intermediation and of government growth.

In modern democracies policy making is obviously only partially determined by decisions based on political participation. A larger part of the actual policy outcome is the result of pressure politics rather than of legitimate procedures. The capacity of an interest group effectively to engage in pressure politics is determined by political power rather than by mass support. The former generally requires considerable control over scarce resources (including information) or special functions.

While the capacity of an interest group to get organized, to maintain effective organization, and to mobilize mass support are closely related to its size, its capacity to control scarce resources and special functions is more difficult to determine.

(1) Basically, the control of scarce resources is determined by the distribution of property and the regulation of property rights in a society.

(2) The control over special functions is determined by the organization of production and distribution in a society and the related division of labor.

(3) Direct size effects occur to the extent to which the control over scarce resources or special functions necessitates prior mobilization of members or supporters.

(4) There are, however, considerable indirect size effects for the scarcity of resources and the importance of functions is related to the number of suppliers of resources or functions.

Given these conditions there are two types of interest groups with good chances of effectively engaging in pressure politics: those that are related to property and more generally to capital, and those connected to skilled labor. Note, however, that the interests of unskilled labor may often be effective because of organizational integration with skilled labor as is the case in the German *Einheitsgewerkschaft*. Normally, interests that are neither related to property and capital nor to skilled labor have little chance of effectively applying pressure politics. Moreover, the potential effectiveness increases with increasing scarcity of resources and of possible supply of special functions. Finally, the more that groups can monopolize the provision of scarce resources or special functions, the more effective they will be.[7]

The control of scarce resources or special functions not only provides a high potential for political (and economic) power, but it also reduces the costs of pressure politics. Dependence forces other interests and governmental agencies to support the interests of those in control of the supply to scarce resources and special functions—even if there is no explicit and actual demand for compliance. This implies that the more an interest group controls scarce resources or special functions, the less it has to rely on a high capacity of organization and mass mobilization in order to be effective.

Summarizing the argument of this section, we can conclude that the amount of government activity is determined by the number of interest groups that can be effectively organized and that can either gain control over scarce resources or special functions or that can sufficiently mobilize mass support. This conclusion, however, is cut somewhat short because the argument neglects the costs of government activity. For the sake of simplicity we will introduce these costs later and will first explain governmental growth under the assumption that the costs of government do not significantly change organized interest intermediation.

Socioeconomic Development, Interest Organization, and Government Growth

We have demonstrated that the increasing density of economic organization and the increasing societal differentiation typical for the development of capitalist societies create increasing social and economic market failure. In this section we will demonstrate that the same factors enhance the organization of interests and thus create an increasing demand for government activity.

As far as the density of economic organization is concerned we can assume that the increasing organization of capital in terms of large firms and the corresponding concentration of the means of production in terms of oligopolistic structures create, as a by-product, effective political organization. Large firms with significant control over production and scarce resources may use their power economically and bypass the market mechanism. They can also use the same power politically and impose pressure on government. Consequently, the increasing density of economic organization is always paralleled by an increasing potential for political pressure. This potential in turn may be used politically to reach higher profits or better conditions than those provided by the market. We may hence conjecture that with the increasing density of economic organization, effective demand for government activity from the capital side increases too.

While the increasing density of economic organization primarily enhances effective political organization of capital, increasing societal differentiation does the same with respect to labor. Societal differentiation consists mainly of the decomposition of societies into a larger number of different interest strata corresponding to the division of labor. Due to their relatively small size, these interest strata bear considerable potential for effective organization. The chance that these interest strata are organized if there is a sufficient purposive incentive is rather high. Since societal differentiation is paralleled by social and economic market failure, motivation is high for most interests to become organized. Moreover, societal differentiation accounts for an increasing control of special functions by organized interests.

Societal differentiation is primarily based on the division of labor, which creates special functions in production and distribution. Hence societal differentiation parallels to a high degree functional differentiation and the distribution of special functions. This implies that those interests that are due to societal differentiation gain a high capacity for organization, and those due to functional differentiation gain considerable control over special functions. In other words, interest groups affected by the division of labor reach both a high organizational capacity and considerable political power. Moreover, as the division of labor increases, the number of interest groups with high potential for effective pressure politics increases too (Widmaier, 1978).

Altogether, socioeconomic development of capitalism is associated with an increase in the demand for government activity to compensate for nonaccepted market allocation. Furthermore, once government activity is an established alternative to market coordination, we can expect demand for government activity whenever government can provide more benefits or higher profits than market coordination. Hence increasing density of economic organization and increasing societal differentiation will, via increasing organized demands, result in increasing government activity and a continuous growth of government.

This development, however, favors specific kinds of interests only—namely the interests of concentrated capital and the interests of specialized and highly skilled labor. Small capital and unskilled labor, as well as interests that are not directly involved in production and distribution, but rather are associated with consumption (of goods and bads) such as ecologists, young people, and old people, are relatively deprived with respect to organizational capacity and the control of scarce resources and special functions, especially if they are large.

Interest groups with little pressure power have to mobilize mass support in order to be effective. Contrary to pressure politics, the mobilization of mass support is rendered more difficult by increasing societal differentiation. The differentiation of positions, needs, and values reduces societal consensus, and the reduction of societal concensus obviously is combined with a declining chance to mobilize and to maintain mass support. In addition to this, most interests on the consumption side and most interests associated with little specialized and skilled labor have to rely for the most part on purposive incentives in order to form and to maintain an organization. These interests thus remain underrepresented in organized interest intermediation—and government intervention can only partially compensate for social market failure.[8]

However, this situation contains a dialectical feature. To the extent to which government intervention is controlled by special and particular interests controlling scarce resources or special functions, the output of government activity and the outcome of market coordination significantly deviate from the distribution of needs and preferences in a society. This deviation in turn contains purposive incentives for the neglected interest groups to organize. If these incentives are sufficiently high—that is, if the deviation of government allocation from societal preference is sufficiently high—some interest groups may increase their organizational capacity to an extent that also increases the effectiveness of demand. Government activity under the influence of the interests that control scarce resources or special functions hence increases the effectiveness of the neglected interests and thus creates new demands for government activity. In other words, to the extent to which the outcome of government activity deviates from societal preference, new demands for government activity are created.

New demands involve interests of a larger number of people with limited organizational capacity; such new demands are for the most part not intermediated conventionally. Rather, the concerned interests rely on a social movement type of organization with a small caucus of activists and punctual mobilization of mass support. Typical examples are the student movement of the late 1960s in the United States and some European countries, the ecologists, and the peace movement that currently is in formation in several European countries. These interests often work within established organizations (churches and parties) and through unconventional behavior (protest, strikes, and occupation of property). This strategy, which resembles the strategy of working-class organization in the last century, involves rather low costs and may be highly effective if sufficient mass support can be mobilized.[9]

Although such new demands partially reduce the deviation of government output from societal preference, they are not sufficient finally to adjust government output to societal preference. The reason for this lies in the nature of purposive incentives: The motivation of members and supporters to further contribute to the common interest necessarily declines to the extent to which demands of interest groups, whose organizational capacity and political power are primarily based on purposive incentives, are satisfied. This implies that even when government increases its activities and expands its scope, it will hardly produce an equilibrium in which government output fits societal preference; whatever government does, it is likely to reproduce in some way or another dissatisfaction with government output.

Thus while continuously growing, government activity also creates continuous new demands for government activity. If we carried this argument to the end, we would have to predict that the continuous growth of government would last until the market and the private sectors vanished. Such a prediction would fit well into the gloomy view of Joseph A. Schumpeter, but would nevertheless be wrong. Our argument so far has neglected the costs of government activity and their impact on the organization of interest.

The Costs of Government and
Their Implication for
Interest Organization

As in the case with other features of government growth, the relationship of costs and expansion of government activity is somewhat dialectical. The reason for this is simply the fact that government activities are collective goods. Accordingly, the costs and benefits of government activity are dissociated from each other; those that benefit from government activity do not necessarily need to bear the costs of the activity. On the contrary, we may reasonably assume that those interests that are powerful enough to forward effective demand for government activity also are powerful enough to carry a favorable distribution of costs into effect. This implies that costs of government activities are usually externalized by its beneficiaries and imposed to a large extent on neglected interests. This externalization of costs has two important effects: It decreases demand for government activity on the part of powerful interests and it increases, with considerable lag, the organizational capacities of the neglected interests.

The fact that interest groups do not have to pay the appropriate price for the government activities they demand is likely to increase the demand forwarded by these interests. This results in an escalation of government activity and its costs. Although the costs of government activity can be widely dispersed, they nevertheless impose considerable loads on a number of interest groups that do not adequately profit from government activity. These loads constitute additional purposive incentives that increase the capacity of some of these interest groups to get organized and to mobilize support either to put forward demands for compensatory benefits or to resist increasing taxation. Effective demands for compensatory benefits will further accelerate the growth of government activity and aggravate the cost problem. Effective resistance against taxation will limit a government's capacity to enlarge its activity or will enforce it to impose higher costs on the beneficiaries. In both cases the escalation of government activity is slowed down. If government is forced increasingly to impose the costs of its activities on the beneficiaries, demand for further activities from this side will decrease. If tax resistance increases, government increasingly meets overload problems which prevent the adjustments of supply and demand. Note, however, that increasing tax resistance often influences government financial capacities only with great time lags because government can increase its financial capacity by increasing its debts and by printing additional money.

These two conditions are not equally probable because the established power structure of organized interest intermediation hinders the adjustment of demand to the supply capacity of government. Sufficiently powerful interests will not easily reduce the demand for government activity based on the limited supply capacity of government. It will be inclined to maintain demand and to attempt to carry repressive measures against less powerful interests into effect. Increasing repression, however, adds to the government overload because it increases the costs of government and, more important, it creates increasingly purposive incentives for relatively deprived interests to increase their organizational capacity. Finally, the escalation of government activity has

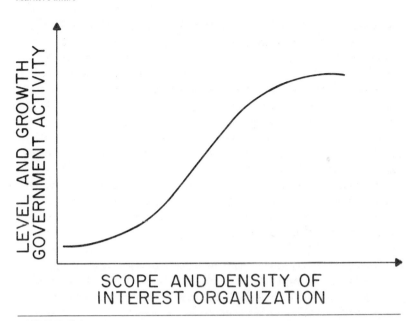

SCOPE AND DENSITY OF
INTEREST ORGANIZATION

FIGURE 13.1

to slow down for the simple reason that government is overloaded and access to government is overcrowded by conflicting interests.

At this point we have to modify our hypotheses on the relationship of societal interest organization and government growth. Considering the costs of government activity and its impact on the organization of government interests, a hypothesis based upon Figure 13.1 seems more appropriate. The slowdown of the escalation of government activity does not imply that the latter approximates a condition of equilibrium. Rather, such a condition cannot be reached because the postulated reduction of government growth does not result from adjustment of demand for government activity, but it is simply created by government overload. Government is no longer capable of meeting demands because its supply capacity is increasingly limited.

At this point, we have to consider differences between governmental activities in terms of financial benefits and in terms of regulatory activities. Fiscal benefits and regulations as the major sources of government intervention meet different conditions with respect to scarcity. We may generally assume that the financial resources of government are scarcer than regulatory resources, and that demand for fiscal benefits is generally higher and grows faster than that for regulatory activities. If this is true the overload problem will first and more strongly appear with respect to the capacity of government to provide financial benefits. Consequently, the supply of financial benefits will decline relatively faster than that of regulatory activities (Economic Council of Canada, 1979).

A relative decline in financial benefits provided by government will create increasing dissatisfaction. In order to reduce this dissatisfaction, government will quite logically offer increasing regulatory activities instead. By doing so government can increase its activities while externalizing a considerable part of the costs; the costs of regulation have partially to be paid by the regulated in terms of direct expenses and losses from restrictions of transactions. This fact enables government to ease further its activities without facing correspondingly rising costs and increasing opposition against regulation. Government will be increasingly involved in conflicts with socioeconomic interests as it increases its regulatory output. Increasing regulation imposes increasing political costs on government that finally severely restrict its capacity to regulate. This development is often accelerated by court interventions that force government to increase regulatory output beyond the desired amount. In the end the government's capacity to regulate is as limited as its capacity to provide financial benefits; government is confronted with both a fiscal and a regulatory crisis that severely restricts its capacity to intervene and to compensate for social and economic market failure.

The relative incapacity of government to meet demand does not, as we have said before, imply that demand on government will be adjusted to the supply capacity of government. Rather, it results in increasing dissatisfaction with government output and in increasing and increasingly complex pressure on government. This in turn aggravates the overload problem for government.

In the perspective of the analysis presented thus far, government, impelled by the dynamics of the socioeconomic development of capitalism, has grown so much that it finds itself in a crisis, and it cannot solve this crisis because it can no longer grow as fast as it did before. Such a conclusion can only hope that the overload crisis of government creates one of those unique historical situations in which fundamental change is not predicted but nevertheless is possible. This conclusion, however, carries our argument to excess. First of all, the fact that government can no longer meet demand for government activities will in the long run enhance a reduction in demand. As effective interest intermediation declines, so do the capacities of many interest groups to maintain powerful organizations. The motivation of group members to contribute to the costs of organization will fall as success seems uncertain. This will to some degree reduce the overall demand on government.

More important, government itself can develop capacities to control and to integrate organized interest intermediation. The growth of organized interest intermediation and the growth of government are based on socioeconomic development, but they have taken place under specific institutional conditions. In most Western democracies the latter have facilitated the pursuit of organized pressure on government. The political institutions of Western democracies are historically the political institutions of a liberal society and have not been designed to manage high demands on government. Unlike spontaneous market coordination, government steering requires a purposive aggregation of interests and preferences. In democratic regimes this interest aggregation needs to be highly consensual since a low degree of consensus creates political instability, which in turn prevents purposive interest aggregation.

These conditions can hardly be met by the political institutions of the liberal democracies if they are confronted with a high scope of politics and a high degree of societal differentiation. The representative institutions of government, namely elections and parliament, can only integrate a rather low number of issues and can hardly provide a systematic and consensual government program. This inevitable selectivity involves a strong tendency to cyclical and inconsistent interest aggregation. Due to societal differentiation, parties and party systems are confronted with problems of conflict and consistency, which often prevent a purposive and systematic interest aggregation as well. A high scope of politics is usually associated with a segmentation of the administrative apparatus of government. To the extent to which government activity is determined or shaped by bureaucracies, segmentation of political-administrative decision making hinders consistent and purposive government steering. Bureaucratic segmentation and the high differentiation of the electorate and parties increase the chances of organized interests effectively to carry through their demands because segmentation and differentiation prevent direct competition between organized interests. There are, of course, important differences among Western democracies; some such as Switzerland are more integrated institutionally than others such as the United States. Overall, the Western democracies are badly equipped to cope with high demand and highly organized pressure.

In order to reach a better control of government activity and to keep it within a manageable and reasonable scope, institutional reforms are necessary that increase government's capacity to integrate demand and to resist pressure from organized interests. The above-mentioned institutional problems indicate the dimensions of such reforms. Moreover, government has to intervene in interest organization and its intermediation in order to manage demand for government activity at its source. Attempts to establish neocorporatist structures in several European countries mark the first steps in the right direction. Although current attempts for controlling organized interest intermediation and for institutional reforms have not gone very far and are still weak, the logic of our argument suggests that they will become stronger in the future. The more the costs of excessive demand on government increase and exceed the costs of reforms, the higher the chances for reforms become.

From Theoretical Arguments
to Empirical Research:
A Dynamic Model
of Government Growth

The arguments presented in this chapter are at present of a theoretical nature and raise considerable problems for empirical testing. Some of the concepts are not yet operationalized and some operationalizations lack a data base. Still, we believe that there are possibilities and strategies that can transform our theoretical arguments into an empirically testable model. Therefore we would like to conclude this chapter with a few brief remarks on the operationalization and measurement of the theoretical concepts we have employed. This will have the character more of a research agenda than a report on results.

Since our concept of the growth and the size of the public sector is initially rather broad, it requires more than just monetary measures of growth. We have to take into account the regulatory activities of governments as well, since both are important in our argument and specifically linked to each other. (This requires at a later stage a division of the government growth level into a budgetary-fiscal part and a regulatory part since we would like to model the substitution and trade-off effects between these two components.) The inclusion of measures of government regulatory activities unfortunately constitutes a much bigger problem compared to the already considerable difficulties involved in collecting budgetary data.

For example, it is not sufficient to count the number of bills passed by parliaments since in a number of states these kinds of activities are done on the level of government or executive orders (Lehner and Dean, 1981). Furthermore, it may be impossible to study all sectors of government regulation activity. A comparative case study will probably be more insightful because the measurements would consider the specific institutional circumstances in which regulations are issued. One is likely to commit fallacies stemming from aggregating across a variety of institutional settings. A compromise might be a two- or three-sector comparative longitudinal study since it would minimize both the problem of an aggregational fallacy and the difficulty of generalizing from one sector to the whole array of state activity. The time period since World War II will supply us with a time series long enough to study the dynamics of the hypothesized relationships.

More specifically, in order to test our theoretical framework we need data on the number and intensity of state regulations in selected sectors. These could be obtained by interviewing experts in those sectors. The indicators should not only cover regulatory measures taken by the state, which are repressive or conflicting, but also those of a cooperative nature. Together with those indicators we will have to collect or assemble more conventional data on government growth (increasing size of budgets, public employment, transfer payments, government income, deficits, and so on).

Having covered the growth and size of the public sector in its regulatory and financial component, we have to address our data collection efforts to the question of how to measure the degree and density of interest organization in a given sector. The number of organizations is one indicator, the number of people in those organizations another. The latter is very often more questionable because it is difficult to estimate potential membership. Furthermore, the strength of the commitment members have to these partic ular groups has to be evaluated. In addition, the intensity or radicality with which organizations pursue their interests has to be taken into account. The collection of this information requires a relatively intimate knowledge about a sector. This constitutes another argument for why we suggest a two-sector comparative study, at least to begin with.

In general one could argue that the size of a sector is a crucial determinant of the degree it is or can be organized. This holds both for the economic organization (e.g., business) and the social organization (e.g., workers and consumers). The smaller the number of firms and the greater their regional concentration, the more effectively they can press governments to make favorable allocation decisions. Similar processes operate for social groups; the more specialized functions a group controls and the smaller it is, the more it will be organized and the stronger its impact on government decision making. A number of empirical studies have demonstrated that these hypotheses hold in general. For example, it was shown that size and concentration of industries are significant variables in explaining variations in the tariff protection they are able to receive from the state (Glismann and Weiss, 1980).

A final data collection effort concerns the indicators measuring the outcomes or consequences of public growth, that is, variables such as resistance to taxation and regulation, political conflicts on benefits and costs of state activity, and to a certain degree expectations of government. We envision that these data will come from a variety of sources including survey data, membership data of antitax movements, reports on the rise and fall of antitax parties, strike activities, and other forms of protest manifestations. These data have to be collected mostly from journalistic sources. Fortunately, to some extent such collections exist. One example are the political events data of the *World Handbook of Political and Social Indicators* (Taylor and Jodice, 1982).

Normally, we would expect resistance and protest only in a situation where the disadvantages or costs of state actions are higher than the benefits.

This basically means that well-organized groups, in pressing for state actions, will transfer the costs to less-organized groups. Therefore, to a certain degree the situation stabilizes itself; since these groups are generally less organized, we also expect less protest. A critical situation arises only when conditions allow for organized collective protests from these otherwise poorly organized sections of society.

Summarizing these intentions on the empirical side, we realize that the task is formidable but not impossible to achieve. The growth of empirical research on the growth of the public sector will, we hope, generate results and data collections that will be useful in our efforts to test empirically the theoretical framework outlined in this chapter.

NOTES

1. As an example, the anti-inflation policy in the 1970s in Germany and other Western countries had substantial unintended structural effects on the functioning of the market in terms of concentration and changes in the structure of occupation (Hankel and Lehner, 1976).

2. Our understanding of the socioeconomic and political consequences of technological development is, of course, strongly influenced by J. K. Galbraith (1973) and J. A. Schumpeter (1942). Sociological studies on the stratification of modern industrial societies demonstrate the strong differentiating impact of division of labor on social structure (Giddens, 1975).

3. We acknowledge that alternative mechanisms of allocation may not be more effective in relating needs to buying power and the distribution of goods and services in a society.

4. In order to be efficient, governmental allocation has to be based on consensual decision making, which is obviously rendered the more difficult the more preferences and needs are differentiated.

5. Note again that dissatisfaction will occur whether or not market allocation is economically efficient, for an individual's evaluation of market outputs is determined by his own needs and perceived possibilities of getting needs satisfied rather than by the wisdom of economic theory and an understanding of the meaning of "Pareto-optimality."

6. As to the problematic of the organization of special interests, our argument is primarily based on Olson (1964) and Wilson (1973). Following Wilson there are basically three types of incentives that organizations can provide to actual and potential members:

(1) Purposive incentives—incentives that stem directly from the purpose of an organization. Psychologically, we can speak of an intrinsic motivation.
(2) Social incentives—nonmaterial (intangible) goods, such as status, public esteem, or power.
(3) Material incentives—tangible goods, such as money, jobs, or other benefits. Their value can be expressed in terms of money, as well as the withholding of desired goods and services.

Social and material incentives, both of which express elements of an extrinsic motivation, may be collective or selective incentives—they may either be collective goods for all members of the actual or potential organization or they may, even within the organization, be private goods that are paid in return for special functions or services provided to the organization.

7. Quite clearly, in modern societies there is always a considerable number of interests

having at least some control over scarce resources or special functions. Therefore, the potential effectiveness of each of these groups is also determined by its relations to the other groups. This is not only and not even primarily a question of relative power between potentially powerful groups, but much more one of the patterns of interactions among these groups. Relative power is only of crucial importance in cases in which the interests of groups directly compete. In these cases the power of those groups in a society that control scarce resources or special functions may be mutually balancing and checking. Altogether, this could drastically reduce the total power of interests controlling scarce resources or special functions in relation to government. Often, however, interests are not directly competing and thus do not mutually balance or check each other. Apart from contents, the degree to which interests are directly competitive depends on the sheer number of existing groups: The larger the number of groups the less they are engaged in direct competition. The reason for this is simply that among many groups the gains and losses of each group are not directly and clearly associated with the losses and gains of each other group. Furthermore, institutional arrangements concerning demand aggregation and collective decision making often prevent or minimize competition among organized interests. Finally, potential competition of interests with respect to the production of public goods can often be reduced by increasing the total amount of goods and services produced by government. Hence we cannot expect pressure power resulting from the control over scarce resources and special functions to be severely limited by competition of interests.

8. In order fully to compensate for market failure, government intervention would have to be based on a power distribution that corresponds with the distribution of needs in the society. This is, obviously, never the case.

9. As far as the mobilization of mass support is concerned, we are dealing with a somewhat dialectical situation. On one side mass support is obviously the more effective the larger it is. This implies that an interest organization's chance effectively to mobilize support increases with its size. On the other hand, the mobilization of mass support faces similar, although less severe mobilization problems (free-rider problems) than the organization of interest itself. This implies that the capacity of mobilizing mass support has a tendency to decline with the size of an interest group. Considering both sides, we may reasonably assume that the capacity of interest organizations effectively to mobilize mass support reaches some satisfaction level.

REFERENCES

ATKINSON, A. B. (1974) The Economics of Inequality. Oxford: Clarendon Press.
BARNES, S. H., M. KAASE, ET AL. (1979) Political Action: Mass Participation in Five Western Democracies. Beverly Hills, CA: Sage.
BUCHANAN, J. M. (1974) The Limits of Liberty. Chicago: University of Chicago Press.
BUDGE, I., J. A. BRAND, M. MARGOLIS, and A. L. M. SMITH (1972) Political Stratification and Democracy. London: Macmillan.
DEUTSCH, K. W. (1974) Government and Politics. Boston: Houghton Mifflin.
Economic Council of Canada (1979) Responsible Regulation. Ottawa: Ministry of Supply and Services.
GALBRAITH, J. K. (1973) Economics and the Public Purpose. Boston: Houghton Mifflin.
GIDDONS, A. (1974) The Class Structure of the Advanced Societies. New York, London: Harper & Row.
GLISMANN, H. H. and F. D. WEISS (1980) On the Political Economy of Protection in Germany. Working Paper 113, Kiel Institute of World Economics, November.
HABERMAS, J. (1973) Legitimationsprobleme im Spätkapitalismus. Frankfurt: Suhrkamp.
HANKEL, W. and F. LEHNER (1976) "Die gescheiterte Stabilitätspolitik und ihre politischen Bedingungen." Hamburger Jahrbuch für Wirtschafts- und Gesellschaftspolitik.

INGLEHART, R. (1977) The Silent Revolution. Princeton, NJ: Princeton University Press.

IONESCOU, G. (1974) Contripetal Politics: Government and New Centers of Power. London: Hart-Davis.

JANOWITZ, M. (1976) Social Control of the Welfare State. New York: Elsevier.

_____ (1970) Political Conflict. Chicago: Quadrangle.

LEHNER, FRANZ (1979) Grenzen des Regierens. Königstein: Athenäum.

_____ and J. DEAN (1981) Politisch-ökonomische Spielräume und Grenzen der Bankerequlierung und ihrer Reform in der Bundesrepublik Deutschland, der Schweiz, Kanada und den Vereinigten Staaten von Amerika. Ruhr University, Bochum. (unpublished)

OBERSCHALL, A. (1973) Social Conflicts and Social Movements. Englewood Cliffs, NJ: Prentice-Hall.

OFFE, C. (1975) Strukturprobleme des kapitalistischen Staates. Frankfurt: Suhrkamp.

_____ (1972) "Politische Herrschaft und Klassenstrukturen," in C. Krees and D. Senghaas (eds.) Politikwissenschaft. Frankfurt: Fischer.

OLSON, M. (1964) The Logic of Collective Action. Cambridge, MA: Harvard University Press.

SCHUMPETER, J. A. (1942) Capitalism, Socialism, and Democracy. New York: Harper and Row.

TARSCHYS, D. (1978) "The growth of public expenditures: nine models of explanation." Scandinavian Political Studies 10, 1: 9.

TAYLOR, C. L. and D. A. JODICE (1982) World Handbook of Political and Social Indicators. New Haven, CT: Yale University Press.

WIDMAIER, U. (1978) Politische Gewaltanwendung als Probleme der Organisation von Interessen. Meisenheim am Glan: Hain.

WILSON, J. Q. (1973) Political Organizations. New York: Basic Books.

CHAPTER 14

THE GROWTH OF THE TAX STATE
The Industrial Democracies, 1950-1978

MANFRED G. SCHMIDT

The role of government in most of the advanced industrial democracies increased dramatically in the three decades following World War II. The "tax state," defined in terms of the extractive capacity of general government (Goldscheid, 1917; Schumpeter, 1976; Grauhan and Hickel, 1978), was in most cases enormously expanded. The major component of this expansion was growth in welfare expenditures (OECD, 1978; Castles, 1982). Nevertheless, the development took place on the basis of very different initial conditions and at varying rates from country to country. In countries such as France, the Netherlands, and Britain, development occurred within the context of a public economy that was already of considerable size of 1950. Taxes and social security contributions as a percentage of GDP increased particularly rapidly in Sweden, the Netherlands, Norway, Ireland, Denmark, Belgium, and Canada, but the rate of change in Japan, the United States, and Switzerland has been rather modest. Both the percentage share and the rates of change are reported in Table 14.1. Reasons for these variations have been the topic of some controversy; see Tarschys (1978), Cameron (1978), and Schmidt (1982a: 89-94) for reviews of the literature.

Economists have tended to argue that the size and rate of expansion of the tax state vary positively, either linearly or nonlinearly, with levels of economic wealth, rates of economic growth, population increase, degrees of urbanization, and technological innovation, and that they vary inversely with

AUTHOR'S NOTE: The research for this report was supported by a grant from the Deutsche Forschungsgemeinschaft. Sections of the present chapter are an abridged version of an analysis that has been fully documented in Schmidt (1982a, 1982b).

TABLE 14.1 The Tax State and the Political Complexion of Governments in Twenty-One Capitalist Democracies (1950-1978)

	Size of the Tax State				Expansion			Dominant Tendency in Government		
	Tax State 1950	Tax State 1960	Tax State 1975	Tax State 1978	Tax State 1950-1960	Tax State 1960-1975	Tax State 1973-1978	1950-1960	1960-1975	1974-1978
	(percent GDP)				(percentage points)					
Australia	20.5[2]	25.5	31.6	31.9	5.0	6.1	3.2	1	2	3
Austria	28.0	31.0	39.1	44.5	3.0	8.1	6.5	3	3	5
Belgium	24.0[1]	27.5	40.6	42.7	3.5	13.1	6.3	2	2	2
Canada	24.7	26.0	37.1	35.8	1.3	11.1	-0.4	1	1	1
Denmark	21.8	27.5	45.3	49.0	5.7	17.8	3.3	3	3	4
Finland	30.4	31.6	39.8	40.2	1.2	8.2	1.7	2	2	2
France	32.8	34.0	40.5	42.3	1.2	6.5	3.7	2	1	1
FRG	31.5	35.4	41.0	43.3	3.9	5.6	2.1	1	3	4
Iceland	27.6[5]	27.8[5]	26.6	27.9[8]	9.4[6]	-1.2[7]	1.8[8]	1	2	2
Ireland	23.4	24.5	36.8	32.2[8]	1.1	12.3	-2.7[8]	2	2	2
Israel	14.4	28.7	38.9[4]	—	14.3	10.2	—	4	4	3

Italy	21.0[2]	29.8	35.2	37.0	8.8	5.4	3.2	1	2	2
Japan	21.7[3]	20.2	23.6	24.3	-1.5	3.4	1.1	1	1	1
Luxemburg	32.5[3]	32.5	50.6	50.0[8]	0.0	18.1	9.8[8]	3	2	3
New Zealand	27.0[1]	28.4	31.4	33.6[8]	1.4	3.0	9.2[8]	2	2	3
Netherlands	32.8	33.1	52.6	54.4	0.3	19.5	5.2	2	2	2
Norway	29.7[2]	34.5	49.7	52.1	4.8	15.2	2.5	5	3	5
Sweden	25.9	34.9	52.6	60.3	9.0	17.7	11.7	4	5	3
Switzerland	25.1	25.1	32.1	34.0	0.0	7.0	5.2	2	2	2
United Kingdom	32.6	29.3	41.1	38.8	-3.3	11.8	1.9	2	3	4
United States	23.9	28.2	30.6	32.6	4.3	2.4	1.4	1	1	1

NOTES: Tax State = Revenues from tax and social security contribution of general government as percentage of GDP. (Source: *OECD National Accounts Statistics*, various volumes, and *United Nations National Accounts Statistics*, various volumes).

Dominant tendency in government = (for details of measurement see Note 2)

    1 = Bourgeois hegemony
    2 = Bourgeois dominance
    3 = Balance
    4 = Social democratic dominance
    5 = Social democratic hegemony

1. 1953 2. 1951 3. 1952 4. 1974 5. 1961 6. 1951-1960 7. 1961-1975 8. Preliminary estimates.

the size of the agricultural sector of the economy. According to this view the expansionary impetus stemmed from the reaction of the authorities to the pressures of rapid economic growth and technological change, to the revolution of rising expectations fueled by the experience of postwar prosperity, and to the social problems generated by rapidly changing social structures and institutions (see, for example, Musgrave and Musgrave, 1973, and Wittman, 1978).

Marxist writers have suggested that the increase in state revenues and expenditures is a function of inherent strains that are the consequences of the development of capitalism and particularly of the class conflicts accompanying the process. To a large degree the expansion of the tax state is seen as a mechanism by which the capitalist state formulates and implements policies designed to secure the long-term reproduction of a capitalist mode of production (Foley, 1978; Gough, 1979). Marxists have emphasized the limits of growth for the tax state. While there is a growing need for measures of state intervention, the fundamental expansion of the extractive capacity of the state is impeded. State activities must neither violate profit-maximizing strategies nor undermine incentives to work. Otherwise, partial investment strikes, increased capital export, and reduction of work discipline are likely to lead to economic decline, increased unemployment, and a reduced volume of revenue.

The Marxist analysis is valuable in diagnosing the common structural problems of the economies under study, but its focus on the general nature of such problems and the limited degree to which the theoretical concepts are operationalized provides less valid cross-national explanatory power with respect to the variation in the sizes and the rates of expansion in the public sectors of the capitalist democracies. Nor are the general modes of economic explanation fully compatible with the actual variation in these states. For example, neither neoclassical nor Marxist economists are able to explain the slow growth of the tax revenue in the United States, Japan, and Switzerland, where transformations in social fabric were very rapid and rates of economic growth were comparatively high.

The prevailing economic and socioeconomic explanations of the growth of the tax state have been challenged by several sociologists and political scientists. Anthony King (1973: 418), for example, has argued that the comparatively small public sector in the United States was only a reflection of the dominant values and preferences inherent in American public opinion. Recent contributions of studies on political-economic linkages also lend further support to a sociological and political explanation. Studies on political business cycles have provided evidence for the view that governments pursue more expansive policies as their popularity deficit comes close to a critical threshold for reelection and as the election approaches (Frey, 1979; Frey and Schneider, 1979). For a critical reassessment in comparative perspective, see Schmidt (1982c). Many authors in the comparative public policy area have emphasized the vital importance of ideology and partisan control of governments as determinants of economic policy in general and of the development of the tax state in particular. The degree of expansion in tax revenue varies with the political complexion of the government. Social democratic governments are on the whole more willing than bourgeois governments to intervene actively in the market (Cameron, 1978; Tufte, 1978; Schmidt, 1980; Stephens, 1979). With a somewhat different sample and time period, Kohl (1981) found an opposite result, but it would seem fair to conclude that politics is an important determinant of tax state development, especially when the structures of party systems, the degree of cohesion of the bourgeois tendency, and the amount of left-wing tendency are simultaneously taken into account. For example, the state interventionist policies of a bourgeois government confronted by a strong, united left-wing party in opposition and a highly organized trade union movement would be substantially different from the policies of a purely conservative government with much wider room to maneuver in parliamentary and other arenas.

Finally, in outlining the major hypotheses in this field, it is necessary to return to Cameron's seminal study on the growth of the public economy in eighteen capitalist countries between 1960 and 1975. Cameron's argument is important because it adds an international economic aspect to the explanation of growth. While the social democratic complexion of government is a sufficient, although not a necessary, condition for an expansive tax state, the relative openness of the economy is ultimately the major determinant of the expansion of the public sector. A sequence of economic, sociological, and political characteristics that derived from the openness of the economy, such as high industrial concentration, high unionization, and strong labor confederations, and the domestic requirements produced by a strong integration in the world market result in large increases in spending supplements and an expansion of the public sector (Cameron, 1978).

The class politics hypothesis, by which is stated that public policies are ultimately the result of power relationships and conflicts within the society, is a hybrid of these political and economic models. Theoretically, it proceeds from the Marxist assumption concerning the laws of motion of the capitalist mode of production; but by pointing to the role played by the structures, strategies, and outcomes of the class struggle engendered by that mode of production, it concedes that policies may be relevant to the shaping of macroeconomic policy.

In the subsequent analysis of the determinants of the growth of the tax state, it is our intention to examine which of the hypotheses provides the best understanding and which fits the data best. We test the hypotheses in the context of a research design utilizing cross-national secondary data for all twenty-one countries that have had both advanced capitalist economies and democratic political procedures since 1950. In order to avoid the pitfalls commonly associated with cross-sectional analysis, our study will combine comparative analysis of the size and rate of expansion of the tax state with a set of time-series analyses of the individual countries. Three time periods are used: (1) 1950-1960, the period of postwar reconstruction; (2) 1960-1975, the period of Cameron's investigation; and (3) 1974-1978, a period of economic crisis.

The dependent variables are the size and rate of expansion of the tax state as measured by current revenues from tax and social security contributions to general government as a percentage of gross domestic product.[1] Measurement of the other economic and social variables follows conventions of comparative public policy analysis. In addition, two sets of political indicators were developed. The political composition of governments is measured by indicators of the duration and strength of bourgeois parties (Liberal, Conservative, Center) and of left-wing parties (Social Democratic and Communist) in government.[2] Indicators of the relative size of both tendencies and of the relative cohesiveness of each were constructed in order to account for both the overall power distribution and the political room for maneuver for the incumbent tendency.[3] In an attempt to assess the nature of extraparliamentary political action, indicators of union strength, levels of industrial conflict, and the development of corporatist structures have been used.[4] Given the low number of cases, a full specification of the models can be approximated only by a set of bivariate analyses and a set of multivariate analyses with no more than two independent variables.[5]

The explanations advanced are probabilistic. They do not fully account for each under investigation, even if the proportion of the variation explained is fairly high. In addition, the causal mechanisms shaping the rates of expansion vary over time. Generally speaking, three patterns emerge. The "politics of convergence" is the most appropriate label for what happened in the period of postwar reconstruction. The 1960s and early 1970s might be characterized by the label the "primacy of party politics." The pattern governing the growth of the tax state from 1974 could be labeled the "primacy of extraparliamentary politics." Genuinely political variables are important predictors of the variation in the growth of the tax state. This result would seem to lend support to the view that further research on political and sociological economics is promising.

The Politics of Convergence

The complex relationships between the tax state and international economic dependence, class politics, party system structures, and political composition of governments for the 1950s are substantially different from what one might have expected from the literature. The latecomers, that is, states with comparatively small tax revenues in the early 1950s, such as Israel, Australia, and Italy, had the highest rates of expansion. Governments that already presided over an extensive tax state, on the other hand, tended to be much more hesitant to increase the tax and social security burden ($r = -0.67$). One can plausibly argue that the expansion of the tax state among the latecomers was a reaction of the governments to gaps in the provision of public goods and services. These gaps had become politically and economically more dangerous with the developing imbalances in the capitalist structure. Such imbalances included increasing competition from abroad, a factor obviously enhanced by the degree of integration into the world market, and the growing problem of reconciling legitimation and accumulation requirements of the state in a democratic capitalist society.

It was, however, under specific economic and domestic political conditions that those requirements and imperatives were actually translated into policy. To a degree, and with varying complex relationships, the expansion tended to be more pronounced, the more the external dependence increased ($r = 0.52$), thereby necessitating rapid assertion of control over the domestic repercussions of enhanced integration into the world market. Similarly, we find a positive association with economic growth rates ($r = 0.41$), presumably because the expansion of the economic resource base allowed for a greater growth in the public sector without strong opposition. On the political side there is a relation between expansion of the tax state and left-wing control of the major offices of state ($r = 0.49$), and, in at least some countries, it appears that a larger public sector was a more feasible objective, where organizational and ideological splits within the bourgeois political tendency allowed governments a greater room for maneuver.

Looking at the individual countries demonstrates the mixed picture in respect to the impact of partisan control of government. While the general tendency is a greater expansion in the extractive capacity of the state where the political composition of government is skewed to the left, three out of five of the leaders in this process, Australia, Iceland and Italy, were characterized by bourgeois hegemony (see Table 14.1). Of the three nations in which social democracy was either hegemonistic (Norway) or dominant (Israel and Sweden) in the 1950s, the latter two were also among the leaders and Norway came seventh, just after Denmark, which itself had a long tradition of social democratic government. On this basis there is some support for the view that partisan control does really matter, but it is by no means as conclusive as has been suggested in some parts of the literature. Moreover, it seems clear that, at best, social democratic political ascendancy is a sufficient rather than a necessary condition for the expansion of the tax state.

A similar conclusion is appropriate with respect to Cameron's explanation in terms of the impact of integration into the world economy. Although it is the case that governments tended to expand their extractive capacity in order to control the domestic consequences of a rapid increase in external dependence, some nations deviated from this trend. Thus it seems necessary to specify more fully the economic and political structures and processes that intervene in complex interrelationship between international dependence, the political complexion of governments, and policy outputs. In the 1950s differential economic growth rates, the need to make up for lost time, and rapid increase in the openness of the economy seem to be the most important intervening variables (see Figure 14.1).

The Primacy of Party Politics

The rates of expansion of the tax state between 1960 and 1975 exceeded by far those typical of the postwar period of reconstruction. During this period a large proportion of the resources extracted from the economy was shifted into welfare, education, and health programs (Castles, 1982). The findings reported in Table 14.2 concerning the expansion of the public sector between 1960 and 1975 again offer support for both the party-control-does-matter hypothesis and an explanation in terms of international economic dependency. The major differences in comparison with the 1950s are that structures of class conflict gain more importance as determinants of tax state expansion, that convergent tendencies disappear, and that economic growth rates no longer appear to be systematically related to the development of the public sector, although one can plausibly argue that the economic prosperity was the major background variable extending the range of choices available for governments in this period. In comparison to the tax state development in the 1950s, the most dramatic change is the cessation of the catching-up phenomenon and the appearance of the evidence that it was governments possessing a major extractive capacity in the early 1960s that tended to expand the extent of the public sector in the subsequent period ($r = 0.36$).

While the political composition of government and the relative openness of the economy continue to be conducive to the expansion of the tax state, there emerged in the 1960s a new set of intervening factors, which are important predictors of variation among the capitalist democracies. These factors include the degree of cohesiveness of the bourgeois tendency, the power distribution between the Left and the bourgeois milieux, and the relative strength of organized labor. Politics does make an enormous difference in the development of the tax state in the 1960s and early 1970s.

What is evident is that organizational and ideological splits within the bourgeois tendency, whether governmental power was held by bourgeois or

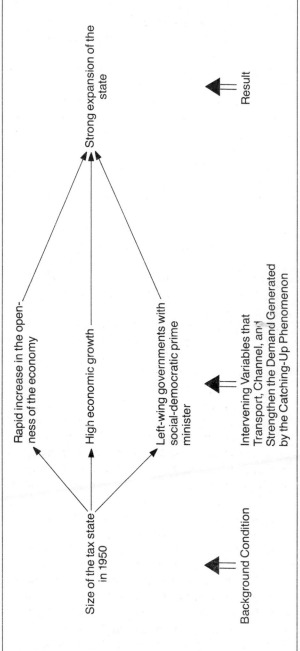

FIGURE 14.1   Politics of Convergence — The Growth of the Tax State in the 1950s (summary)

TABLE 14.2 Macrosocial Determinants of the Growth of the Tax State (Bivariate Relationships)

Hypothesis	Independent Variable	Expected Relationship	Actual Relationship 1950-1960	Actual Relationship 1960-1975	Actual Relationship 1974-1978
Party control does matter	Dominant tendency in government[1]	positive	.18	.29	.35
	Left-wing-party Prime Minister	positive	.49	.42	.13
	Left-wing-parties in office	positive	.31	.26	.20
Structure of party systems and political tendencies	Left seats	positive	.24	.34	—
	Dominant party in party system[1]	positive	.21	.51	.49
	Cohesion of bourgeois tendency (1 = weak, 0 = strong)	positive	-.21	.40	-.10
	Cohesion of left-wing tendency (1 = weak, 0 = strong)	positive	-.21	.34	.13
Extraparliamentary distribution of power	Left vote	positive	.25	.30	.53
	Corporatism (1 = weak, 2 = medium, 3 = strong)[1]	positive/inverse	—	.13	.43
	Strike	negative	—	-.35[2]	-.40[3]
	Union density[1]	positive	—	.36[2]	.46[4]
	Importance of trade unions confederation in collective bargaining	positive	—	.43	.50
Institutions	Federalism (=1)/centralism (=0)	inverse	-.09	-.32	-.16
Openness of the economy	Import and export as percent GDP at t − 1	positive	-.35	.53	.33[5]
	Import and export as percent of GDP, change between t and t − 1	positive	.52	.17	—

Economics and social structure				
Economic growth rates (per capita, constant prices)	positive	.41[6]	−.11[6]	−.60
Size of agricultural sector at t − 1	inverse	.19[6]	−.32	−.38[5]
Change in size of agricultural sector between t and t − 1	inverse	−.08[6]	.30	—
Size of wage and salary dependent labour force at t	positive	−.17	.14	.54[5]
Change in size of wage and salary dependent labour force between t and t − 1	positive	−.63	−.07	—
Rate of inflation (average between t and t − 1)	inverse	.14	−.34	−.24
Tax state in previous period				
Tax state at t − 1	inverse	−.67	.36	.21
Number of cases		21	21	20

NOTES: 1. The coefficients are Spearman's rank order correlation coefficients. All other coefficients are Pearsonian product-moment correlation coefficients. Since our sample is identical with the population we did not report significance levels. Those who really go in for significance tests will remember that with 21 cases the critical value of the coefficients at the 0.1 level is some ± .3 and some ± .37 at the 0.05 level.
2. Data were taken from Korpi and Shalev (1979). The indicators cover the total postwar period.
3. For the measurement of the strike-indicator see Note 4.
4. Pearson's r. The data on union density are for the mid-1970s.
5. 1975 data for import/export.
6. Number of cases: 20.
7. Data for Israel were not available.

leftist parties, created fewer impediments to the expansion of the public economy than where a large and politically united bourgeois tendency possessed strong veto power within the political system ($r = 0.40$). Thus a government made up of social democratic and left-wing parties, committed to reform policies, comprehensive labor market intervention, and macroeconomic demand management, which was confronted with an organizationally and ideologically split bourgeois opposition (e.g., Sweden until 1976, Norway, and Denmark), had much more room for maneuver than the Social Democratic-Free Democratic Coalition in West Germany from 1969 onward. Even under bourgeois rule the lack of cohesion of the bourgeois tendency facilitated the expansion of the tax state. This was particularly true in those cases where one of the parties in a bourgeois coalition government had close links to the trade unions and comparatively strong working-class support. Here, governments would be more sensitive to demands for enhanced state intervention (e.g., Belgium and the Netherlands). Moreover, in those cases where a bourgeois coalition engages in consensus building and where the practice of mutual overbidding results in an expansion of the state expenditures, an increased extractive capacity of the state develops (e.g., Denmark and Norway under bourgeois coalitions in the late 1960s).

At least in some countries, of which Denmark, the Netherlands, and West Germany might be the best examples, the development of the tax state was further reinforced by the combined influence of two factors. On the one hand these countries experienced a resurgence of class conflict in the 1960s and early 1970s, with the effect that, over a period of time, the burden labor imposed on capital was shifted to the state. Moreover, this reappearance of class conflict also tended to disrupt formerly stable modes of conflict resolution, with the breakup of the Dutch system of "pillarisation" being the most dramatic example. On the other hand, the growing importance of so-called postmaterialistic values in many Western nations also created an impetus for government intervention, particularly with respect to expanding educational provision. Where intensified class struggle was conjoined with new values and faced by weakened decision-making structures, the pressures for a strong upsurge in the extent of the tax state were irresistible (see Figure 14.2).

The Primacy of
Extraparliamentary Politics

We have argued that the vast expansion of the 1960s and the early 1970s was strongly facilitated by the favorable economic conditions in this period. Rates of economic growth were, generally speaking, high and rates of unemployment and inflation were relatively low. Governments were therefore in a position to expand the extractive capacities of the state without causing dangerous political opposition from those who ultimately had to pay the bill.

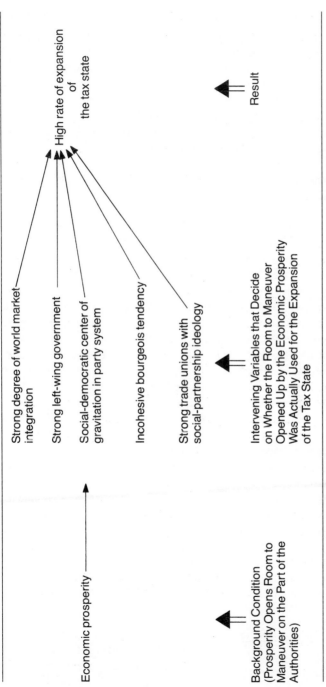

Economic prosperity ——————▶

Strong degree of world market integration

Strong left-wing government

Social-democratic center of gravitation in party system

Incohesive bourgeois tendency

Strong trade unions with social-partnership ideology

High rate of expansion of the tax state

Result

Intervening Variables that Decide on Whether the Room to Maneuver Opened Up by the Economic Prosperity Was Actually Used for the Expansion of the Tax State

Background Condition (Prosperity Opens Room to Maneuver on the Part of the Authorities)

FIGURE 14.2   The Growth of the Tax State Between 1960 and 1975 —The Primacy of Parliament and Party Politics

The question that must now be examined is what happened to the tax state in the crisis of the 1970s, when, for the most part, growth rates declined and rates of unemployment and inflation went up.

The governments of the advanced democratic states adopted very diverse strategies to cope with the new situation. Some of them—for example, Austria, Sweden, and New Zealand—continued to expand the tax state at the same rate as before or even at a faster pace. Some—for example, Norway and Denmark—slowed down the rate of expansion. Others—for example, the United States and Japan— more or less halted growth of the tax state. Only in Canada and Ireland did the size of the tax state actually manifest a decline. Apart from the states in the first group, the governments seem to have paid tribute to the conventional notion that too rapid an expansion of the public sector could provoke reaction by social groups aimed at restoring their accustomed share of income and output, and that such competition for scarce resources could be a major source of inflationary pressure and could aggravate the risk that future growth prospects would be diminished by conflict over resource allocation.

When we examine the impact of political and socioeconomic factors on tax state development during this period, we are confronted with the problem that our measurement of the dependent variable tends to inflate the figures whenever the economy is depressed. This is the case because it relates total revenues to GDP, and because in periods of economic crisis unemployment insurance, the social wage, and early retirement schemes expand the costs of social security both in absolute terms and relative to GDP. Thus it is hardly surprising that, overall, nations with low levels of economic growth tended to expand the tax state strongly and that nations with a more resilient economy mainifested the opposite tendency. Thus it was low growth countries, such as Sweden, New Zealand, and Switzerland, that reported the strongest expansion of the public economy in this period; whereas Norway, whose high economic growth was largely predicted on oil wealth, only increased the share of the tax state as a percentage of GDP by some 2.5 percentage points (see Table 14.1). The general strength of this tendency is indicated by the fact that some thirty-six percent of the total variance in the expansion of the tax state during this period is statistically explained by economic growth rates alone.

However, an examination of the residuals suggests additional insight into the policy process characterizing the crisis period. Once we have accounted for that proportion of the variance explained by economic growth, there remain important political factors at work. Relative to what one would expect on the basis of economic growth rates, the expansion of the tax state was markedly overproportionate under social democratic rule, for example, Austria and Sweden until 1976, and in countries where the dominant tendency in government was balanced, for example, Luxembourg and New Zealand. One of the major reasons for the expansion of the tax state in these countries is the policy stance adopted by the governments. State intervention was geared to keeping the rate of unemployment down, more often than not, by substantially increasing employment in the public sector (compare OEDC Economic Surveys). In contrast, in certain countries where the bourgeois tendency was either hegemonic or dominant (for example) Canada, — the expansion of the public sector was much more muted relative to economic growth rates.

Contrary to widely shared belief, it is apparent that consciously adopted policies of state intervention may foster high economic growth. The altogether favorable economic performance in Austria is, for instance, largely a consequence of compensatory demand management combined with incomes policy, enormously flexible wage policies on the part of the trade unions, comparatively low labor costs, a hard currency policy approach, and a wide variety of selective labor market measures. The Norwegian case points in much the same direction. During the mid-1970s Norway was able to combine a very high growth rate with one of the largest public economies among the capitalist democracies. While Norway's good fortune in possessing adequate domestic energy resources facilitated this development, it is quite clear that the government's demand management, labor market, and industrial policies contributed to the outcome (OECD Economic Surveys).

As a final point concerning the impact of economic factors during the crisis, it should be noted that our findings also affirm the importance of several socioeconomic factors such as the relative importance of the openness of the economy ($r = 0.33$) and the size of the agricultural sector ($r = 0.33$). However, this explanation is incomplete insofar as it fails to specify the linkages through which the pressures and imperatives inherent in economic circumstances are fed into the policy formulation process and ultimately translated into policy outputs. To understand these linkages, we must focus our attention on a number of political factors.

The picture with respect to the impact of the political composition of governments is far from straightforward. The party-control-does-matter hypothesis is not systematically supported. There is no clear dividing line between the policies pursued by governments of different political makeup. The differential performance of governments with strong social democratic parties helps to illustrate this point. In the period 1973 to 1978 Austria and Norway were ruled exclusively by their respective social democratic parties, while in Denmark, Germany, Sweden and the United Kingdom, the Social Democrats were the dominant parties of government. However, as we have already seen, it was only in Austria and Sweden that there was a substantial concomitant increase in the size of the tax state, a performance largely reflecting those countries' reliance on active demand management and labor market policies. In contrast, the expansion of the tax state was much more muted in Norway, Denmark, in West Germany, and in the United Kingdom.

There would seem to be evidence for the view that the low degree of expansion of the tax state in certain social democratic countries was a consequence of government reaction to the threat imposed by tax protest movements, such as the Anders Lange Party in Norway and the Progress Party in Denmark. In Germany the Social Democratic/Free Democratic coalition was afraid that it might lose decisive parts of its electoral base to a new tax protest party, which Herman Fredersdorf, a former member of the SPD, planned to organize (Murphy et al., 1979). Tax protest movements made the governments in these countries extremely sensitive to tax policy issues, since further distributive or redistributive policies on the part of the Social Democrats risked their potential demise at the hands of a coalition of conservative elements plus disaffected former supporters (Wilensky, 1976, 1981).

While the expansion of the tax state in the economic crisis of the 1970s is largely independent of which party is in power, the extraparliamentary distribution of power is the most important explanatory variable. The increase in the size of the public sector was systematically related to characteristics of the extraparliamentary political arena. It was higher

- the higher the left vote and thus the more the power distribution between the left milieu and the bourgeois milieu was balanced ($r = 0.53$);
- the greater the strength of trade union organization ($r = 0.46$);
- the more the power of the labor movement was institutionalized in corporatist arrangements ($r = 0.43$);
- the lower the strike volume ($r = 0.40$);
- the higher the share of wage and salary dependent labor as a percentage of the civilian labor force ($r = 0.54$).

Given the limits imposed by the preliminary status of the data and given the further limits imposed by the nonavailability of comparable data for Israel, our results tend to suggest that in the mid-1970s the expansion of the tax state was largely conditioned by the impact of the extra parliamentary power distribution on the course of governmental policy—to a great extent irrespective of which party was in power. Such a finding would be broadly compatible with the trends apparent in other areas of macroeconomic policy in the 1970s, such as in labor market policies and inflation control (Schmidt 1980, 1982b; see Figure 14.3).

Political and Economic Consequences of the Expansion of the Tax State

According to a widely shared view, the growth of the tax state has generated more problems than it has solved (Rühle and Veen, 1979; Flora, 1979).

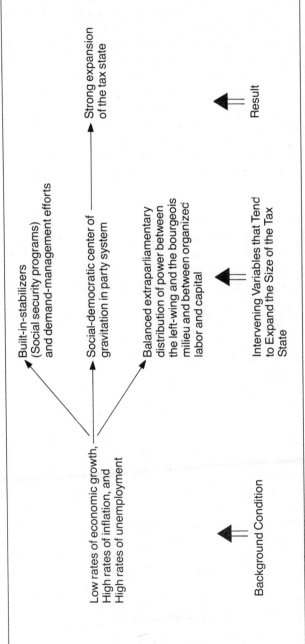

Built-in-stabilizers
(Social security programs)
and demand-management efforts

Social-democratic center of
gravitation in party system

Balanced extraparliamentary
distribution of power between
the left-wing and the bourgeois
milieu and between organized
labor and capital

Low rates of economic growth,
High rates of inflation, and
High rates of unemployment

Strong expansion
of the tax state

Result

Intervening Variables that Tend
to Expand the Size of the Tax
State

Background Condition

FIGURE 14.3   The Primacy of Extraparliamentary Politics—The Expansion of the Tax State Between 1974 and 1978

It is, for example, frequently argued that a large and expansive public sector is basically responsible for those economic problems, new political conflicts, and governability problems that have come onto the political agenda in the 1970s and the early 1980s.

Within the limits of this chapter it is not my intention fully to evaluate the economic and social costs and benefits of the growth of the tax state. However, I would like to challenge the pessimistic view referred to above with some empirical results from our analysis. The focus will be on the impact of the tax state on those four problems that also typically rank high in the preference order of conservative and liberal critics of the public sector: the level of industrial conflict, redistributive effects, the rate of unemployment, and last but not least, the rate of inflation.

Judged by the available data and investigations on comparative strike volumes (Hibbs, 1978; Flora, 1979; Korpi and Shalev, 1979), there can not be much doubt that the wide range of distributive and redistributive policies in nations with large tax states helped to contain the level and intensity of open industrial conflicts. Generally speaking, strike volumes are remarkably lower in nations with large tax and welfare states than in states where governments have pushed less in the direction of generous welfare provisions. The growth of the tax state and the growth of welfare state provisions shifted a substantial proportion of distributional conflicts from the extraparliamentary arena over to parliamentary and bureaucratic arenas. Thus the growth of the tax state has contributed to depoliticize and dampen disruptive conflicts between labor and capital though, at least in some countries, at the price of a new welfare-tax backlash phenomenon (Wilensky, 1976, 1981).

While the growth of the tax state did have enormously important political consequences, it is more than uncertain whether the nature of its economic impact was as redistributive and as destabilizing for the private sector as conservative critics would make us believe. For example, our analysis of recently published OECD figures on redistributive patterns of tax systems in OECD countries would seem to support the view that the redistributive effect of a large tax state is much more limited and much less a common phenomenon than is widely assumed (OECD, 1980). For example, the correlation between the size of the tax state and some tax progression indicators quite often yield very low or, at best, moderately high relationships.[6] These cross-national results reflect to some extent an underproportionate degree of progression and redistribution in countries with relatively large tax states, such as Austria, West Germany, and the Netherlands, and overproportionately high progression and redistribution effects in Australia and New Zealand, which are both characterized by smaller public sectors.

To what extent has the size of the tax state had an impact on the successful political control of pending economic system problems in capitalist soci-

Rates of
Inflation
(Consumer Price Index,
average 1974–1980)

	20–30 per cent	30–40 per cent	40–50 per cent
greater than 15	Iceland	Ireland Israel Italy United Kingdom	
10 to 15	Australia New Zealand	Finland France	Denmark Sweden
5 to 10	United States Japan	Belgium Canada Austria	Netherlands Norway Luxembourg
0 to 5	Switzerland	Germany	

Size of
the
tax state
(average
1970–73;
in percentages)

Sources: OECD Economic Outlook;
OECD Economic Surveys

FIGURE 14.4   Tax State and Rates of Inflation

eties? Did all of those governments possessing a large tax state, and thus control many levers for steering the economy, really employ their resources in such a way as to bring the basic and structurally given tendencies of economic instabilities under control? To what extent is there evidence for the opposite view that a large and expansive tax state generated high levels of inflation and high rates of unemployment? In order to answer these questions, we will plot the average rates of unemployment and the average rates of inflation between 1974 and 1980 against the average size of the tax state in the period before the worldwide economic recession of 1970 to 1973. The choice of such a research design is based, on the one hand, on the conservative hypothesis that the detrimental economic impact of the tax state would be particularly pronounced in periods of worsening economic conditions. On the other hand, we would argue that conditions of reduced economic growth are a particularly appropriate setting for a test of the view that governments which possessed a large tax state managed successfully to control the economy.

Rates of
Unemployment
(average 1974–1980)

	20–30 per cent	30–40 per cent	40–50 per cent
greater than 5.0	Australia	Belgium Canada Finland France Ireland Italy United Kingdom	Denmark Netherlands
2 to 5		Germany Israel	
less than 2.0	Iceland Japan New Zealand Switzerland	Austria	Luxembourg Norway Sweden

Size of
the
tax state
(average
1970–73;
in percentages)

Sources: OECD Economic Outlook;
         OECD Economic Surveys

FIGURE 14.5   Tax State and Rates of Unemployment

The data displayed in Figures 14.4 and 14.5 demonstrate that there is
neither much evidence for the political-control-of-the-economy-hypothesis
nor for the conservative view. Only in some countries, for example, Denmark and Sweden, did a large tax state go hand in hand with relatively high
and increasing rates of inflation, and only did some countries with a relatively small tax state, for example, Switzerland, have a low rate of inflation.
In addition, high rates of inflation were more often than not a common feature of countries with small or medium sized tax states, such as Iceland,
Australia, New Zealand, the United Kingdom, and the United States.

A broadly similar picture emerges in the labor market consequences of
the differential size of the tax state. It is only a minority of states that fit the

predicted covariation of rates of unemployment and the size of the tax state. Both low and high rates of unemployment covaried very frequently with both small, medium-size, and large tax states.

We would thus conclude that both the conservative criticism of the state and the political-control-of-the-economy-view are far from being compatible with the data. It is not our intention here to account for the variation in the rates of inflation and the rates of unemployment in both statistical and substantive terms. We demonstrated elsewhere that rates of unemployment and rates of inflation in the mid-1970s are largely, though not exclusively, determined by differential power relationships in extraparliamentary and parliamentary political arenas. To a surprisingly large extent this relationship is independent of both the size of the economy and the political complexion of governments (Schmidt 1982a, 1982b).

Summary

Our analysis would imply that the mechanisms shaping the rates of expansion of the tax state in advanced industrial democracies vary over time. A rapid expansion of the tax state in the fifties was the outcome of the politics of convergence process, while the primacy of party politics was the major characteristic in the 1960s and early 1970s. On the other hand, the expansion of the tax state in the period of economic crisis from 1974 onward was basically shaped by what one might call the pattern of the primacy of extraparliamentary politics. The crucial point that emerges is that in many capitalist democracies, the links between the economy and public policy are, to varying extents and in a variety of complex ways, mediated by intervening societal and political factors. Perhaps the most important finding is the degree to which those mediating factors are of the kind suggested by the party politics and the class politics paradigm, with the latter one being more important for studies of policy making in periods of economic crisis, whereas the former one seems to be more appropriate for investigations of public policy in periods of economic prosperity. The analysis of some of the political and economic consequences of the size of the tax state would seem to indicate no systematic evidence for the view that rates of unemployment and rates of inflation were systematically related to the size of the tax state. On the other hand, the evidence accumulated in comparative public policy studies would lend support to the hypothesis that a large tax state has significantly helped to contain problems of extreme social inequality and political disorder. This result would seem to imply that the views held by many contemporary conservative and liberal critics of oversized tax states are not supported by cross-national public policy studies.

NOTES

1. The actual measurement is generally based on the latest available OECD Economic Surveys and, for Israel, on UN publications. Measures of the development of the tax state are computed by first differences (i.e., by subtracting the size of the tax state in 1960 from the figures for 1975). It should be pointed out that due to changes in data collection and definition, the data from the period 1950 to 1960 are not strictly comparable with the data from the beginning of the 1960s onward. We would further like to point out that the major disadvantage of our measures of the extractive capacity of the state is the exclusion of revenues from nontax and non-social-security contributions and borrowing, tax aids and tax credits. Unfortunately, no cross-nationally comparable figures for these items were available for the twenty-one nations under study.

2. The political composition of governments was measured by three indicators: (1) the percentage of months the left-wing-parties or the bourgeois parties were in government in a given period. This indicator measures the mere presence of the respective political tendencies in government. (2) the number of months in a given period in which the post of a prime minister (or functional equivalent) was held by leftist parties or bourgeois parties. This indicator measures which tendency had the major role in government. (3) The third indicator is derived from the left-wing parties' share of cabinet seats in a given period. The original values were converted into a rank-order scale of the dominant tendency in government in order to take account of the fact that such a comparatively low level of measurement is generally more compatible with the theoretical language and the theoretical knowledge of political scientists than interval scales or cardinal scales. The scale runs from 1 to 5: 1 means bourgeois hegemony government (share of cabinet seats equals 100 percent); 2 means bourgeois dominance government (the share ranges from greater 66.6 percent to less than 100 percent); 3 means balanced government (the bourgeois parties' share and the left-wing share are each larger than one-third and equal to or less than two-thirds of the total cabinet seats); 4 means social democratic dominance government (in analogy to rank 2); 5 means social democratic hegemony government (share of cabinet seats on the part of the social democratic and other left-wing allies is equal to 100 percent).

3. The relative size of the bourgeois and the left-wing tendency is measured by the average left vote in a given period, including the last national election preceding this period. The cohesiveness of the bourgeois tendency was dichotomized: 1 means weak cohesiveness, that is, if more than one bourgeois party scores at least ten percent of the vote in the majority of the elections within a given period; 0 means cohesiveness (any other case which does not meet the criteria stipulated under 1). The cohesiveness of the left-wing party spectrum was scored 1 (strong cohesiveness) whether nonsocial democratic left-wing parties scored less than ten percent of the vote in the majority of the elections within a given period, and 0 for any other case that did not meet the criteria stipulated under 1. It should be pointed out that by this decision rule France and Italy score 0 even if the PCI is the dominant party among the left-wing parties. In order to account for the political complexion of the center of gravity within the party system, an indicator of the dominant party was used. It takes on three values which are rank-ordered on a left-right scale: 1 means a bourgeois party is dominant, that is, if it is stronger than the major left-wing party by at least five percent of the popular vote in the majority of elections; 2 means balance or no dominant party, that is, if the criteria stipulated for rank 1 and rank 3 are not met; 3 means that a left-wing party is dominant (classified in analogy to rank 1). The latter four indicators were used in order to account for structures of the party system and for the distribution of power between the major political milieus (in the case of the left-vote-indicator) that are both of crucial importance for the differential room to maneuver on the part of the governing political tendency. The data were taken from Mackie and Rose (1974), Souler et al. (1977), and Keesing's *Archiv der Gegenwart*. Since in most of the nations under study the size of the Social

Democratic parties by far exceeds those of other left-wing parties, the left-wing measures employed correlate very strongly with the measures of social democratic party strength.

4. Union density was measured by the share of the dependent labor force organized by trade unions both for the total postwar period (Korpi and Shalev, 1979) and for the period between 1974 and 1977 from International Labor Organizations publications (yearly average of working days lost per total civilian employment). "Corporatism" is a theoretical concept relating to a particular mode of policy formation and a particular mode of regulating class conflicts in advanced democratic nations which is distinct from a competitive (regulation largely without the state) and an authoritarian mode (concerted action between the state and capital under exclusion of the trade unions). The corporatism indicator was rank ordered. Strong corporatism is the label for all those countries in which the trade union leadership and the employers associations are committed to a social-partnership ideology; in which the state, the trade unions, and the employers associations cooperate in some economic policy areas; in which the strike volume between 1974 and 1978 is very low (ratio of working days lost to total civilian employment lower than 0.1 for the average of the years from 1974 and 1978); and where no authoritarian incomes policy was enacted by the state. Switzerland and Japan deviate from the typical West European liberal corporatism. Switzerland displays characteristics of a societal corporatism with comparatively low involvement of the state. Japan is a case of a paternalistic capitalism and a private corporatism. Both arrangements are broadly functionally equivalent to the typical liberal corporatism. Weak corporatism relates to countries where employers and trade unions are not cooperative (indicated by frequent lockouts, high strike involvement, strong socialist and communist wings in the labor movement, weak industrial democracy) and where incomes policies were usually enacted from above. Medium corporatism is a residual category.

5. It goes without saying that indicators relating to identical or similar dimensions are frequently strongly interrelated. Apart from these intercorrelations, the only major problem of multicollinearity is that of the strong relationship (some 0.6) between the openness of the economy and the indicators of extraparliamentary distributions of power between organized labor and capital. For a causal model which takes account of the interrelation, see Cameron (1978).

6. The correlation between the size of the tax state and the OECD tax progression indicator was 0.20 for 1974 (N = 16); the relationship between the tax state size and an indicator for tax progression, measured as the percentage difference in income tax and employees' social security contributions at selected levels of earnings, was 0.49 in 1978 (N = 19). The latter correlation was based upon a tax progression indicator for single persons whose earnings were twice as high as the earnings of the average production worker and single persons whose earnings were only 66 percent of the average. A coefficient based upon a similar indicator for families with two children with earnings at 200 percent of average earnings and families with average earnings was 0.29 (N = 19).

REFERENCES

ARRIGHI, G. (1981) "Der Klassenkampf in Westeruopa im 20. Jahrhundert," pp. 53-75 in Folker Fröbel, Jürgen Heinrichs and Otto Kreye (eds.) Krisen in der kapitalistischen Weltökonomie. Reinbek bei Hamburg: Rowoholt.
CAMERON, D. R. (1978) "The expansion of the public economy." American Political Science Review 72, 4: 1243-1261.
CASTLES, F. G. (1982) "Politics, public expenditure and welfare," in Francis G. Castles (ed.) The Impact of Political Parties. London: Sage.

FLORA, P. (1979) "Krisenbewältigung oder Krisenerzeugung: Der Wohlfahrtsstaat in historischer Perspektive," pp. 82-136 in Joachim Matthes (ed.) Sozialer Wandel in Westeuropa. Frankfurt and New York: Campus.

FOLEY, D. K. (1978) "State expenditure from a Marxist perspective." Journal of Public Economics 9, 2: 221-238.

FREY, B. S. (1979) "Politometrics of government behavior in a democracy." Scandinavian Journal of Economics 81, 2: 308-322.

_____ and F. SCHNEIDER (1979) "Ein politischökonomisches Modell: Theorie und Anwendung für die Bundesrepublik Deutschland," pp. 406-417 in Werner Pommerehne and Bruno S. Frey (eds.) Ökonomische Theorie der Politik. Berlin, Heidelberg, New York: Springer.

GOLDSCHEID, R. (1917/1979) "Staatssozialismus oder Staatskapitalismus," in Rudolf Hickel (ed.) Die Finanzkrise des Steuerstaates: Beiträge zur Politischen Ökonomie der Staatsfinanzen. Frankfurt: Suhrkamp.

GOUGH, I. (1979) The Political Economy of the Welfare State. Basingstoke: Macmillan.

GRAUHAN, R. R. and R. HICKEL (eds.) (1978) Krise des Steuerstaats? Opladen: Westdeutscher Verlag.

HIBBS, D. A., Jr. (1978) "On the political economy of long-run trends in strike activity." British Journal of Political Science 8, 1: 153-175.

KING, A. (1973) "Ideas, institutions and the policies of governments: a comparative analysis." British Journal of Political Science 3, 2: 291; 3, 3: 409-423.

KOHL, J. (1981) "Trends and problems in postwar public expenditure development in Western Europe and North America," pp. 307-344 in Peter Flora and Arnold J. Heidenheimer (eds.) The Development of Welfare State in Europe and America. New Brunswick and London: Transaction Books.

KORPI, W. and M. SHALEV (1979) "Strikes, industrial relations and class conflict in capitalist societies." British Journal of Sociology 30, 1: 164-187.

MACKIE, T. T. and R. ROSE (1976) The International Election Statistics. London: Macmillan.

MURPHY, D., F. RUBERT, F. MILLER, and J. RASCHKE (1979) Protest: Grüne, Bunte und Steuerrebellen. Reinbek bei Hamburg: Rowohlt.

MUSGRAVE, R. A. and P. B. MUSGRAVE (1973) Public Finance in Theory and Practice. Tokyo: McGraw-Hill.

Organization for Economic Cooperation and Development, Economic Surveys. Paris: OECD. (annual)

_____ Economic Outlook. Paris: OECD. (biannual)

_____ (1980) The Tax/Benefit Position of Selected Income Groups in OECD Member Countries 1974-1979. Paris: OECD.

_____ (1978) Public Expenditure Trends. Paris: OECD.

RÜHLE, H. and H. J. VEEN (eds.) (1979) Wachsendestaatschaushalte. Stuttgart: Verlag Bonn Aktuelle.

SCHMIDT, M. G. (1982a) Wohlfahrtstaatliche Politik unter burgerlichen und sozialdemokratischen Regierungen. Ein internationaler Vergleich. Frankfurt and New York: Campus.

_____ (1982b) "Political and economic determinants of macroeconomic policy in advanced capitalist democracies," in Francis G. Castles (ed.), The Impact of Political Parties. London: Sage.

_____ (1982c) "Politische Konjunkturzyklen und Wahlen: Ein internationaler Vergleich," in Rainer-Olaf Schultze (ed.) Bundestagswahl '80. Heidelburg: C. F. Müller.

_____ (1980) CDU and SPD an der Regierung: Ein Vergleich ihrer Politik in den Ländern. Frankfurt and New York: Campus.

SCHUMPETER, R. (1976) "Die Krise des Steuerstaates," in Rudolf Hickel (ed.) Die Finanzkrise des Steuerstaates. Frankfurt: Suhrkamp. (reprint)

STEPHENS, J. D. (1979) The Welfare State and the Transition to Socialism. Basingstoke: Macmillan.

TARSCHYS, D. (1978) "The growth of public expenditures: nine models of explanation." Scandinavian Political Studies 10, 1: 9-31.

TUFTE, E. R. (1978) Political Control of the Economy. Princeton NJ: Princeton University Press.

WILENSKY, H. L. (1981) "Leftism, catholicism, and democratic corporatism: the role of political parties in recent welfare state development," pp. 345-382 in Peter Flora and Arnold J. Heidenheimer (eds.) The Development of Welfare States in Europe and America. Brunswick and London: Transaction.

———— (1976) The New Corporatism, Centralization and the Welfare State. Beverly Hills and London: Sage.

WITTMAN, W. (1978) Die öffentlichen Finanzen. Reinbek bei Hamburg: Rowohlt.

ABOUT THE CONTRIBUTORS

DONNA BAHRY, assistant professor of politics at New York University, is author of articles in *Comparative Political Studies, Slavic Review*, and other journals. Her interests include comparative public policy, Soviet and East European politics, and methodology in aggregate data analysis.

GEOFFREY BRENNAN is professor of economics in the Center for the Study of Public Choice, Virginia Polytechnic Institute and State University. He has written a significant number of articles in public finance and related fields and is coauthor, with James Buchanan, of *The Power to Tax*. Together they are currently working on several other books.

KARL W. DEUTSCH is director of the International Institute for Comparative Social Research, Wissenschaftszentrum-Berlin and Stanfield Professor of International Peace, Harvard University. He is author of *Nationalism and Social Communication, The Nerves of Government, Tides Among Nations,* and many other contributions to the theory of modern social political analysis.

RICHARD C. EICHENBERG is assistant professor of government at Florida State University. His research interests include defense policy and the political economy of defense spending, comparative public policy, and international relations. He is currently working on European public opinion on defense and public spending.

WALTER ELTIS is fellow of Exeter College and lecturer in Economics in the University of Oxford. He has published widely in academic journals, has been managing editor of the *Oxford Economic Papers*, and is author of three books, the most important of which is *Britain's Economic Problem: Too Few Producers* (coauthor with Robert Bacon). He contributes regularly to the London *Sunday Times* and the *Wall Street Journal*.

FRANK GOULD, lecturer in economics at the Polytechnic of Central London, has published a number of articles examining economic, political, and social aspects of public expenditure development in industrialized countries. Currently, he is investigating problems of management and control of public expenditures in both developed and developing countries.

MARTIN O. HEISLER is senior lecturer in the Institute of Politics at the University of Aarchus and is a member of the Departments of Government and Politics and of Sociology at the University of Maryland. He is author of *Politics in Europe* and numerous articles, book chapters, and papers on social policy, ethnic relations, and other topics. His interests include the political and economic impact of the welfare state on society and the political economy of ethnic and regional conflict.

JÜRGEN KOHL is an assistant in the Department of Sociology, the University of Bielefeld. He is author of *Staatsausgaben in Westeuropa* and contributor to *Soziologischer Almanach* and *The Development of Welfare States in Europe and America*. His research interests include modernization and social indicators research.

FRANZ LEHNER is professor of political science at the Ruhr University, Bochum. He is author of *Grenzen des Regierens* and other publications in political economy and public policy. His main interests are in political economy and comparative policy analysis.

RICHARD A. MUSGRAVE is H. H. Burbank Professor of Political Economy, Emeritus, Harvard University, and adjunct professor of economics, University of California at Santa Cruz. He is the author of *Theory of Public Finance* and *Public Finance in Theory and Practice*, as well as of numerous other publications in the fiscal field. In 1981 he was recipient of the Frank E. Seidman Distinquished Award in Political Economy.

B. GUY PETERS is director of the Center for Public Policy Studies and Professor of Political Science at Tulane University, and Honorary Fellow, Centre for the Study of Public Policy, University of Strathclyde. He is author of *The Politics of Bureaucracy,* of *Can Government Go Bankrupt?* (with Richard Rose), and of numerous articles on comparative policy and administration.

JONATHAN PINCUS is fellow in Economic History, Institute of Advanced Studies, Australian National University, and Visiting Research Associate at the Center for the Study of Public Choice, Virginia Polytechnic Institute and State University. He is author of *Pressure Groups and Politics in Antebellum Tariffs* and of *Government and Capitalism: Public and Private Choice in Australia, 1901-1975*.

JOHN S. PITZER is employed at the Office of Economic Research, Central Intelligence Agency. He conducts research on the Soviet economy, especially national income accounting.

RICHARD ROSE is Director of the Centre for the Study of Public Policy and Professor of Public Policy at the University of Strathclyde. He is author of *Can Government Go Bankrupt?* (with B. Guy Peters), *Do Parties Make A Difference?*, *Managing Presidential Objectives*, *Governing Without Consensus*, *Politics in England*, and a large number of other publications. He is currently engaged in the study of the growth of government in the United Kingdom since 1945.

MANFRED G. SCHMIDT, Privat-Dozent in political science at the University of Konstanz, is author of *Staatsapparat und Rustungspolitik in der Bundesrepublik Deutschland, 1966-1973, Empirische Politikwissenschaft* (with Ferdinand F. Muller), *CDU and SPD an der Regierung*, and numerous articles in comparative public policy.

GERTRUDE E. SCHROEDER is professor of economics at the University of Virginia. She specializes in the centrally planned economies and is author of many articles on various aspects of the Soviet economy, especially national income accounting.

CHARLES LEWIS TAYLOR is professor of political science, Virginia Polytechnic Institute and State University, and Associated Research Fellow in the International Institute for Comparative Social Research, Wissenschaftszentrum-Berlin. He is author of the *World Handbook of Political and Social Indicators* (with Michael C. Hudson and David A. Jodice) and other books and articles in the fields of social and political measurement, political stability, and Western European politics.

HENNY van der WIELEN is assistant head of the Research Department of the Central Bank in the Netherlands, where she is working on public finance. She is a graduate in economics of the Vrye Universiteit of Amsterdam.

ULRICH WIDMAIER, Research Fellow in the International Institute for Comparative Social Research, Wissenschaftszentrum-Berlin, is author of *Politische Gewaltanwendung als Problem der Organisation von Interessen* and other publications in mass political activity. His main research interests are political economy, macro-quantitative political analysis, and global simulation.